Education in the Broader Middle East:
borrowing a baroque arsenal

Education in the Broader Middle East
borrowing a baroque arsenal

Edited by
GARI DONN & YAHYA AL MANTHRI

SYMPOSIUM
BOOKS

Symposium Books Ltd
PO Box 204, Didcot, Oxford OX11 9ZQ, United Kingdom
www.symposium-books.co.uk

Published in the United Kingdom, 2013

ISBN 978-1-873927-86-1

© Symposium Books Ltd, 2013

All rights reserved. No part of this publication may be reproduced, stored in a retrieval system or transmitted in any form or by any means, electronic, mechanical, photocopying, recording or otherwise, without the prior permission of the publisher.

Printed and bound in the United Kingdom by Hobbs the Printers, Southampton
www.hobbs.uk.com

Contents

Introduction, **7**

CHAPTER ONE
Gari Donn & Yahya Al Manthri. Education Policy Transfers – Borrowing and Lending Education Policy: a conceptual expedition into baroque arsenals, **9**

CHAPTER TWO
Sajid Ali. Education Policy Borrowing in Pakistan: public–private partnerships, **23**

CHAPTER THREE
Mohammed Alrozzi. The Politics of Foreign Aid and Policy Borrowing in Palestine, **41**

CHAPTER FOUR
Brooke Barnowe-Meyer. Qatar's Independent Schools: education for a new (or bygone?) era, **63**

CHAPTER FIVE
Tanya Kane. Higher Education in Qatar: does a US medical school break the baroque arsenal?, **85**

CHAPTER SIX
Sana Al Balushi & David Griffiths. The School Education System in the Sultanate of Oman, **107**

CHAPTER SEVEN
Özlem Yazlık. International Influences on Adult Literacy and Basic Education in Turkey, **127**

CHAPTER EIGHT
Salha Abdullah Issan. Gender and Education in the Arabian Gulf States, **145**

CHAPTER NINE
Jane Knight. Crossborder Education in the Gulf
Countries: changes and challenges, **171**

Notes on Contributors, **203**

Education in the Broader Middle East: borrowing a baroque arsenal

GARI DONN & YAHYA AL MANTHRI

Introduction

A number of years ago, in the heat of a Muscat summer, we started to discuss the ways in which education policy is trans-located around the globe. At that time, there had been World Trade Organisation, European Union and World Bank visitors to the Sultanate of Oman. A series of seminars had been arranged to facilitate discussions between these key agencies and personnel from Ministries in Oman. We knew that the outcome would be further elaboration of Oman's Basic Education Reform and extended support for education developments in Oman. What we did not know was the range of countries similarly addressed by intensely mobile international agencies.

We spoke to colleagues in other Gulf States and heard that they, too, had been approached by the World Trade Organisation, the European Union and the World Bank. They, too, had been in discussions about education reform and had been asked to consider the introduction of various education policies to enhance science, mathematics and technology in the school curriculum and to address the importance of English as the main language of instruction.

Back in Edinburgh, on a cold and wet winter day, the idea took hold to write a book on what was happening globally. We had already written on the subject of globalisation and higher education in the region. Now we wanted to widen this to education throughout the countries of the broader Middle East. It seemed, to us, that these 'key players' from the Bank and development agencies were enacting a form of 'educational supremacy'. They were travelling the globe, often questioning and sometimes deriding what existed in-country whilst expounding the values and virtues of a globally driven fabrication of national curriculum, assessment and educational reform, indeed, of education itself.

We knew that the 'key players', acting under the principles of the market and neo-liberalism, had encouraged the Gulf States to transform their education systems, from historical and indigenous to current and global. Whilst we had no problem with changing historical and out-of-date systems of education, we did wonder at the speed at which new forms of governance, quality, curriculum and assessment were introduced.

We knew from various UNESCO conferences that Oman was a very special example of a country travelling at speed, from pre-history to postmodern currency. Yet we were aware of the problems of assuming that we knew too much about travelling policies, about 'borrowing' policy and the 'lending' of educational ideas. After all, we were aware that no sooner had one innovation been trialled, tested and deemed 'eminently suitable' for a country's education reform programme, than it was declared 'outdated' and another found support. Given the turbulent nature of educational reform globally, and especially in the countries of the broader Middle East, ours had to be a very careful journey.

This publication is part of that journey. It has brought together academics and postgraduate students, practitioners and Ministry officials, all of whom are wedded to developing an understanding of what is happening to education in the region of the broader Middle East. Our contributors address all stages of education, one chapter highlighting the underlying key concerns of gender. We cover many countries and recognise that there could be many more included. In drawing attention to education in Pakistan, Palestine, Oman, Turkey and Qatar we are indicating the wide range of education-policy 'borrowing' and, most importantly, the effects of this exchange. Other countries in the broader Middle East, we suggest, will have similar concerns and that may well be the subject of future studies. Finally, one major development globally and regionally is Crossborder Education; this is addressed in our final chapter.

We hope that these chapters assist in bringing others on similar journeys, for we are certain that the countries of the broader Middle East are not alone in having purchased glitzy, glossy and tantalisingly wonderful educational reforms, only to find how quickly they became 'outdated'. In other words, they became a 'baroque arsenal' of educational goods, services and models of practice which, having been discussed, designed and generated many years before in countries elsewhere, were sold and delivered to the probably unsuspecting countries of the broader Middle East. Through our chapters, we argue that many of the countries of the region did not suspect that their purchases were, more frequently than not, the 'off-loading' of failed educational experiments in countries of 'the centre'. We discuss what this means not only for educational reform projects, but also for the impact upon regional political stability. As we say, ours has to be a careful journey.

CHAPTER ONE

Education Policy Transfers – Borrowing and Lending Education Policy: a conceptual expedition into baroque arsenals

GARI DONN & YAHYA AL MANTHRI

Introduction

Across the world, in almost all states, there are increasing numbers of education-policy reforms. These cover the trend towards the decentralisation of administration and management of schooling, innovations in curriculum design, development and implementation, as well as new forms of ownership of schools and of higher-education institutions. It seems that every other day policy makers announce one policy or another to 'reform' their existing education systems.

These changes seem to be a constant feature for education policy in the broader Middle Eastern region. The reforms are often borrowed (or lent) with the ideas behind them tending to have been tested elsewhere, usually in a developed country. Middle Eastern policy makers would say: 'We should borrow tested education reforms to achieve excellence in educational outcomes; or from a different stand point we should lend the tested ideas to the nations in need of development.' All of this is done to 'quick fix' education systems to deliver results. Yet time and again these reforms result in further social and political desperation leading to an urgent need to find yet another education policy reform.

It is important, therefore, that these policy transfers – either borrowed or lent – be investigated. For it appears that no matter what reform is implemented, there continues to be a 'problem' with education systems in the broader Middle East. In many ways the 'problem' is less to do with 'education' per se and more to do with the generation and sustainability of 'knowledge' and a country's relationship to the 'knowledge economy'. The World Bank took the lead in addressing this phenomenon of new forms of knowledge and noted:

> The knowledge economy relies primarily on the use of ideas rather than the physical abilities and on the application rather than the transformation of raw materials or the exploitation of cheap labor. It is an economy in which knowledge is created, acquired, transmitted and used more effectively by individuals, enterprises, organisations and communities to promote economic and social development ... .The knowledge economy is transforming the demands of the labor market in economies throughout the world. (World Bank, 2003, p. 1)

It is now widely acknowledged that 'knowledge', and its application, has become the most important commodity within the 'networked society' (Castells, 2002). Indeed, as Castells noted, almost two decades ago (1996), new forms of information and communication technology (ICT) are at the very roots of new productive sources, of new organisational forms and of the formation of a global economy (Castells, 1996, p. 32). In a networked global economy, ICT and advanced informational structures are a prerequisite to sustained 'development'. We suggest that organisations and societies best able to generate and manage the knowledge developed from their education systems also enhance their chances of growing and being economically and politically stable (Rizvi & Lingard, 2000). This is mainly because they transfer educationally driven knowledge of, for example, ICT in the school curriculum (Rizvi et al, 2005), into their production and distribution systems thereby becoming 'the centre' of a global knowledge economy (Altbach, 2008). The societies which have to import, or borrow (Phillips & Ochs, 2003), knowledge and educational products (curriculum, assessment, quality assurance processes, qualifications frameworks, accreditation, styles of learning and teaching etc.) are disadvantaged twice. Firstly, by virtue of their relationship to knowledge production and distribution, these societies find themselves on the 'periphery' of global knowledge structures; secondly, by having continually to import knowledge, they maximise the economic gain of countries of the 'centre' and minimise their own financial resources.

Therefore, how far a country, and a region, supports indigenous knowledge development is often seen as a precursor to its integration into 'the centre'. In other words, education in all its forms – including schooling, tertiary, vocational, lifelong learning – holds the key responsibility for transferring knowledge and maintaining competitive advantage (Ozga & Jones, 2006) and creating 'knowledge workers' who are adaptable and self-improving (Spring, 2008).

Often the knowledge economy discourse is most visible through reforms in Higher Education and these are frequently the result of collaboration between a country's relevant Ministries with the World Bank and other International Organisations. Various World Bank Task Force Reports define higher education as the key pillar for economic growth of a country and a source of developing human capital. Alongside this characterisation resides the rhetoric, the 'soft policy' formulation, of how to achieve such development: through decentralisation, new governance structures, accountability, transparency, revision of the curriculum, emphasis on science, technology, mathematics, and the introduction of English language throughout all stages of learning. Most frequently, these material and rhetorical policy changes are the result of defining a nation's education needs in relation to what happens elsewhere, be that globally, internationally or regionally. International organisations, such as UNESCO with its Global Monitoring Reports (GMR) and its Performance Indicators (PISA, TIMSS et al) appear to provide substantive evidence to support an 'educational need' for 'improvements'. Such conceptualisation supports pressures from key global policy players to transport educational policies, structures, procedures and practices from 'the centre' to 'the periphery' (Altbach, 2008).

Our previous writing on policy borrowing has indicated that borrowed policies rarely 'travel well' and add little – if anything – to the educational requirements of countries 'at the periphery' (Donn & Al Manthri, 2010).

> Countries at the periphery are placed in a position of becoming consumers of the knowledge created, generated and delivered from elsewhere. And as soon as that knowledge is consumed, further knowledge development occurs: what was 'new and innovatory' today becomes commonplace and dated tomorrow. Knowledge, like the products it generates, becomes outdated, old-fashioned, baroque. (Donn & Al Manthri 2010, p. 180)

In this previous writing, we argued that most frequently, educational products have greater value in their sale rather than in their importation and arrival. This is often due, we suggested, to the 'baroque' and outdated nature of the educational products transported around the globe. These education products may well be seen as 'the new approach', a 'new understanding' and may well arrive with glossy packaging, developmental programmes and in-built learning and teaching assistance. But once *in situ*, such educational products do not necessarily sit well. They may not resonate with the domestic needs of a country's educational reforms. Glossy they may be. Well sold they may be. Useful they may not turn out to be. Like Kaldor and others argued in the case of superannuated armaments (Kaldor, 1981), our educational products can be seen as outdated before they even arrive: glitzy they may be but in fact they are a baroque arsenal, promising much and delivering little.

Our thesis and that argument is developed in this publication. Our contributors explore the view that policy borrowing is fundamentally about borrowing 'a baroque arsenal' of outdated and costly educational products: these wend their way from an already rich centre to countries on the periphery, in the broader Middle East. Their acquisition by the countries of the periphery, we have argued, further weakens the educational performance, knowledge generation and hence, inevitably, the economic sustainability of these countries.

Borrowing a Baroque Arsenal

To explore the efficacy of this approach to policy borrowing, the following chapters focus upon education-policy developments in Pakistan, Palestine, Qatar, Oman and Lifelong Learning in Turkey, with gendered education in the states of the Gulf Cooperation Council and with borderless education in the States of the Gulf. In various ways, our contributors address the concern that whilst we see huge financial investments in education, these countries of the broader Middle East remain locked into the 'periphery'. A number write of 'policy brokers', a 'magistracy', a 'cohort of people, key players and policy makers' (Donn & Al Manthri, 2010, p. 156) who travel the world, defining agendas, setting frameworks, objectives, targets and goals for 'quality' education. Our contributors outline the relevance of 'the magistracy' as they provide concrete evidence of the way it operates in the countries of the broader Middle East.

In previous writing (2010) we suggested that the meetings of G8/BMENA (Broader Middle East North Africa) may well be seen as part of this 'magistracy'. We argued that these meetings encourage and support agenda setting and the delineation of 'suitable' and 'appropriate' educational rhetoric, as well as the continuous travelling and importation of knowledge, curricula, assessment, institutional arrangements and styles of management, all of which are embedded in almost-identical educational systems, schooling and training courses, in both public/state and private Higher Education Institutions around the region.

In fact, and as we noted previously, there is growing realisation amongst scholars and the wider public of an emerging 'global education policy field' – a form of supra-state space where broader consensus around preferred education policy priorities is emerging (Rizvi & Lingard, 2010). There are various possibilities through which these policies make their way into the national spaces. One way to understand this transfer is to conceptualise it not just as a policy borrowing and lending phenomenon but to interweave the positive benefits for seller nations and the frequently negative impacts of buyer states. It thereby becomes apparent that the context of policy borrowing and lending is firstly financial, secondly political and, much further down the scale of rationales, thirdly, educational.

This so-called 'global education policy field' has affected several educational reforms over the years and particularly since the 1990s. These include policies that are prevalent across the globe, such as: privatisation, decentralisation, achievement of universal educational targets, higher-education reforms and the proliferation of educational statistics of all sorts (Ali & Tahir, 2009). These concerns are evident in Pakistan and are addressed by Sajid Ali in Chapter 2. They are also of prime importance for understanding recent education reforms in Palestine, Turkey, Qatar and Oman. In Chapter 3 Mohammed Alrozzi addresses the role of international organisations in assisting educational development in Palestine, whilst in Chapter 4, Sana Al Balushi and David Griffiths provide insight into the global reach of international indicators as they impact on teacher training in Oman's Basic Education Reform. In Chapter 5 Ozlem Yazlik discusses the role of literacy in social and economic development in Turkey, and in Chapters 6 and 7 Brooke Barnowe-Meyer and Tanya Kane examine different aspects of reform and policy implementation in Qatar. More generally in Chapter 8, Salha Issan examines gendered understandings of educational reforms across all six countries of the Gulf Cooperation Council (GCC).[1] Finally in Chapter 9, and with a view very firmly to the future, Jane Knight writes on Crossborder Education, drawing our attention to the possibilities for educational hubs in the broader Middle East region.

Pakistan (Chapter 2)

Pakistan, neighbouring China, India, Afghanistan and Iran, is located at a strategically important geo-political nexus. The complexity of this context is compounded by Pakistan being Islamic (in part), pro-Western (in part) and South Asian (in part). Further, as Ali argues, the Pakistani state is under considerable global pressure to align its policies – especially its education policies – with reference to a dominant set of definitions about 'efficient' and 'efficacious' 'quality education': in other words, Ali notes, this is a global education policy field (Ali, 2009) within which Pakistan finds its place.

In this 'policy space', the pressure for appropriate education reform is exerted through both material and discursive means. Whilst in the Pakistani context, it does face national resistance, Ali suggests that this is usually weak and often is of only a discursive nature. Ali argues that the discursive nature of any resistance to political reform of education is evident in many – perhaps, most – developing countries, this being due to a heavy reliance on international aid for financing their development programmes. Such aid may come from the World Bank, the IMF, regional development banks or country development budgets and tends to support projects for improving governance, capacity building, elementary education, reconstruction, teacher training and curriculum reform.

In the case of Pakistan, Ali draws attention to the inculcation of new methods of financing aid and its delivery, notably through 'public–private partnerships'. As Ali notes, the idea of public–private partnership indicates recent re-positioning of the state to ensure public service. It is seen as an appropriate means of financing education reforms from both global and local perspectives. The emergence of such partnerships in Pakistan's education policy space, it is suggested, reinforces what has been felt elsewhere in the world: that the state is unable to provide basic services to its population without the involvement of the private sector. Ali notes that this broad ideological paradigm has several strands which touch upon the policies of decentralisation, privatisation, community involvement and good governance. All strands are evident in the international literature on education reform and emanate from the post-2000 Washington Consensus view that the financial methods of neo-liberalism can be applied, quite properly, to education.

Ali argues that these processes of globalisation, often based on inequality in provision, are mostly transitory, and usually support a trend towards privatisation. They have led to a 'hollowed out state' or a 'competition state' in which the absolute power of the state over its affairs is drastically and dramatically reduced.

Palestine (Chapter 3)

This increasing global reach and reduction of national autonomy is something all our broader Middle Eastern countries experience. Reduced local state power may appear to be part of a beneficent borrowing and lending arrangement. It may even be seen as worth having, regardless of the exceptional hardship and dubious success in the implementation of reform programmes.

In his chapter on Foreign Aid and Policy Borrowing in Palestine, Mohammed Alrozzi outlines the impact of a 'world view' embedded in support for diminished local and enhanced global authority, power and control. Those holding the reins of this perspective are clearly aligned with neo-liberal forms of globalisation. Alrozzi argues that this 'world view' – supported by International Non-Governmental Organisations (NGOs), Intergovernmental Institutions and donors – is tailored to maximise capital and achieve macro-economic growth. But, this chapter suggests, it also increases inequality amongst peoples, communities and nations. It undermines national cultures, national sovereignty and regional aspiration. This becomes increasingly important, it is argued, for fragile countries such as the Palestinian Territories which has, possibly, one of the world's most aid-dependent education systems.

Alrozzi writes that since the Oslo Accords in 1993, the Ministry of Education and Higher Education (MoEHE) has struggled to establish its own mechanisms for planning, budgeting, coordinating and reviewing policies. In particular there has been the challenge to develop a Palestinian curriculum for schools. The chapter addresses the role of foreign aid in the development of the education system and in the creation of that curriculum. It notes that especially from 2005, there has been a new policy space with enhanced availability of increased resources alongside high civilian expectations. Yet the high levels of donor aid for education have meant that there has been a nuancing of what is 'possible for education' in the Palestinian Territories. Global pressures, it is apparent, impact on both material and rhetorical education-policy processes, notably those addressed by UNAID and in the field of Technical and Vocational Education and Training (TVET). Indeed, as Alrozzi argues, despite the tremendous effort to support TVET in the Palestinian Territories, little has actually been achieved.

Turkey (Chapter 4)

Similar concerns are raised by Ozlem Yazlik with regard to Adult Literacy and Basic Education (ALBE) policy in Turkey. Through an in-depth analysis of current education policy documents in Turkey, she asks what concept of literacy underpins these ALBE policies? She wonders whether learners and teachers are 'positioned' by such policies and whether the programmes and outcomes are delineated well outside not only Turkey but also the geo-economic region of the broader Middle East.

In her starting point, Yazik recognises that the dominant model of literacy is technical and skills-based; literacy is seen as a means of developing and enhancing economic participation in society. She draws attention to New Literacy Studies which, coming from the tradition of ethnography, are based on people having different literacies in different domains of life – such as the home, the workplace, the school and the community.

In Turkey literacy education, Yazik argues, has played an important role in the development of the nation-state. Since 1923, it is noted, different forms of 'modernisation' have been equated with the contents and practices of modern material culture and scientific progress associated with the West. Since the 1960s, in particular, she suggests that the 'functionalist' definition of literacy has underpinned government approaches to literacy, language and learning in Turkey; the policy changes appear to hold an economistic vision of literacy and their vital role for employability and economic growth. This assumption is characteristic of the skills-based model of literacy: however, she concludes, there are signs of deepening critiques of this approach, critiques which focus upon the non-economic yet vitally human and important possibilities for and of literacy.

Oman (Chapter 5)

An important way to assess the introduction of international education policies is through identification of the kinds of educational projects that have been financed by international organisations. As Al Balushi and Griffiths argue, in examining the case of education reform in Oman, the development of Basic Education Reform (BER) was instigated through World Bank support in the mid-1990s. The guiding principle behind the design of the new BER of the Curriculum was to include relevant knowledge and skills-based content to help prepare young Omanis for life and work under the new conditions created by the global economy. They note that globalisation places a higher economic value on particular types of knowledge and skills so, in recognition of this, the Ministry of Education followed practices in other countries in the region, and around the world, in developing new subject areas such as information technology and life skills.

Its subsequent implementation created numerous problems not least because the curriculum – based on the assumption that to function effectively and produce high-quality learning, the same values and operational principles should be universal – involved English language (the language of the global economy), a reduction in Islamic Studies and a stronger background in mathematics and science. One consequence of these changes was that 'liberal arts' subjects, which tend to serve society's longer-term goals, diminished. Many now see the current unease with the BER curriculum as a result of a policy borrowed yet actually inappropriate for the needs of that Gulf State.

The uneasy acceptance of the imported BER and curriculum subjects was strained especially in changes to pedagogy. The authors draw attention to new management techniques and the role asked of teachers. Teachers in Oman had historically been trained in rote-learning methods and whole-class teaching methods. The new BER and its curriculum asked teachers to move towards student-centred and individualised approaches to learning with a focus upon inquiry, analysis and higher-order thinking skills. Perhaps unsurprisingly, many teachers have experienced difficulties in making the hoped-for transition. Maybe more surprisingly, given intense concern in society generally – and not just about these new approaches for teaching – the Ministry has entered into collaborations with external agencies and organisations. Al Balushi and Griffiths wonder whether such external collaborative relationships do support and encourage teachers in building their much-needed professional capacity.

Qatar (Chapter 6)

Indeed, as Barnowe-Meyer reports, the situation is not very different in Qatar. She writes of the country's K–12 education system, which has undergone a series of remarkable transformations in the past half-century, especially the introduction of the 'independent schools' in 2004. These schools are built upon policies of school autonomy, accountability, variety and choice and owe their origins to the Charter Schools of the USA.

Barnowe-Meyer traces support for these schools to a magistracy, a powerful international set of proponents from the USA, the United Kingdom, New Zealand and Germany, who have suggested that market-style mechanisms of choice and competition have made struggling schools more flexible, innovative and diverse. In a drive to free Qatari schools from 'bureaucratic regulation and monopolistic inefficiency of a highly public education system' the magistracy – spearheaded by the Rand Corporation – supported the transfer of Charter Schools/ Independent Schools to Qatar. Yet, as this chapter makes clear, there was little reference paid to the failings of the Charter School movement in the USA, which include poor student achievement, discrimination, financial mismanagement and little evidence of curriculum innovation or quality instruction. Indeed, as Barnowe-Meyer argues, these appear to be just those attributes *not* required by an educational reform.

Yet, Qatar has rapidly transitioned its remaining public schools to independent institutions and, alongside, there is an over-reliance upon the market, magisterial 'expertise' and a uniquely US version of 'democracy'. Indeed, as Barnowe-Meyer argues, these schools and their placement in Qatar produce profound evidence in support of a 'baroque arsenal'. She writes that rather than representing best educational practice, the charter school model of the USA – and by association, the independent-school model in Qatar – more aptly serve as stark examples of 'the baroque arsenal'. They are educational goods, services and models of practice 'discussed, designed and generated years before their delivery', then marketed and sold to states across the globe, despite lingering questions regarding their potential for true reform.

Qatar (Chapter 7)

Tanya Kane, writing of Higher Education also in Qatar, holds a different view of a US-imported model of education in that oil-rich Gulf State. She draws attention to the importance of a US model of crossborder institutional development which, far from being 'baroque', outdated and undermining, may well be a means of cultivating knowledge and skills, attitudes and dilemmas which, although they emerge from a Western perspective, enable an interweaving of local concerns within global contexts.

In this version of 'denationalistion' she suggests that whilst logics, frames and practices are increasingly associated with growing knowledge economies and a global scale of policy making, governments are being forced to evaluate how well indigenous education systems are preparing their students in an increasingly centralised and Westernised world.

Qatar, perhaps alone of all the Gulf States, has taken seriously the role education plays in the development of an indigenous knowledge economy. In 1995 the Qatar Foundation was established on a 1000-hectare campus, called Education City. It was intended to develop people's abilities through investment in human capital, innovative technology, state-of-the-art facilities and partnerships with elite organisations. One collaboration has been with Cornell University Medical School (WCMC), which established a Qatar base, with the medical curriculum being strategically delivered by a team of medical faculty, resident in Qatar. Cornell's distinctive institutional arrangement, Kane notes, shapes the educational programme and has resulted in 'an innovative pedagogical form'.

Through a careful analysis of the collaboration between Qatar and Cornell, Kane wonders whether this transnational educational partnership may be breaking the baroque-arsenal mould and providing an alternative model for the region. She argues that the Qatari model does not buy in outdated practices and products but, through its co-venture status, enables WCMC-Q to contribute to advances in medicine geared to the region's health-care challenges. Whilst we would like this to be the case, and can see some evidence for this view, there are severe constraints (not only financial) on the model being rolled out elsewhere in the broader Middle East.

Gender in the Arabian Gulf States (Chapter 8)

One challenge which is of great importance to broader Middle East countries is the inclusion of females at all levels of education and the inclusion of males in higher education. In Pakistan, Oman and other Gulf States, for example, the number of females in higher education vastly outstrips that of males. However, generally, there are concerns about the reduced numbers of females entering and remaining in education and reaching high levels of attainment: once in school and being retained there, there is evidence that females succeed. The issue is to get girls to school.

In her chapter on Gender in the Gulf States, Salha Issan draws attention to the gender disparities in attainment which run alongside issues of access and opportunity in schooling and tertiary education. The six Gulf States appear to have economic success based upon imported domestic products and inward investment. Yet, most importantly, there are also high levels of migrant-workers' remittances sent elsewhere and an almost total absence of a knowledge economy.

Through a cameo overview of all six GCC states, Issan argues that progress in educational attainment is 'stymied' by a lack of democratic institutions: she notes that excessively restrictive rules on the formation of civil-society organisations make it extremely difficult for women's advocates to organise effectively and lobby for women's choices and their 'democratic rights'.

Crossborder Education (Chapter 9)

One educational development which will be less problematic in its roll-out is presented by Jane Knight in her chapter on Crossborder Education. She notes that internationalisation is one of the main forces shaping higher education as it meets the challenges of the twenty-first century. These challenges – complexity, diversity and differentiation – have to address the immense increases in student numbers as well as the widening range of academic and vocational programmes and educational services provided by a growing list of public and private, state and corporate providers.

Knight suggests that crossborder education, which refers to the movement of people, knowledge, programmes, providers, policies, ideas, curricula, projects and services across national or regional jurisdictional borders, is developing apace in the Gulf countries. Indeed, as her chapter indicates, there have been three generations of movement: firstly, students and scholars; secondly, programmes and providers; and thirdly, the current development of education hubs. This latter, she suggests, need to be more than just a brand if they are to be sustainable. Sustainability requires knowledge and service-based economies which will, over time, provide a competitive edge for the nation and for the region.

As crossborder education increases in the Gulf countries and adapts to new global, regional, national and local challenges, it is necessary, Knight argues, to continually monitor its rationales, intended and unintended consequences, and its ultimate impact. So whilst new developments in crossborder education provide many opportunities – increased access to higher education, strategic alliances between countries and regions, the production and exchange of new knowledge through academic/industry partnerships, the mobility of graduates and professionals, human-resource and institutional-capacity building, income generation and improvement in academic quality – there are also many risks. Low-quality staff and programmes, foreign qualifications not being recognised by domestic employers and the overuse of English as the medium of instruction are just three of many problems drawn to our attention.

Conclusion

There is growing realisation among scholars of an 'emerging global education policy field', a supra-state space where broader consensus towards preferred education policy priorities are emerging (Rizvi & Lingard, 2010). The educational reforms that are successful in one context and hence replicated in other contexts – the so-called *'best practices'* – reflect once tangent of this emerging global-education policy field. Another tangent is represented by the emerging trend of *global comparative indices* such as the progress on Education for All (EFA) targets, Millennium Development Goals (MDG) targets, performance on international tests like the Programme for International Student Assessment (PISA) and Trends in International Maths and Science Study (TIMSS). It is argued that these tend to pressurise governments towards a form of global standardisation of education (Spring, 2008).

Our contributors have written of 'hard' policy concerns – of new organisational forms in and re-structuring of schooling, TVET, lifelong learning and higher education; they have noted the importance of the 'soft' policy rhetoric involving definitions of 'quality', 'access', 'equity', 'retention', 'capacity building' and 'accreditation'.

In our view, when accepting a vision of global education reform, the countries of the broader Middle East, in the periphery, have become purchasers of knowledge. They have imported definitions almost regardless of the geo-politically located views of the 'relevance' of certain forms of education. These definitions are generated elsewhere – in the centre – and, through their importation from the centre to the periphery, they come to be financially supported by the periphery. After all, their transfer does not occur without money: it occurs through 'development' loans, aid and direct budgeted costs. The periphery is therefore incredibly important for the centre: just as the centre is important for the periphery. But whereas one, the centre, relies on the other for the onward transport of education products and processes of – we argue – questionable relevance, the other, the periphery, provides the funding and the space for the importation of policy and, almost inevitably, the architecture of policy failure. This is, indeed, an exchange mechanism of a baroque educational relationship, and – given recent financial circumstances – of a possibly baroque global economy.

Note

[1] The Gulf Cooperation Council (GCC) was founded in 1982 to provide countries in the region with coordination as they developed trade and fiscal monetary policy cooperatively and worked together in implementation. The six Gulf States are Bahrain, Kuwait, Oman, Qatar, Saudi Arabia and the United Arab Emirates.

References

Ali, S. (2009) Governing Education Policy in a Globalising World: the sphere of authority of the Pakistani State. PhD thesis, University of Edinburgh.

Ali, S. & Tahir, M.S.A. (2009) Reforming Education in Pakistan: tracing global links, *Journal of Research and Reflections in Education*, 3(1), 1-16.

Altbach, P.G. (2008) Globalisation and Forces of Change in Higher Education, *International Higher Education*, 50 (Winter).

Castells, M. (1996) *The Rise of the Networked Society. The Information Age: economy, society and culture.* Oxford: Blackwell.

Castells, M. (2002) *The Rise of the Networked Society*, 2nd edn. London: Wiley-Blackwell.

Donn, G. & Al Manthri, Y. (2010) *Globalisation and Higher Education in the Arab Gulf States.* Oxford: Symposium Books.

Kaldor, M. (1981) *Baroque Arsenal.* New York: Farrar, Straus & Giroux.

Ozga, J. & Jones, R. (2006) Travelling and Embedded Policy: the case of knowledge transfer, *Journal of Education Policy*, 21(1), 1-17.

Phillips, D. & Ochs, K. (2003) Processes of Policy Borrowing in Education: some explanatory and analytical devices, *Comparative Education*, 39(4), 451-461.

Rizvi, F., Engel, L., Nandyala, A., Rutkowski, D. & Sparks, J. (2005) *Globalisation and Recent Shifts in Education Policy in the Asia Pacific: an overview of some critical issues.* Bangkok: UNESCO Asia Pacific Regional Bureau for Education.

Rizvi, F. & Lingard, B. (2000) Globalisation and Education: complexities and contingencies, *Educational Theory*, 50(4), 419-426.

Rizvi, F. & Lingard, B. (2010) *Globalising Education Policy.* London: Routledge.

Spring, J. (2008) *Globalization of Education: an introduction.* New York: Routledge.

World Bank (2003) *World Development Indicators.* Washington, DC: Oxford University Press.

CHAPTER TWO

Education Policy Borrowing in Pakistan: public–private partnerships

SAJID ALI

Introduction

There is a growing realisation among scholars of an 'emerging global education policy field' which is a sort of supra-state space, where a broader consensus around preferred education-policy priorities, is developing (Rizvi & Lingard, 2010). Educational reforms that are successful in one context and are subsequently replicated in other contexts – the so called 'best practices' – are also becoming part of this emerging global education policy field. These models of best practice are subsequently lent to countries that require assistance in reforming their education system. Generally, these reforms emerge in the developed countries and are lent to developing countries in a centre to periphery relationship (Altbach, 2004).

The emerging trends of global comparative indices, such as progress on Education for All (EFA) and Millennium Development Goals (MDG) targets as well as performance related to international tests like the Programme for International Assessment (PISA), have also strengthened the global education policy field by providing global comparisons, within which global standards for education are embedded (Spring, 2008). Countries throughout the developed and developing world are benchmarked against these standards and if a country does not display high scores on these standards, a call for reform is generated. These global comparisons create the need for 'catch-up' by developing countries, leading them to borrow tested education-reform solutions from elsewhere.

The transfers of education policy do not only follow this very straight and direct route of policy borrowing always. Roger Dale (1999) provides a good range of mechanisms through which policy influences transfer from one space to another: borrowing is one of them. It is however, not guaranteed that the reforms developed and tested in one context will also work out in another setting. These policy ideas, which travel across countries, are not simply taken up by the national policy actors, but become embedded within the national policy dynamics (Jones & Alexiadou, 2001). However, the negotiation between arrived and embedded policy depends on the negotiating power and capacity of the state – its sphere of authority (Ali, 2009). It is important to understand particular reforms, borrowed and implemented in specific contexts, to fully comprehend the phenomenon.

This chapter addresses education-policy borrowing in Pakistan. It will first provide a brief context of education in Pakistan and deliberate on recent educational development. Later it will focus on a major education policy that has been borrowed from the so-called global education policy field: that is, the policy of public–private partnership. Its emergence in the international context and arrival within the Pakistani education-policy space will be discussed, followed by a view on its reception and outcome. The concluding section will provide a commentary on the overall outcome of the borrowed policies, their transformation – including policy negotiation – and the possibilities for becoming embedded policy within the current Pakistani education-policy context.

Education Policy Context of Pakistan

Pakistan is located at a strategically important location within South Asia neighbouring China, India, Afghanistan and Iran. It came into existence in 1947 and was separated from East Pakistan (present day Bangladesh) in 1971. The current population is estimated to be around 177 million with an average growth rate of 2.07% (Pakistan. Ministry of Finance, 2011). The Pakistan Social and Living Measurement (PSLM) survey 2010-11 shows that the literacy rate among population over ten years old is 58% (M-69%; F-46%). The current net primary-enrolment rate is 66% (M-71%; F-61%) (Pakistan. Federal Bureau of Statistics, 2011). As far as the system of education is considered, it is broadly categorised into public and private, within which there are further variations. There are 225,135 schools, including both the public and private sector, offering education up to higher secondary level (Pakistan. Ministry of Education, 2008). The total numbers of students enrolled in these schools are 33,688,629. Despite these enormous figures, there are still around 5 million children in Pakistan who are out of school (UNESCO, 2012).

In terms of higher education, there are 129 universities including 72 public and 57 private, with an enrolment of 803,507 students (Pakistan.

Ministry of Education, 2008). Since 2001 the government has invested heavily in advancing the higher-education sector, which has resulted in an increase in the number of universities, in enrolment, scholarships, graduates (from national and overseas institutions), research grants, and, importantly, the building of a research culture. The overall budget of the Higher Education Commission (HEC) has been on the rise since 2001, although the development budget has been recently curtailed due to the unsettling economic condition of the country. (See Table I below for a comparative view).

	2005-6	2006-7	2007-8	2008-9	2009-10	2010-11
Recurring	10.5	14.3	12.5	15.8	21.5	20.3
Development	10.9	14.4	15.4	16.4	11.3	9.2
Total	21.4	28.7	27.9	32.2	32.8	29.5

Table I. Development and non development expenditures on higher education (Rs. billion). Source: Pakistan. Ministry of Finance (2011) *Economic Survey of Pakistan 2010-11*.

The growth in the HEC budget matches an increase in the number of universities and graduates at a higher education level. During 2005-9, the higher-education sector saw 400,000 graduates every year, which is a 30% increase during this period (Pakistan. Ministry of Finance, 2011). Since 2002, HEC has sent around 4313 candidates for MPhil and PhD degrees abroad, and another 8873 students have been sponsored for the research degrees within the country. During 2010, some 750 doctoral degrees were awarded by Pakistani universities, which shows an enormous growth compared with the situation in 2000 (Pakistan. Ministry of Finance, 2011; HEC website various reports at www.hec.gov.pk).

Since this chapter focuses upon policy borrowing in Pakistan and its effects on overall education policy, a brief historical understanding about the involvement of foreign assistance in Pakistan is required. Foreign assistance comes in a number of forms: these include loans, grants and technical expertise. It is an instrument which brings foreign innovations, reforms and ideas into the national policy space. The following table (Table II) shows the extent of external economic assistance to Pakistan over the years:

At present there are some 97 education-development projects funded by external agencies in various parts of Pakistan with a good number of them (13) dealing with improving governance (Mujahid-Mukhtar, 2011). Other prominent areas receiving foreign assistance are Capacity Building (40); Elementary Education (22); Reconstruction (20) and Teachers' Training (16). Foreign assistance raises questions about external influence and policy borrowing. Ali and Tahir (2009) explain various global policy influences that are evident in the education

Sajid Ali

policies of Pakistan. In addition Ahsan (2005) points out that assistance to Pakistan is attached very much to the geo-strategic situation of the area where Pakistan is situated. The case of Afghanistan during the 1980s and 2000s provides a good example to support this assertion. For example, aid for education in Pakistan is not simply to improve educational indicators, but a means to curtailing supposed extremism (Curtis, 2007).

Period	Committed Loans	Disbursed Loans	Committed Grants	Disbursed Grants	Total Commitment	Total Disbursed
	A	b	C	D	a+c	b+d
1951-60	618	192	794	650	1,412	842
1960-65	1,805	1,232	1,106	1,162	2,911	2,394
1965-70	2,233	2,324	704	719	2,937	3,043
1970-78	6,152	5,096	815	634	6,967	5,730
1978-83	5,667	-	1,566	-	7,233	-
1983-88	9,130	5,158	2,777	2,025	11,907	7,183
1988-93	11,736	9,540	2,177	2,541	13,913	12,081
1993-97*	9,183	9,214	928	1,008	10,111	10,222

*Includes provisional data for year 1996-97.
Source: Pakistan. Federal Bureau of Statistics (1998) *50 Years of Pakistan.*

Table II. Foreign economic assistance to Pakistan (US$ million).

For better contextual understanding, it is also important for readers to be aware of the current education reforms happening in the country. The National Education Policy 2009 (NEP, 2009) was developed after a three-year consultative process and can be accessed at the Ministry of Education's website (http://www.moe.gov.pk). In 2010 a constitutional amendment (18th Constitutional Amendment) was passed, which has brought significant changes in the education sector. The amendment made it compulsory that all children aged 5-16 receive free education. In addition, responsibility for education has now been devolved from the federal to provincial governments. As a consequence of this, the federal Ministry of Education has been dissolved. Apart from these, some of the prominent education policy moves visible in the country include the promotion of privatisation and decentralisation; an emphasis on the achievement of EFA and MDG targets; and a focus on the improvement in governance systems through measurement and new management practices. According to Carnoy's analysis (2006) these developments show an increased influence of globalisation on education, and also hint at the process of education policy borrowing in Pakistan (Ali & Tahir, 2009).

This section has outlined the structure of Pakistan's basic and higher education sectors and has aimed to demonstrate the reliance on foreign assistance in Pakistan, which provides the background to understanding education-policy borrowing. It has been argued that various educational reforms in Pakistan tried out since the 1990s are linked to the influences of globalisation (Ali & Tahir, 2009). The following part of this chapter will extend this discussion by focusing on a significant policy preference, that of public–private partnerships. It will be seen that these have surfaced gradually in Pakistan and now hold a dominant space in the field of education policy-making and policy implementation.

Public–Private Partnerships (PPP)

The idea of public–private partnership reflects the hybrid governance arrangements between various state and non-state actors over number of educational development initiatives across the globe (Robertson et al, 2012). It indicates the recent re-positioning of the state to ensure public services in a joined-up fashion. The processes of globalisation have led to what is referred to as a 'hollowed out state' or 'competition state' (Jessop, 2002), which alludes to the reduction of a state's absolute power over its affairs. Globalisation has affected the state from the top and bottom and it now has to negotiate its power with supra-national, as well as sub-national, actors and agencies (Scholte, 2000). As a result, the sphere of authority of the nation-state has been reshaped (Rosenau, 1999, 2000).

The World Bank titled its annual development report in 1997 'The State in a Changing World' and through that narrative, and others subsequently, contributed to the global movement of curtailing the state's scope and authority (World Bank, 1997). Due to this re-calibration, the state has gradually withdrawn from its absolute claim over provision of basic public services like education and health. It has allowed, and at times encouraged, the involvement of private actors in the provision of basic public services, generating the idea of public–private partnerships (PPP or 3Ps). Over the past decade many forms of public–private partnerships have been practised in a variety of sectors. The Canadian Council of Public Private Partnership defines PPP as follows:

> A cooperative venture between the public and private sectors, built on the expertise of each partner, that best meets clearly defined public needs through the appropriate allocation of resources, risks and rewards. (http://www.pppcouncil.ca)

The partnership results in a range of options, many of which are practised in Pakistan. They are based on the degree of private-sector involvement allowed, required and promoted at any given time.

Alongside the benefits, as perceived by various key players, there are also risks. In my view, the picture below describes it appropriately:

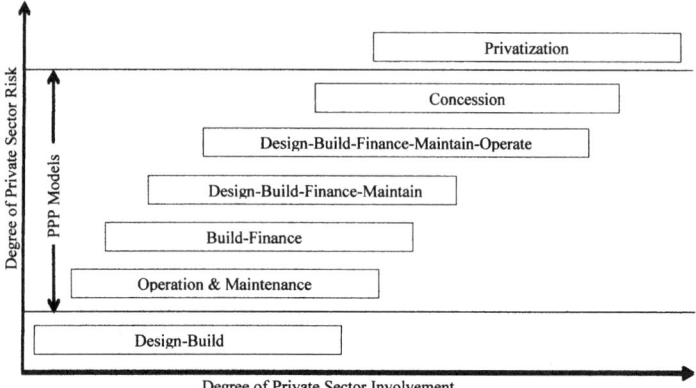

Figure 1. The scale of public–private partnerships: risk transfer and private sector involvement. ©The Canadian Council for Public–Private Partnerships.

The complexity of partnerships also alludes to the fact that the distinction between public and private itself is not very clear. Robertson et al (2012) consider that although people have tried to distinguish between the two sectors and economists have stricter definitions, in reality it is hard to delineate a substantial boundary between public and private.

The realisation that the state could not meet the heavy social responsibilities of providing welfare to its citizens grew enormously during the 1980s, particularly in the United Kingdom and the USA under the leadership of British Prime Minister Margaret Thatcher and US President Ronald Regan. The growth in labour-union activism troubled these heads of state, leading them to institute policies of increased centralisation and private involvement in state functions. The demise of the Soviet Union also served as a swift blow to the promise of state intervention and encouraged the belief in the suitability of a reliance on markets as better managers of future growth. This ideological push continued to grow across the globe in both developed and developing countries. The 1997 World Development Report by the World Bank sets out the following fundamental tasks for the state (World Bank, 1997, p. 4):

- Establishing a foundation of law
- Maintaining a non-distortionary policy environment, including macroeconomic stability
- Investing in basic social services and infrastructure

- Protecting the vulnerable
- Protecting the environment.

Most importantly for this examination, the report emphasised that the 'state need not be the sole provider' of infrastructure, social services and other goods and services (p. 4). Rather, the state should focus on regulating service provision, maintaining quality and equity.

Green (2005, p. 6) sceptically notes that the moves to privatise education have been discursively understated by the usage of the term 'partnerships', as it sounds politically more appropriate. He lists several partnership initiatives used by the UK Government in engagement with the private sector. These initiatives include:

- Private Finance Initiatives (PFIs)
- PPP's faces of the Office for Standards in Education (Ofsted)
- Academies
- Independent specialist schools
- Former Education Action Zones (EAZs) and Excellence in Cities and Clusters (EiCs) programmes
- Private schools in partnership with state schools
- State schools run by private firms
- Historical links between schools and charities and the church
- Local Education Partnerships (LEPs)
- Interventions by the DfES into the work of LEAs forcing a range of 'partnerships'.

Green (2005, p. 6) further notes that this 'trend is global' and similar concepts are prevalent in many parts of the world, particularly the United States, Canada, Australia, New Zealand, parts of Middle East, Europe, Asia, Africa and South America. In fact, as Savas (2000) argues, the term partnership is being used instead of privatisation because of its positive connotations and general acceptability. The arrangements under public–private partnership, however, represent programmes similar to those previously categorised as contract and privatisation.

The phenomenon of public–private partnership or some form of privatisation, as some would argue, is also on the rise in developing countries, so it is important to understand the meaning of 'private' in this situation. There is a range of activity that is generally categorised as 'private'. On the one hand we see private schools running on commercial basis to earn profit; on the other we have private schools operating on a non-profit basis and with philanthropic intentions (Srivastava & Walford, 2007, p. 7). Sometimes the low-cost private initiatives are in fact considered a means of providing mass education to even deprived communities (Tooley & Dixon, 2007, p. 15). Ball (2007, p. 122) asserts that 'partnerships are a major part of the project to reform and 'modernise' local governments and public bodies, by 'cultural re-engineering'. Partnerships are the new way for governments to introduce the private into the public sector and this has become the global discourse, building upon the back of neo-liberal ideology. While these arrangements have existed for quite some time in Pakistan, what is uncomfortable at the moment is the intention of the government to shift the responsibility for educational provision to parents and communities, despite it being constitutionally the responsibility of the state (Farah & Rizvi, 2007).

Public–Private Partnership in Pakistan

Defining private education in the Pakistani context touches upon various discourse and policy narratives. The Ministry of Education in Pakistan has noted these as being:

> Sources of funding: public, private, commercial, community supported etc.
> Specialisation: madrassa, technical and vocational
> Quality: ordinary public schools, low-cost private school, elite schools
> Medium of instruction: Urdu medium, English medium, Mother tongue
> (Ministry of Education, 2006; Aly, 2007)

When one considers public–private partnerships in the Pakistani context, different stakeholders appear to hold a variety of understandings simultaneously. These partnerships arouse various emotions, some viewing them very negatively and others appreciating their contributions to education policy and the possibilities presented for implementation. If we try to classify schooling arrangements in Pakistan over a continuum, we would see at one end the fully public schools and at the other, fully autonomous private schools. The latter are not required to adhere to a national curriculum or the school calendar (Farah & Rizvi, 2007). In between, there are various arrangements including the involvement of various stakeholders – the government, non-governmental organisations (NGOs), community-based organisations (CBOs), communities, philanthropists, religious seminaries, and so on. Farah and Rizvi (2007) point to at least three reasons that have led to the growth of partnerships in Pakistan, including the inability of the government to finance educational provisions to all; international pressure and policy recommendations by donor agencies; and the rise of NGOs and CBOs since 1980s (around 45,000 in 2002 according to Asian Development Bank [ADB] estimates).

In fact, in order to locate the current position of the public–private partnerships in the Pakistani education system, it would be useful to provide a historical analysis of past education policies concerning the issue of privatisation. This is to emphasise the importance of 'periodisation' when analysing policy borrowing: according to Spreen (2004, p. 102) this helps us to understand the historical context within which the policy lands. For this purpose the following policy documents are considered:

- Pakistan Education Conference, 1947
- Proceedings of Education Conference, 1951, including Six-Year National Plan of Education Development, 1951-57
- Commission on National Education, 1959
- Commission on Student Problems and Welfare, 1966
- The Education Policy, 1970
- The Education Policy, 1972-80
- National Education Policy and Implementation Plan, 1979
- National Education Policy, 1992
- National Education Policy, 1998-2010
- Education Sector Reforms, 2000-5
- White Paper on Education in Pakistan, 2007
- National Education Policy, 2009

There appears to be at least four phases of governmental policies towards the role of the private sector in education in Pakistan. The initial phase from 1947 until 1959 shows a relatively positive attitude towards private education on behalf of the government. It generally encouraged the role of the private sector and showed willingness to improve the situation to support growth in the private sector. However, the overall responsibility for the provision of education was seen to be within the remit of the state. In the subsequent phase from 1966 until 1970 the role of the private sector was seen as a problem rather than a source of enhancing quality or efficiency, hence the 1966 Commission Report outlined difficult issues with the private sector and the ways of handling them. Although the government refrained from stopping the work of private providers, it continued to highlight problems with them. In 1972, the government brought an end to earlier criticisms and nationalised all private schools, except religious education institutions. In this way the state took a very negative stance towards the privatisation of education. Not only the creation and management of schools, but also the production of textbooks, were invested in the functions of the state. The fourth phase emerged from a 1979 policy, which reversed the nationalisation and also encouraged private-sector inclusion in education. The 1992 and 1998 education policies went even further and offered various incentives and tax exemptions for private entrepreneurs to establish private schools. A few examples from the 1992 Education Policy are presented below:

- The Government is looking forward to a richer participation of the private sector in education development. The incentives built into the Policy, and the Provincial and National Education Foundations,

Sajid Ali

now in the making, should facilitate the growth of education in the private sector and, in particular, the rural areas
- Grants-in-aid and tax rebates shall be provided to private institutions.
- Companies with a paid-up capital of Rs. 100 million or more shall be required under the law to establish and run educational institutions up to secondary level with funds provided by them.

The education sector reforms under the Musharraf government between 2000-6 favoured public–private partnerships as a strategic choice for attaining educational goals committed under EFA and MDGs. The Education Sector Reform Plan (ESR) (2001-4) provided many incentives for the private sector to 'flourish' in the education sector (Pakistan. Ministry of Education, 2002, p. 63). The incentives included tax exemption, exemption of customs duties for the import of educational equipment, provision of land or subsidised land, along with subsidised utilities. The ESR either initiated or strengthened the partnership programmes which included: the Afternoon School System Up-Grade of Schools through Community Participation Project (CPP); the Adopt-a-School programme; IT programmes in government schools; capacity-building of School Management Committees (SMC); and Education Foundation Programmes.

Level of Institutions	Total	Public (%)		Private (%)	
Pre-Primary	1,081	287	(26.5)	794	(73.5)
Mosque School	14,123	14,035	(99.4)	88	(0.6)
Primary	122,349	105,526	(86.2)	16,823	(13.8)
Middle	38,449	14,334	(37.3)	24,115	(62.7)
Secondary	25,090	10,550	(42.0)	14,540	(58.0)
British System	281	11	(3.9)	270	(96.1)
Intermediate and Degree Colleges	1,882	1,025	(54.5)	857	(45.5)
General Universities	49	31	(63.3)	18	(36.7)
Technical / Professional	1,324	426	(32.2)	898	(67.8)
Vocational / Poly Technique	3,059	916	(29.9)	2,143	(70.1)
Non Formal Basic Education (NFBE)	4,831	2,008	(41.6)	2,823	(58.4)
Deeni Madaris (religious schools)	12,153	354	(2.9)	11,799	(97.1)
Others	3,120	2,241	(71.8)	879	(28.2)
Total	227,791	151,744	(66.6)	76,047	(33.4)

Table III. Number of private and public educational institutions by level.
Source: Pakistan. Ministry of Education (2006) *National Education Census 2005*.

The growth of the private sector due to these policy initiatives has increased substantially. At present more than 30% of education institutions are in the private sector (Pakistan. Ministry of Education, 2006). Table III shows the overall strength of public and private institutions across the country at various levels. It is interesting to note that apart from primary and university education most other levels of education are dominated by the private sector.

Table IV shows official educational expenditures on education over the years. The table also estimates expenditures by the private sector, which is a considerable amount.

Year	GDP (mp) (Rs million)	Public Expenditure on Education (Rs Million)	Private Expenditure on Education (Rs Million)	Total Expenditure on Education (Rs Million)	Public EE as % of GDP	Total EE as % of GDP
1999-2000	3,826,111	71,129.944	11,908.746	83,038.690	1.86	2.17
2000-1	4,162,654	75,887.064	16,709.797	92,596.861	1.82	2.22
2001-2	4,401,699	78,924.971	21,510.848	100,435.819	1.79	2.28
2002-3	4,822,842	89,827.384	26,311.898	116,139.282	1.86	2.41
2003-4	5,640,580	124,274.476	31,112.949	155,387.425	2.20	2.75
2004-5	6,581,103	139,968.001	35,914.000	175,882.001	2.13	2.67
2005-6	7,713,064	170,708.773	40,715.051	211,423.824	2.21	2.74
2006-7	8,706,917	211,778.919	45,516.102	257,295.021	2.43	2.96

Notes:
(1) GDP (at market price) values at current factor cost taken from *Pakistan Economic Survey* (2005-6, 2006-7).
(2) Private Sector Expenditure on Education projected on the basis of data contained in *FBS Census of Private School* (1999-2000) and MoE-NEC (2005-6).

Table IV. Actual gross domestic product (GDP) and expenditure on education (EE) 1991-2007. Source: Pakistan. Ministry of Education. Policy & Planning Wing (2007) *Reforms: education sector 2004-2007,* p. 21.

However, these figures are not able to show the PPP arrangements and contribution. So, to make further sense of these initiatives, we should look at various models of PPP in education as they have existed in Pakistan. This will be followed by a critical evaluation to ascertain the extent to which PPP is a home-grown or imported policy and what results it has produced in achieving stated educational objectives in Pakistan.

Models of PPP in Education in Pakistan

Table V provides a snapshot of some prominent public–private partnership programmes that have been launched in Pakistan, particularly since the 1990s. The programmes have focused mainly on

Sajid Ali

addressing the access issue, particularly for deprived communities and segments of the population such as girls. All of these partnerships involve various partners like government, NGOs, private organisations and communities. The two most significant points as far as the focus of this chapter is concerned are that most of these initiatives have been financially supported by international donor agencies, prominently the World Bank. Secondly, it is also evident that the supposed ownership of these initiatives ultimately lies in the private sector. Farah and Rizvi (2007) conclude that although these partnerships have yielded positive results they are 'often unequal and retain many aspects of hierarchical governance. Moreover, they are transitory (i.e. they are formed for a limited period) and are often intended to support a transition to privatisation (i.e. towards the school being owned, financed and managed by private or community groups or individuals)' (p. 350).

PPP Programme	Dominant focus	Partnership between	Financial support by	Likely ownership after project
Community Support Programme, Balochistan, 1992	Increase girls' enrolment	NGO, Village Education Committee (VEC), Government	USAID, World Bank	Government with conditions
Adopt a School Programme, Sindh, 1998	Quality	Adopter (private or NGO), Government	Adopter, Government	Adopter (private)
Fellowship School Programme, Balochistan, Sindh, 1997	Access	Government, Community	World Bank through Government: per child subsidy model	Community: private model
Social Action Programme (SAP) Community Schools, whole Pakistan, 1992	Access	Government, Community	World Bank, Government of Pakistan	Community: private model
Coaching Centres – AKES, Northern Areas, ongoing	Quality: post-primary	Community, NGO	USAID	Community: private model

Promoting Private Schooling in Rural Sindh (PPRS), 2008	Access, quality	Sindh Education Foundation (SEF), Private entrepreneur	World Bank	Private
Integrated Education Learning Programme (IELP), Sindh, 2009	Quality	SEF, Private Schools	World Bank	Private
Foundation Assisted Schools (FAS), Punjab, 2004	Access, quality	PEF and Private Schools		Private
Technical Training Centre Daharki, Sindh	Technical Education	Engro-led private consortium, Government	Engro-led private consortium	Private
Technical Training Centre, Daultala, 1992	Technical Education	Pakistan Petroleum Limited (PPL)	PPL	Government

Table V. Models of PPP in Pakistan.

Discussion: the importance of PPP and is it baroque? Has it achieved what it claims or has it led to educational apartheid?

Understanding public–private partnership in Pakistan from the lens of policy borrowing is a complex issue. It is indeed quite hard to determine precisely when and whether the policy was actually imported or if it emerged as a response to local needs. Indeed I tend to agree with Spreen (2004) who argued that 'in this era of global circulation of ideas, movements, and people, it is difficult to pinpoint precisely when and how a concept arrives' (p. 110). Nevertheless the historical developments of the idea within the Pakistani context as presented above suggest that the idea of private involvement in public educational provisions have been operative in Pakistan since its inception. However, the idea had gone through significant transformation both in terms of its ideology and quantum. The official policy documents since 1990s started utilising and, in fact, promoting, public–private partnerships to achieve the EFA commitments that government found hard to fulfil given its limited resources. Here, the idea of 'magistracy of influence' by Lawn and Lingard (2002, p. 292) is quite relevant to consider to see how educational policy gets shaped in the era of globalisation. Taking an example from European education policy they argue that the interaction of national and international policy elites plays a significant role in shaping education policy ideas in any country. The magistracy of influence is 'a policy elite that acts across borders, displays a similar habitus, have a feel for the same policy game and are, in a sense, bearers of an emergent European educational policy and policy space' (p. 292). The shifts in policy in Pakistan towards privatisation after the 1980s may have been a result of the magistracy operative in Pakistan, where bureaucrats, academics, consultants, donors, NGO representatives and politicians start to exchange ideas beyond formal channels and gradually build common discourse and consensual ideas like public–private partnerships.

Table V above showing various models of PPP operating in Pakistan also demonstrates that since 1990 the donor agencies, and particularly the World Bank, have taken a keen interest in supporting various PPP initiatives in Pakistan. Ali (2008) argues that the donor agencies in Pakistan enjoy a very influential position in determining national education policy based on their financial and knowledge resources. In fact, financial loans by the World Bank have been considered as an example of policy imposition as loans carry explicit policy conditionalities (Dale, 1999). In the case of PPP in Pakistan it is visible that donor financing is quite instrumental in trying out various models of PPP, suggesting a policy push that needs to be adopted by the government (see Table V, and also Table II). There is also some research work, sponsored or supported by international organisations, which has built a discursive knowledge base, consistently demonstrating that the involvement of the private and non-governmental sector in education is a cost-effective option (see for example Farah, 1996; Aslam, 2007; Andrabi et al, 2008; ASER-Pakistan 2010, 2010). In reading their various scholarly and policy texts, it has to be acknowledged that the record of government schools in Pakistan has remained dismal. Throughout the past decade and more, private schools have been considered providers of better-quality education.

Looking simplistically, the policy of PPP has global traces and appears a borrowed policy for Pakistan under the aegis of international organisations. However, a critical scrutiny would reveal that PPP as a favoured international policy was introduced by Pakistani policy makers to address some local issues (perhaps under the influence of magistracy discussed earlier). For example, the subsequent policies in Pakistan have miserably failed to ensure access to all school-going children. The government has also lacked resources for fulfilling these targets. The international favour for PPP perhaps provided an opportunity for the policy makers to address their deficiencies through this novel idea. The 1998 Education Policy asserts that 'the government alone could not carry the burden of the whole education process [and hence the] private enterprises will be encouraged to open education institutions, particularly in rural areas' (Pakistan. Ministry of Education, 1998, p. 108). This is exactly what (Silova, 2004, p. 75) refers to as 'adopting the language of new allies', whereby the local policy elites adopt the international discourse to their own objectives and the apparently international policy, may, in fact be a choice preferred by the local policy elites. In fact the context of Pakistan within which the PPP policy arrived is very different from the context where this policy originated: the United Kingdom or the USA. In Pakistan, until 1972, private schools were initially officially supported by the state through Grants-in-Aid programmes. Then all schools were nationalised and gradually de-nationalised. It has been noted in previous sections that the government also lacked resources to finance education even if it wished to do so. We also see the enormous growth of NGOs participating in the provision of social services. While PPP in the United Kingdom or other developed countries is pre-dominantly concerned with quality, PPP in Pakistan has focused pre-dominantly on access. Given these contextual realities, PPP did not simply land in Pakistan. While PPP is part of a global education policy field, it interacts with local specificities, history and politics to become embedded in education policy (Ozga & Jones, 2006). In fact Table V shows that the policy is being tried out through various projects so as to come up with a contextually relevant model of PPP in Pakistan.

The outcomes of PPP initiatives shared in Table V above, show relatively positive outcomes particularly in terms of teachers' and students' attendance and time spent on tasks (Farah & Rizvi, 2007). In addition the LEAPS study (Andrabi et al, 2008) and ASER reports (ASER-Pakistan 2010, 2010) show that low-cost private schools are providing a relatively better quality of education. These positive outcomes need to be scrutinised against various other concerns such as: Is PPP in Pakistan a move to the gradual privatisation of education? If so, who will the private/semi-private schools be answerable to: the public or owners? Will low-cost private schools or PPP initiatives sustain better quality? What will the power relationship be among various partners: private organisations, governments, donors, NGOs? These are often-debated questions which arise in relation to the discussion on PPP and which are still without settled answers. Indeed the trend of privatisation in Pakistan has shown a substantial increase, and current contribution of the private sector stands at just over 33% (see Table III above). It is also alarming that the government's decision to promote PPP is driven by financial concerns. Though Pakistan has remained in a difficult financial situation, the budgetary and political priorities of the government suggest that education is a low-priority area. Having this as a low priority has led to the un-regulated privatisation of the education sector, which has already created a situation some refer to as 'educational apartheid' (Rahman, 2004; Siddiqui, 2007). Education, rather than becoming a resource for promoting equality of opportunity in society, becomes a source of inequality itself, even for graduates. It is time for the government to think seriously about its PPP policy, and especially to consider how it can become advantageous for its citizens.

References

Ahsan, M. (2005) Politicization of Bilateral Aid and Educational Development in Pakistan, *Educational Studies,* 31(3), 235-250.

Ali, S. (2009) *Governing Education Policy in a Globalising World: the sphere of authority of the Pakistani state.* Edinburgh: University of Edinburgh.

Ali, S. (2008) National Policy Global Imperatives: role of international agencies in education policy in Pakistan. Paper presented at the British Association for International and Comparative Education (BAICE) Annual Conference: 'Internationalisation in Education: culture, context and difference', 4-6 September, Glasgow.

Ali, S. & Tahir, M.S.A. (2009) Reforming Education in Pakistan: tracing global links, *Journal of Research and Reflections in Education,* 3(1), 1-16.

Altbach, P.G. (2004) Globalisation and the University: myths and realities in an unequal world, *Tertiary Education and Management*, 10(1), 3-25.

Aly, J.H. (2007) *Education in Pakistan.* A White Paper Revised: document to debate and finalize the National Education Policy. http://www.moe.gov.pk/nepr (accessed 14 March 2007).

Andrabi, T., Das, J., Khwaja, A. I., Vishwanath, T., Zajonc, T. & LEAPS Team (2008) *Pakistan – Learning and Educational Achievements in Punjab Schools (LEAPS): insights to inform the education policy debate.* Washington, DC: World Bank.

ASER-Pakistan 2010 (2010) *Annual Status of Education Report 2010.* Lahore: South Asian Forum for Educational Development.

Aslam, M. (2007) *The Relative Effectiveness of Government and Private Schools in Pakistan: are girls worse off?* Cambridge: RECOUP, DFID and University of Cambridge.

Ball, S.J. (2007) *Education Plc: understanding private sector participation in public sector education.* London: Routledge.

Carnoy, M. (2006) *Globalization and Educational Reform: what planners need to know.* Paris: UNESCO.

Curtis, L.A. (2007) U.S. Aid to Pakistan: countering extremism through education reform. *Heritage Lectures,* 8 June (1029), 1-5.

Dale, R. (1999) Specifying Globalisation Effects on National Policy: a focus on the mechanism, *Journal of Education Policy,* 14(1), 1-17.

Farah, I. (1996) *Roads to Success: self-sustaining primary school change in rural Pakistan*, rev. edn. Oslo and Karachi: IMTEC and AKU-IED.

Farah, I. & Rizvi, S. (2007) Public-Private Partnerships: implications for primary schooling in Pakistan, *Social Policy and Administration,* 41(4), 339-354.

Green, C. (2005) *The Privatization of State Education: public partners, private dealings.* London: Routledge.

Jessop, B. (2002) *The Future of the Capitalist State.* Cambridge: Polity Press.

Jones, K. & Alexiadou, N. (2001) Traveling Policy: local spaces. Paper presented at the Global and the National Symposium, ECER, Lille, September.

Lawn, M. & Lingard, B. (2002) Constructing a European Policy Space in Educational Governance: the role of transnational policy actors, *European Educational Research Journal*, 1(2), 290-307.

Ministry of Education (2006) *Green Papers.* http://www.moe.gov.pk/nepr (accessed 14 March 2007).

Mujahid-Mukhtar, E. (2011) *Situation Analysis of the Education Sector.* Islamabad: UNESCO Pakistan.

Ozga, J. & Jones, R. (2006) Travelling and Embedded Policy: the case of knowledge transfer, *Journal of Education Policy*, 21(1), 1-17.

Pakistan. Federal Bureau of Statistics (1998) *50 Years of Pakistan.* Karachi: Manager of Publications.

Pakistan. Federal Bureau of Statistics (2011) *Pakistan Social and Living Measurement Survey (2010-11) – PSLM 2010-11.* Islamabad: Government of Pakistan, Statistics Division.

Pakistan. Ministry of Education (1998) *National Education Policy: Iqra 1998-2010.* Islamabad: Government of Pakistan.

Pakistan. Ministry of Education (2002) *Education Sector Reforms: Action Plan 2001-2004.* Islamabad: Government of Pakistan.

Pakistan. Ministry of Education (2006) *National Education Census 2005 – Pakistan.* Islamabad: Academy of Educational Planning and Management, Statistics Division Federal Bureau of Statistics. Government of Pakistan.

Pakistan. Ministry of Education (2008) *Pakistan Education Statistics 2008-09.* Islamabad: NEMIS, AEPAM, Government of Pakistan.

Pakistan. Ministry of Education. Policy & Planning Wing (2007) *Reforms: Education Sector 2004-2007.* Islamabad: Government of Pakistan.

Pakistan. Ministry of Finance (2011) *Pakistan Economic Survey 2010-11.* Islamabad: Government of Pakistan.

Rahman, T. (2004) *Denizens of Alien Worlds: a study of education, inequality and polarization in Pakistan.* Karachi: Oxford University Press.

Rizvi, F. & Lingard, B. (2010) *Globalizing Education Policy.* London: Routledge.

Robertson, S., Mundy, L.K., Verger, A., & Menashy, F. (2012) An Introduction to Public Private Partnerships and Education Governance, in S. Robertson, L.K. Mundy, A. Verger & F. Menashy (Eds) *Public Private Partnerships in Education: new actors and modes of governance in a globalizing world*, pp. 1-20. Cheltenham: Edward Elgar.

Rosenau, J.N. (1999) Toward an Ontology for Global Governance, in M. Hewson & T. J. Sinclair (Eds) *Approaches to Global Governance Theory*, pp. 287–301. Albany: State University of New York Press.

Rosenau, J.N. (2000) Governance, Order, and Change in World Politics, in J.N. Rosenau & E.-O. Czempiel (Eds) *Governance without Government: order and change in world politics,* pp. 1-29. Cambridge: Cambridge University Press.

Savas, E. S. (2000) *Privatization and Public-Private Partnerships.* New York: Chatham House.

Scholte, J. A. (2000) *Globalization: a critical introduction.* New York: Palgrave.

Siddiqui, S. (2007) *Rethinking Education in Pakistan: perceptions, practices, and possibilities.* Lahore: Paramount Publishing Enterprise.

Silova, I. (2004) Adopting the Language of the New Allies, in G. Steiner-Khamsi (Ed.) *The Global Politics of Educational Borrowing and Lending,* pp. 75-87. New York: Teachers College Press.

Spreen, C.A. (2004) Appropriating Borrowed Policies: outcomes-based education in South Africa, in G. Steiner-Khamsi (Ed.) *The Global Politics of Educational Borrowing and Lending,* pp. 101-113. New York: Teachers College Press.

Spring, J. (2008) *Globalization of Education: an introduction.* New York: Routledge.

Srivastava, P. & Walford, G. (2007) *Private Schooling in Less Economically Developed Countries: Asian and African perspectives.* Oxford: Symposium Books.

Tooley, J. & Dixon, P. (2007) Private Education for Low-Income Families: results from a global research project, in P. Srivastava & G. Walford (Eds) *Private Schooling in Less Economically Developed Countries: Asian and African perspectives*, pp. 15-40. Oxford: Symposium Books.

UNESCO. (2012) *EFA Global Monitoring Report 2012 – Youth and Skills: putting education to work.* Paris: UNESCO Publishing.

World Bank (1997) *World Development Report 1997: the state in a changing world.* New York: World Bank.

CHAPTER THREE

The Politics of Foreign Aid and Policy Borrowing in Palestine

MOHAMMED ALROZZI

Introduction

An enormous body of literature has been written on globalisation, its impact on various areas of our lives and its covert and overt agents. The movement of goods, knowledge and culture from the centre to the periphery is part of the human experience regardless of whom it involves.

In the distant past, knowledge was brought from the Orient to the West with traders, scholars and immigrant tribes. However, unlike today, this kind of smooth movement was not imposed on nations, or controlled by global rules, targets and legal agreements. It was a 'soft' human activity. Nowadays, we are living in a world where increased connectedness is welcomed, encouraged and, sometimes, is enforced. A new world has emerged, governed by neo-liberal vision and ideology with its focus on free trade and markets, privatisation and decentralisation. This approach is tailored to maximise capital interests and achieve macro-economic growth. However, as many economists and sociologists argue, it increases inequality amongst people, communities and nations. Given, its standardised nature, it is said to undermine national cultures, state sovereignty and socio-political aspiration. Within the globalised world, these ideas and ensuing arguments fast spill over into various areas, including education.

In the field of education there are many ways in which globalisation appears to impact upon policy and its implementation. Policy borrowing is one. An increasing literature on comparative education is being written, focusing on the contexts and stimuli that facilitate policy borrowing. Attention is being paid to its advantages and drawbacks, for both countries that borrow and lend. Literature highlights the role of international non-governmental organisations (NGOs), intergovernmental institutions and donors in policy borrowing. One aspect of policy borrowing, foreign aid, I believe, ensured sustainable communication for many decades, between developing and developed countries and became one of the tools for enforcing laws, reforms and financial adjustments. Thus, the role of foreign aid, international actors and national elites deserves further attention, especially for the recipients in developing and fragile countries. The Palestinian Territories, as one of the most aid-dependent countries, is certainly one such 'fragile country'. It has constructed its educational system in the last two decades, following the Palestinian Authority takeover of responsibility for education, and as a result of the Oslo Accords.

Indeed, the Palestinian education system has emerged in the midst of the on-going crisis of constant conflict and a lack of resources. However, progress has been made in the last decade towards developing a largely secular and modern Palestinian education system. When a fledgling Ministry of Education and Higher Education (MoEHE) was first established in 1994, it took over a neglected and broken-down system. Over the last two decades, the Ministry struggled to establish its own basic mechanisms in terms of planning, budgeting and coordination, as well as by reviewing the education policies of others. Curriculum development was a particular challenge for the MoEHE, as it was the first opportunity to develop a Palestinian curriculum after a long history of domination by other countries.

That is why it is important to explore the recent construction of the educational system around this benchmark, the Oslo Accords. Such an approach enables a coherent study of how foreign aid is becoming one of the tools for change especially though the procedures of policy borrowing.

Barakat (2007) suggests that: 'The struggle over Palestinian education offers interesting insights ... [as] it brings into sharp focus issues raised by role of the education in anti-colonial and modernisation projects throughout the world.' These insights are invaluable and relevant to our current discussion of the politics of policy borrowing.

This chapter aims to explore the issue of policy borrowing by showing how foreign aid plays a significant role in facilitating policy borrowing in education. Moreover, it will outline why policy borrowing is not always beneficial for national governments.

The chapter is composed of two parts. The first focuses on the Palestinian educational system, globalisation and foreign aid. It aims to contextualise and provide an overview of the Palestinian educational system, its recent construction and the background context. It then moves to review the effects of globalisation on education in the Palestinian Territories and the main manifestations of convergence between global and national socio-political and educational forces. Given that the Palestinian Territories are one of the most aid-dependent entities, the issue of aid and its impact on policy borrowing in education will be discussed.

The second part of the chapter defines policy borrowing in education, by addressing the stimuli and conditions that facilitate it. Examples of policy borrowing in the Palestinian Territories are presented. The chapter ends by critically responding to the questions of why local and national governments borrow policies, and draws on examples from Palestinian education. In so doing, it highlights a range of issues about borrowing, including some of the problems and various wide-ranging concerns.

Constructing the Palestinian Educational System: a background history

After the Oslo Accords [1] in 1993, Palestinians took over responsibility for education in part of the occupied Palestinian territories [2] which became self-governed by the Palestinian Authority (PA). This was the first instance in which the Palestinians had assumed responsibility for the administration of their educational system. Prior to that, the education of Palestinians had been undertaken by a succession of regimes including Ottoman, British, Jordanian, Egyptian and Israeli as well as by a United Nations agency (UNRWA) [3] set up in 1949 to ensure the education of refugees (Mazawi, 2000, p. 371). The Oslo Accords were an important benchmark in the history of the education system, especially in the environment of post-conflict reconstruction. The Accords provided a special chance for radical change as the old political regimes had been challenged and subsequently were replaced by a new 'political space'. Equally important, for this opportunity, is the weakness of bureaucracy, the availability of new resources and the high expectations of the community after a conflict (World Bank, 2005, p. 26).

Following the conflict that brought radical changes to politics and policy, Palestinians started to build their own education system. Developing a suitable, coherent and appropriate curriculum was a central step toward reconstruction of the education system. This process, which is typical to any post-conflict reconstruction context, comes about through reviewing textbooks, implementing reform gradually and revising the assessment system (World Bank, 2005). Exploring the education policies around the benchmark of the Oslo Accords, which separates two different education eras, will provide a sound understanding of the main determinants and factors that influenced the construction of the present developing system. In the environment of the Palestinian Territories, it is necessary to situate policy borrowing and lending in the context of the need to establish new and dramatically rehabilitating educational systems.

Globalisation of Education

Steiner-Khamsi (2004) stresses the point that from time to time, some 'epidemics' emerge in educational research. These epidemics start with a *virus* that spread quickly amongst scholars, then circulate within the scholarly community, eventually becoming an 'epidemic' when it is commented upon by almost each and every author (Steiner-Khamsi, 2004, p. 2).

In my mind, there is no doubt that the concept of globalisation has become an epidemic that scholars and authors feel compelled to address in their work. This has created vast amounts of literature about globalisation, from widely different perspectives (Steiner-Khamsi, 2004, p. 2). For example, cultural anthropologists tend to explore globalisation across nations in order to understand why it takes place in different ways across cultures (e.g. Comaroff & Comaroff, 2001). Historians are keen to explore earlier processes of convergence, or previous forms of transnational and trans-regional dependencies, similar to 'globalisation', in order to understand the differences in modern globalisation (e.g. Hopkins, 2002; Sen, 2002b). The richness of literature on this area means that there is no uniform definition of globalisation or definite explanation of what globalisation involves (Scholte, 2002).

Globalisation, according to some writers, refers to the 'interconnectedness between people and places, between time and space' (Giddens, 1990). With globalisation, 'borders between countries seem to vanish and individuals are more linked to each other' (Castells, 1999, 2010; Robertson et al, 2007). This process has many dimensions including the technological, economic, social, cultural, political and geopolitical (Castells, 1999).

Although the notion of globalisation is usually linked with free markets, privatisation, entrepreneurship, knowledge economy and the global trade agreements (i.e. an economic phenomenon), there is growing literature on the globalisation of services, cultures and public goods including education. International education agreements and summits are the main vehicles of globalised education. As Donn and Al Manthri (2010) emphasise: 'The result has been a drive towards the achievement of specified outcomes and adoption of standardised curricula and teaching models' (p. 29). Moreover, 'education has come to resemble a private rather than a public good' they suggest.

The effects of globalisation on national governments are explicit and can be seen in the tension between economic and cultural objectives (Rizvi et al, 2005). Moreover, it is apparent in the rhetoric, discourse and practice of education at national levels. As Ali (2009) points out 'globalisation is represented in rhetoric: a discursive rhetoric is built through research, media and rhetorical presentations of politicians.' Given these considerations, the following section highlights some examples of the effects of globalisation relating to the Palestinian situation.

The Effect for Globalisation on the Palestinian Educational System

Although Palestine has been under conflict it is certainly not immune to global trends in education. Indeed, globalisation in its various forms and forces has had tremendous impact upon recent developments in education in Palestine. Palestinians began to establish their first-ever education system from scratch, from a *tabula rasa*, without prior experience in the field. They based their observation on what was happening throughout the world (Mahshi, 2002). It is true that the Israeli system was in place, but it did not reflect the ambitions and needs of post-Oslo Palestinian education. Secondly, donors were very interested in funding and thus intervening in the educational agenda. Thirdly, Palestinian experts were abandoning the traditional methods of learning and teaching and looking for a change in order to meet the fast-developing global trends.

The impact of globalisation has been manifested in the first Five-Year Plan developed by the Ministry of Education and Higher Education (MoEHE) in 2000. The main goals of the Plan were to provide access to education for all children, to improve quality, to develop formal and non-formal education, to strengthen management capacity and to enhance human resources in the education system (MoEHE, 2000). Interestingly, most of the goals reflect the attention given by the international community to quality and access as asserted in the EFA framework, and which was reaffirmed in the World Education Forum in Dakar in 2000. Interestingly, this was the year in which the Education Plan was published. In the Plan, education was viewed as human right, a basis for citizenship, a tool for social and economic development, the basis for values and democracy and continuous renewable and participatory processes (MoEHE, 2000). These themes can be seen in an educational context throughout many international documents and plans. This common language should not be surprising, as one of the requirements of the EFA Framework was to develop the EFA national plan, with set of targets with which to assess progress (UNESCO, 2000; Sommers, 2004; Nicolai, 2007). Moreover, knowing that The Jomtien Conference of 1990 brought together a heterogeneous combination of governmental and non-governmental organisations (Steiner-Khamsi, 2004, p. 169) makes it easier to comprehend the influence of international movements on the plans and policies of national governments. Nicolai (2007) points out that the Five-Year Plan was driven initially by the requirements of donors but later it became the tool and guiding map of the Ministry of Education in the Palestinian Territories.

Similar themes can be observed in the recent Education Development Strategic Plan 2008-12. The new Plan is contextualised within the discourses of international movements and toward achieving MDG and EFA targets (MoEHE, 2008). Moreover it reflects the attention given to Technical and Vocational Education and Training (TVET), which was neglected in the first Plan despite being on the international agenda of OECD since the 1990s (Taylor & Henry, 2007).

Mundy and Murphy (2000) claim that international agents have been the driving force in building an international model of education, and especially at a discursive level. They argue that this model is imposed frequently upon national governments. And as Steiner-Khamsi (2004) notes, this kind of 'pressure from the international community on low-income countries in the form of international agreements', like EFA targets and the MDGs, is not imaginary (Steiner-Khamsi, 2004, p. 5). She suggests this is the case especially as 'development assistance programs' are being run by a coalition of governments, international non-governmental and multilateral organisations. This is not to criticise the smooth exchange of knowledge, practices and policies amongst nations because, as Tilly (2004) puts it, 'humanity has globalized repeatedly'. What differentiates globalisation between the fifteenth and twentieth centuries is the emphasis on 'commerce, commitment, and coercion' in the latter century (Tilly, 2004, pp. 13-14). Sen (2002a, b) outlines that our modern globalisation is featured by competition and driven by global capitalism, which was not in place in the other eras of human history.

This intensification of the processes of internationalisation and the adaptation of local policies to meet international standards, takes place for several reasons. Beerkens (2008) makes a distinction among three reasons for adopting external models when he states:

> compliance with conditions in order to gain access to financial resources (coercive adoption); the adoption of external models as a standard response to uncertainty (voluntary imitation); and gaining legitimacy through the adoption of best practice or conformation to role models (normative adoption). (Beerkens, 2008, p. 24)

However, regardless of the reasons behind internationalisation, developing countries face many challenges in ensuring standardisation in education processes and models. This is especially the case as there are unique constraints – notably the lack of sufficient resources to keep pace with international standards. Developing countries cannot respond in the same way as developed countries to the global policies encouraged by the International Monetary Fund (IMF), the World Trade Organisation, or other international influential actors' guidelines

(Beerkens, 2008; Rawolle & Lingard, 2008). Therefore, the effects of internationalisation are often out of the control of the national government (World Bank, 2002).

The convergence of processes and models depends upon extensive intervention by agents at local and international levels. It has been noted that, generally, the role of multilateral organisations (e.g. United Nations [UN] agencies such as UNESCO and the Organisation for Economic Cooperation and Development [OECD]) and international non-governmental organisations (e.g. Save the Children) is apparent in the promotion of educational reforms based on particular approaches and practices (Steiner-Khamsi, 2004, p. 169). This also applies to the development of education plans for the Palestinian Territories in particular.

In the Palestinian case, the United Nations does indeed play a key role especially through its education-related agencies, notably the United Nations Children's Fund (UNICEF), UNESCO and the United Nations Development Programme (UNDP). However, as each is concerned to implement its own priorities, there are inevitable disjunctures as well as overlaps. In the Education Sector Working Group (ESWG) chaired by MoEHE, UNESCO provided the Secretariat and played an essential role in curriculum development through the International Institute for Educational Planning (Nicolai, 2007). That organisation and the Italian government have been involved in supporting education in Palestine since the beginning of the post-Oslo Accords era (Mahshi, 2002). They work alongside other agencies, some of whom prioritise infrastructure while others prioritise protection, and yet others prioritise nutrition within schools.

As noted previously, globalisation's effect is explicit. In the Palestinian case, this intervening, modelling or forming of the educational policies and practices by international actors would not be possible without bilateral and multilateral aid. This is especially due to the nature of the Palestinian territories as a poor developing 'country' that lacks sovereignty and control over its natural and man-made resources and policies. The demographic characteristic also adds much to this speciality [4] (Brynen, 2000). The subject of aid is increasingly becoming salient and questionable as the Palestinian Territories become one of the most dependent countries, receiving aid with limited positive impact on the ground (Sayigh, 2007; More, 2010). The following sections will address aid in the Palestinian Territories, drawing attention to the main donors and actors in the arena of international development. They will provide an understanding as to how aid contributes to the structure of education policies in the Palestinian Territories.

Aid as a Political Tool

When the Oslo Accords was signed in 1993, donors showed their interest and willingness to support Palestinians. They considered it an opportunity to support the building of a Palestinian governance system, foster economic growth and maintain the peace process through its first hard milestones (More, 2008). At the same time, aid was one of the tools of pressure used to encourage Palestinians to accept the conditions of the Agreement and to make 'painful decisions' (Le More, 2008). Additionally, many donor countries considered funding as an entry point to playing a high-profile role in the so-called Israel-Palestinian conflict. With reference to education, aid has been used to put conditions on the Palestinian Authority. And, as it will be demonstrated later in the chapter, aid is an important medium for policy borrowing, especially for an aid-dependant entity like the Palestinian Territories.

It is estimated that net official development assistance (ODA) received per capita in the Palestinian Territories is one of the highest in the world (MAS, 2011) with an average of US$463 per capita in the last four years. Even more interestingly, in 2008 it was the highest per capita in the world with US$675 per capita (data from World Bank website, 2010).[5]

Figure 1 shows the net ODA to the Palestine National Authority (PNA) since the Oslo Accords and the steep increase in the ODA to the PNA in the last five years.

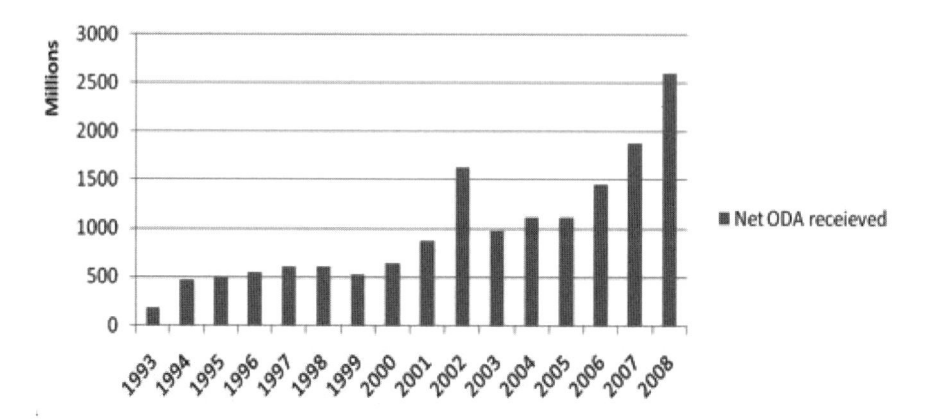

Figure 1. Net ODA received by Palestinian Authority (1993-2008).
Source: World Bank Database. Excel sheet extracted and downloaded from: http://data.worldbank.org/sites/default/files/data/wdiandgdf_excel.zip (accessed 3 November 2010 and triangulated with data in http://www.oecd.org/dataoecd/52/1893167.xls).

When one compares the ODA received per capita by the Palestinian Territories with other countries in similar contexts (where armed conflict is presumed to be a key determinant) interesting data emerges. Iraq, for example, which receives a massive amount of money every year, reached US$9.87 billion in 2008 (World Bank data, 2010), but its net ODA received per capita was approximately the half of the correspondent value as provided to Palestinians. Figure 2 compares between Iraq and Palestinian Territories.

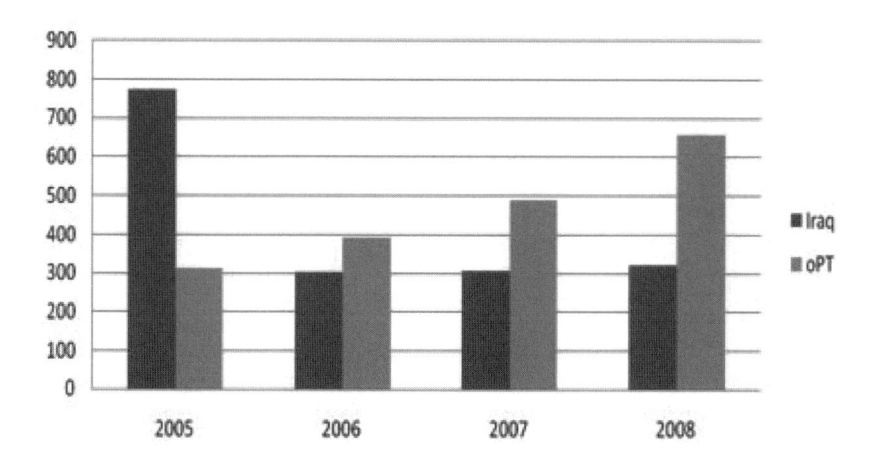

Figure 2. Net ODA received per capita (current US$).
Source: World Bank Database. Excel sheet extracted and downloaded from: http://data.worldbank.org/sites/default/files/data/wdiandgdf_excel.zip

Figure 2 suggests the level to which the Palestinian Authority depends on aid. This is indicated by MAS, Palestine Economic Policy Research Institute, who reported an increase in aid by almost 500% in the last decade (MAS, 2011).

This is supported by the debate on aid effectiveness in Palestine, as featured in studies by various economists. Le More (2008) claims the PNA continues to function only because of support pledged into its budget from international donors. At the same time, the Palestinian Government itself admitted that 'stability and growth in the Palestinian economy remains largely dependent on public expenditure, backed by substantial external aid' (PNA, 2010, p. 7). The high level of aid dependence indicates the importance of aid in forming national policies and the role of donors, in setting the agenda and in decision making. This role will be discussed in more detail in later sections.

Defining Borrowing and Lending

Policy borrowing and lending are two of the many phenomena of globalisation (Popkewitz, 2004, p. vii); more specifically they are media through which policies are globalised. In education research, and especially in the field of comparative education, policy borrowing has been a key concern (Phillips & Ochs, 2004; Waldow, 2009). Recently, an increasing body of knowledge has been generated on the levels of convergence and policy borrowing, with discussions about why national governments borrow policies, how policy borrowing influences national policies and the circumstances in which borrowing usually takes place. This area becomes increasingly important as it enables an understanding of how educational policies and systems are constructed and the impact of globalisation on them.

The diversity of issues included in policy borrowing and the complexity and uncertain nature of the convergence between countries' policies make it very hard to define the exact circumstances of education-policy borrowing. Indeed, there has always been much agonising and disagreement about how to define policy borrowing, the methods of borrowing and the purposes behind it. However a consensus can be reached on one thing: namely, that among the aims of policy borrowing is the intention to learn from foreign experiences, to identify aspects of other countries' policies and consider those that might serve as examples to be applied at a national and domestic level. Authors use many expressions synonymously like copying, appropriation, importation and transfer (Phillips & Ochs, 2004).

The concept of 'educational borrowing' is usually used to denote the process of conscious adoption of external education policies, philosophies and concepts, through which education is transferred to the domestic context (Phillips & Ochs, 2004, p. 774). It can be perceived as the direct and indirect importing and appropriating of ideas, thoughts and concepts, within national systems and across underlying layers. Popkewitz (2004) differentiates between borrowing and copying by asserting that the former 'provides a concept to examine how patterns of thought move through and are transmuted in different layers of the local and global systems' (Popkewitz, 2004, p. ix). In a similar context, Waldow (2009) argues that policy convergence between two countries does not necessarily constitute a proof that borrowing '*transfer*' has taken place between countries (Waldow, 2009, pp. 479-480). It is therefore difficult to use examples of policy convergence between Palestine and the rest of the world as educational transfer. However, examples in this chapter aim to explore the process of borrowing and its influence on the national level. This is not to suggest that chasing a definite example of policy borrowing would be easy. Waldow (2009) points out that '[e]ducational borrowing does not always occur from one nation state to another; international discursive currents that are less easy to pin down as concerns their geographical origin can also serve as a source of policies that can be borrowed' (Waldow, 2009, p. 480).

What Can Be Borrowed?

Ochs & Phillips (2002) summarised aspects of educational policy in education by asking what could be borrowed. These range from *'guiding philosophy'* (e.g. equality of educational opportunities), targets and *'goals'* (e.g. EFA and gender equality), *'strategies'* (e.g. training and additional funding), *'enabling structures'* (e.g. new types of school, general organisational reform) and *'processes'* (e.g. assessment procedures and grade repetition) to *'techniques'* (teaching methods) (Ochs & Phillips, 2002, pp. 329-330).

As demonstrated earlier, policy borrowing takes place at different levels (rhetoric, discourse and practices); through various institutions (government, private sector, NGOs); and is facilitated by multilateral and bilateral aid. Donn and Al Manthri (2010) point out: 'Language and rhetoric have become central features of policy and practice – from a borderless world, the knowledge economy, outcome-based education, to citizenship and entrepreneurship studies' (Donn & Al Manthri, 2010, p. 22). Such discursive statements are salient in understanding the process of borrowing and the impact of borrowing on the national level.

Knowledge-Based Economy

In the Palestinian case, there is strong evidence that education is influenced by the discourse and concepts of neo-liberalism, notably by the rhetoric of a knowledge-based economy. This features in different MoEHE publications. During the Thirteenth Government's term in office, it aimed to work toward a group of goals; one of them being:

> to provide essential economic stimulus to alleviate poverty. Our longer term objective is to build a vibrant, knowledge-based economy capable of producing competitive goods and delivering high quality services. A solid economic foundation will be the basis of our people's prosperity and social welfare. (PNA, 2009, p. 10)

Similar themes are evident in different policy papers, plans and reports to donors. For example, the PNA concluded, in its vision to the future Palestinian State in the Palestinian Reform and Development Plan (PRDP):

> The Palestinian economy is open to other markets around the world and strives to produce high value-added, competitive goods and services, and, over the long term, to be a knowledge-based economy. (PNA, 2007, p. 4)

This notion of a knowledge-based economy and its links to education on a connotative level is not coincidental but political. It aims to achieve many goals; chief amongst which is the aim of attracting international donors and legitimising their reform plans (both will be discussed later).

However, policy borrowing is not taking place only on this level, but also in practice, as discussed in the following section.

TVET and Career Guidance

As a result of donor-aid funding to Palestinian Territories, there are many examples of borrowing and lending of Technical and Vocational Education and Training (TVET). The PNA has included many strategic goals in its Thirteenth Government's programme. The review of these goals is significant as it highlights some of the trends of the borrowing body. One of the goals of the programme is to enhance the skills of Palestinian workers to enable them to compete in the global economy through:

– Rejuvenating the National Vocational and Technical Education and Training Strategy
– Matching vocational and technical training with labour-market needs
– Enhancing the quality of vocational and technical education and training in cooperation with relevant PNA bodies
– Distributing vocational and technical training centres throughout the occupied territory.

(Program of the Thirteenth Government 2009, p. 25)

The interest of the PNA in TVET has not come by accident but through complex processes and decisions. Chief amongst them is the convergence with international key actors who were active in the development and financing of the TVET sector. In addition, TVET has also been on the international agenda of the OECD since the 1990s (Taylor & Henry, 2000). Indeed, many donors support the development of the TVET programme in Palestine. However, each adopts different approaches and targets in different areas, based on their interests as well as their expertise. Some donors construct the infrastructure and facilities of TVET, build the capacity of students and teachers through training, or develop curricula for TVET. Some would target the formal governmental system, while others focus on non-formal training as well as on private institutions. The goals behind the diverse interventions vary. Some international donors link TVET with poverty alleviation and think that it has the potential to contribute to achieving the fundamental targets, MDGs; and eradicating poverty (Maintz, 2004). Others intervene to diversify skills and to serve the local market that need professional technicians. Some others think of it as a medium to ensure engagement of disadvantaged groups, such as those with a disability, through participation in production.

In particular, the Swiss Agency for Development and Cooperation (SDC) supported this sector through focusing on planning at a central level (Niclolai, 2007, p. 81). Likewise, Deutsche Gesellschaft für Internationale Zusammenarbeit (GIZ) is an important key aid agency promoting it.

Another relevant example involving TVET is a career-counselling curriculum, recently funded (February 2012) by the United States Agency for International Development (USAID) in the West Bank (oPt) to support the MoEHE and TVET programme. As a result of the project, USAID handed over TVET's Career Counselling Curricula to the Ministry to be integrated into the national education system. As reported by USAID, the Curricula will provide Palestinian students with career information and skills to help them to prepare for the job market. Moreover, it will give students some idea about work experience and information about possible careers as well as teach them career-path planning strategies. Interestingly, one of the important aspects of the Career Education Curricula, as claimed by USAID, is its unique approach in establishing linkages with the private sector.

The Technical and Vocational Education and Training Program was originally funded by USAID. The programme aimed to strengthen and diversify the skills of young Palestinians through developing the Palestinian technical and vocational education sector, in order to give young Palestinians the skills needed to enter and succeed in the job market and contribute to the development of the Palestinian economy.

Despite the tremendous effort to support TVET, little has been achieved. Nicolai (2007) reported that the TVET has not moved a lot from the starting point, when Palestinians began to construct their education system, although, this has been on the global agenda for the last two decades. Lamis Abu-Nahleh (Mazawi, 2000, p. 374) identified four areas that resulted in this disadvantaged situation:

> a. Politically, as a result of being affiliated to various agencies and lacking and integrative approach.
> b. Organizationally, due to staff employment policies which result in an over-representation of women in the lower administrative echelons.
> c. Economically, being 'almost non-functional' and disconnected from infrastructure and labour market needs; and
> d. Methodologically, as they lack any research-based approach, rending [TVET] programs socially and gender insensitive. (Mazawi, 2000, p. 374)

Why Does the Local Accept the Global?

It is helpful to investigate the reasons behind policy borrowing by asking why do national governments and local non-governmental organisations borrow policies and why do they accept lent policies? What are the contexts and factors that facilitate borrowing? These questions and their answers are vital for our understanding of borrowing in the Palestinian Territories. Waldow (2009) makes the point:

> Educational change is usually explained either as an epiphenomenon of social change, as a result of political and ideological shifts in the country or as a result of the inner dynamics of the process of educational reform itself.
> (Waldow, 2009, p. 479)

David Phillips (2004), one of the key pioneers in writing about policy borrowing, lists a number of stimuli for the borrowing process. This includes political change, systemic collapse, internal dissatisfaction and negative external evaluation, both new and in the aftermath of extreme upheaval, whether war or natural disaster. In addition to that, Steiner-Khamsi (2004) notes that when continuous reforms fail, policy makers become more open to borrowing and thus the likelihood of it increases. In such a case, policy makers resort to external policies due to an international agreement on its ability to reform education (Steiner-Khamsi, 2004, p. 4).

Most of these stimuli and conditions are present in the Palestinian case as, after the Oslo Accords, and in a drive for self-determination, Palestinians took over responsibility for education. At this time of political change the system was suffering from systemic weakness from being under the rule of Israel (Nicolai, 2007). This change came after years of conflict, upheaval and continuous dissatisfaction with the previous educational system that did not, in any way, reflect aspirations held by parents or their hopes for independence.

From a different perspective, Robertson and Waltman (1992) also emphasise the view that politicians' decisions to borrow are frequently influenced by short-term appearances and the pressures that they are under to solve urgent problems for which there is no recognisable solution Indeed, Halpin and Troyna (1995, p. 308) also draw attention to similar concerns.

The aforementioned stimuli denote some of the key factors that facilitate borrowing everywhere. However, in the Palestinian context there is also extreme dependence on foreign aid, various forms of 'conditionality' ensuring that aid is tied to various economic, financial and political mechanisms. Additionally, there is a lack of sovereignty with continuous internal and external debate about the state of political and social reform. These are some of the key reasons behind Palestinian policy borrowing, already described as one of the entities most dependent on aid (MAS, 2011).

Indeed, Phillips and Ochs (2004) consider responsibilities through aid donation as one of the most important stimuli for policy borrowing. This happens regularly as multilateral donors usually put conditions on recipient governments and NGOs in order to receive aid and/or loans. Without adhering to these conditions (donors usually call them 'guidelines'), national governments and local and international NGOs would not be able to secure the funding needed to undertake their activities and to deliver the required 'public goods'. In a highly aid-dependent territory like Palestine, this leaves limited space for decision makers to overcome this dilemma. An active expert in developing curricula reported the interests of donors in funding specific subjects (e.g. curricula of human rights and civic education) but not in other subjects.

A salient example of conditionality can be seen in the allegations from the Centre for Monitoring the Impact of Peace (CMIP) [6] that the Palestinian curricula called for and was inciting violence (Brown, 2001). Since publication, the Centre's reports have been used against Palestinians in political committees in the European Parliament and at other high-level meetings (Brown, 2003). These allegations have tremendous implications for funding the education sector (Brown, 2001). Italy, which supported the curriculum since its early stages, informed the National Palestinian Authority that it would not continue funding the curriculum, referring directly to the CMIP's reports. The World Bank adopted a similar position and shifted its aid contributions, as did many other donor countries (Nicolai, 2007).

In another example of conditionality, in October 2011 the USA cut aid to UNESCO immediately after that UN organisation declared Palestine a full member state. This momentous decision by UNESCO and the reaction of the USA was imbued with many meanings. On the one hand, it asserted the political nature of UNESCO beyond that of a scientific, cultural and educational organisation. On the other, it drew attention to the financial implications a powerful country – such as the USA – can have on an organisation when it is seen not to be doing its bidding.

In UNESCO's response to the cut, a senior official explained to the USA that they have been working for the interests of the USA since its foundation. In her letter to the *Washington Post*, the Director-General of UNESCO, Irina Bokova, wrote in response to the funding cuts:

> UNESCO supports many causes in line with U.S. security
> interests. In Afghanistan and Iraq, we are helping governments
> and communities prepare for life after the withdrawal of U.S.
> military forces ... In Tunisia and Egypt, we are leading
> education reform and training journalists. We target the causes

of violent extremism by training teachers in human rights and Holocaust remembrance. (Bokova, 2011)

On other occasions, national governments and NGOs themselves have proposed ideas for programmes to international donors. This is seen to support a more global consensus and thus is more likely to be funded. This approach is evident in the Palestinian's governments' publications, its reports, strategic plans and proposals to donors. Similarities in language, syntax and concepts can be discerned, quite frequently, between reports from one country and region with those from other countries and regions. It is the case that education decision makers tend to use similar language, perhaps to legitimise their plans. It may be a means of ensuring local policies dovetail with international standards and, therefore, are less likely to be questioned on the local community level. Likewise, Waldow (2009) emphasises that national senior officials often refer to international contexts for support and for the purpose of 'legitimation or de-legitimation of political argument' (Waldow, 2009, p. 478).

International meetings, seminars and symposia often facilitate convergence between multilateral donors from one side and the planners and decision makers on the national level on the other. These symposia give national officials the opportunity to listen and know what donors' areas of priority and interests are for funding in the home and recipient countries.

Robertson et al (2007) stress the role of international NGOs, who act as 'conduits' of convergence between the global agenda and local practices. This rapid dissemination of educational ideas, Phillips and Ochs (2004, p. 776) suggest, has facilitated the likelihood of 'conscious borrowing'.

It can be argued that this synergy would be impossible in the absence of national elites who are open to global influences, discourses and political interventions. In the Palestinian case, an enormous amount of international aid is linked to Mr Salam Fayyad, the current Prime Minister for the Palestinian National Authority (PNA), who is usually perceived as the chief fundraiser for the PNA. Not surprisingly Mr Fayyad has a background in these international agencies. In 1987 he joined the IMF and then served as a representative to the Palestinian National Authority from 1996-2001. Part of his capacity in fundraising refers to the vision he holds for key 'gates to development' that are based on an open market, a knowledge-based economy, privatisation, entrepreneurship, microfinance, removing borders and a general openness to the West. Mr Fayyad is well known for his beliefs in these neo-liberal pillars for development.

Moreover, elites, who received their education from Western universities and later become decision makers in their home countries, have contributed by importing and adapting some of the international ideas and global agendas in education to the local context. The development of the Palestinian curricula for the first time tells us how Palestinians utilise the experience of their elites in wrapping up modern curricula based on a review of educational systems and curricula in more than 60 countries across the region and, indeed, from all over the world. Some Palestinians elites, when working in education-policy positions, censored the curriculum contents, especially those parts less likely to satisfy Israel, the USA and the donors. One of the experts reported that: 'Many of our ideas and thoughts for the content of curriculum were rejected internally (in MoEHE) and replaced by other contents that dissatisfy the local community who thought that curriculum will reflect their national aspiration of independence.'

What is the Problem with Policy Borrowing in Education?

The stimuli of policy borrowing, the context in which it takes place, the process itself and the consequences of borrowing, all convey a great deal about what is problematic with the system. As outlined elsewhere in this chapter, policy borrowing often takes place in exceptional situations of reform, change, dissatisfaction, aid-dependency and country fragility. I suggest that importing and adapting the global into the local in times of these hard conditions is inevitably problematic.

As outlined in the context of adopting and developing TVET in the Palestinian Territories, this sector has not achieved as intended. Although warmly welcomed, its progress has been very limited. This is, in part, because it does not reflect the priorities of the Palestinian people nor does it address their needs. Despite the continuous marketing of TVET in the formal system over many years and the incentives ministries provide to attract more students to TVET, unremarkable progress has been achieved (Nicolai, 2007). This is not to suggest that TVET is not an important approach to development elsewhere, but rather attests to the fact that those involved in policy borrowing often possess at least a degree of ignorance of the context in which policy is being adapted, adopted and implemented. It is argued that adopting global trends usually affects and undermines the local. Global standardisation may not be suitable for the current Palestinian condition.

Indeed, the dominant forces which form educational policies on the global level are structural, procedural and personnel. They are usually from the 'core', from the US and Europe, and are increasingly driven by neo-liberal ideas with their focus on open markets, free trade, entrepreneurship in general, and privatisation and decentralisation in education. Other countries in the 'periphery', including the Palestinian Territories, are not immune from these trends: after all, we live in a globalised world where we 'become acclimated to the language used by the global centre, the centre of hegemonic power' (Altbach, 2002, 2006).

Yang emphasises that 'global education', and the context in which borrowing is actively taking place, became a 'new coloniser' which controls views and ideas and spreads them to developing nations without considering their uniqueness and speciality, in the mistaken belief that they are actually helping people (Yang, 2003, p. 282).

These international actors in education focus on the development of human capital, so they give little attention to the development of social and national capital by not recognising the importance of indigenous knowledge (Ozga & Lingard, 2007, p. 75). This is very risky as it results in reducing national and cultural components in the education systems in countries of 'the periphery'. Instead, elites from the periphery find themselves enticed by and following the machinations of global policies (Robertson et al, 2007, p. 150). For countries with limited resources that depend on foreign aid, like the Palestinian Territories, there exists only limited space for national decision making. This is especially the case as inter-governmental organisations 'convert financial means into political instruments' (Stiglitz, 2002, cited in Beerkens, 2008, p. 25)

Concluding Comments

In the current context of the Palestinian Territories, there seems to be a clear contrast between two sets of principles underpinning educational development. On one hand there are those who see education as a driving force for market interventions in the country. They see the benefit in the growth of curriculum structures and processes that support a national knowledge economy. However, others argue that this approach inevitably threatens equal opportunities and leads to greater social, political and economic inequality.

But it is not a one-way street. Policy borrowing in education can lead to different levels of community resistance. Halpin and Troyna (1995) note in the earlier works of Phillips (1989, 1992) that:

> the political, historical and socio-cultural settings of education policy formulation, development and implementation are fundamental inasmuch as they help both to keep certain policies 'in place' as well as to provide resistance to the implanting of anything more than selective aspects of competing ideas from other systems. (Halpin & Troyna, 1995, p. 304)

The situation of policy borrowing in Palestine is therefore, at one level, unremarkable: it is evident that countries of the global core export to the global periphery education ideas, concepts, concerns, structures and processes. What does make the Palestinian case so different is that there appears to be very little 'voluntarism' in the purchasing of these education packages. It is apparent that donors not only provide aid but that they also define the political agenda as well as educational needs, be these curriculum and assessment, career guidance or TVET. In a world where the conflict in this region is so intensely important, having national control of education policy would appear to make sense.

Notes

[1] The Oslo Accords, officially called the Declaration of Principles (DOP) in 1993 was the first framework for agreement between Israel and the Palestine Liberation Organization (PLO).

[2] Occupied Palestinian Territories is the term used by the United Nations to refer to parts of Palestine occupied by Israel after the Arab–Israeli War in 1967. It consists of the West Bank, East Jerusalem and the Gaza Strip (UN, 2003)

[3] UNRWA: United Nations Relief and Works Agency operates in Lebanon, Syria, Jordan and the West Bank and Gaza Strip.

[4] The Palestinian population has one of the highest growth rates at 4%. About 46% of the population are young (under 14 years old).

[5] The data was downloaded from the official World Bank website and calculations have been done to suggest some findings. http://data.worldbank.org/sites/default/files/data/wdiandgdf_excel.zip

[6] An Israeli-based organisation which has been established, along with the Palestinian curriculum development process, since 1998 (Nicolai, 2007). Many authors refuted the Centre's allegations stressing its political drives and objectives.

References

Ali, S. (2009) Governing Education Policy in a Globalising World: the sphere of authority of the Pakistani state. Unpublished PhD thesis, University of Edinburgh.

Altbach, P.G. (2002) Knowledge and Education as International Commodities: the collapse of the common good, *Journal of International Higher Education*, 28, 19-36.

Altbach, P.G. (2006) *International Higher Education: reflections on policy and practice*. Center for International Higher Education. http://www.bc.edu/cihe/ (accessed 20 April 2011).

Barakat, B.F. (2007) The Struggle for Palestinian National Education Past and Present, in C. Brock & L. Z. Levers (Eds) *Aspects of Education in the Middle East and North Africa*. Oxford: Symposium Books.

Beerkens, E. (2008) University Policies for the Knowledge Society: global standardization, local reinvention, *Perspectives on Global Development and Technology*, 7, 15-36.

Bokova, I. (2011) Don't Punish UNESCO, *Washington Post*. http://www.washingtonpost.com/opinions/dont-punish-unesco/2011/10/23/gIQAfZXYAM_story.html (accessed 20 March 2012).

Brock, C. & Levers L.Z. (Eds) (2007) *Aspects of Education in the Middle East and North Africa*. Oxford: Symposium Books.

Brown, N.J. (2001) *Democracy, History, and the Contest over the Palestinian Curriculum*. Washington, DC: Adam Institute.

Brown, N.J. (2003) *Palestinian Politics after the Oslo Accords: resuming Arab Palestine*. Berkeley: University of California Press.

Brynen, R. (2000) *A Very Political Economy: peacebuilding and foreign aid in the West Bank and Gaza*. Washington, DC: United States Institute of Peace.

Castells, M. (1999) *Information Technology, Globalization and Social Development*. UNRISD Discussion Paper 114. New York: United Nations.

Castells, M. (2010) *The Rise of the Network Society*, 2nd edn. London: Wiley-Blackwell.

Comaroff, J. & Comaroff, J.L. (2001) Millennial Capitalism: first thoughts on a second coming, in J. Comaroff & J.L. Comaroff (Eds) *Millennial Capitalism and the Culture of Neoliberalism*, pp. 1–56. Durham, NC: Duke University Press.

Donn, G. & Al Manthri, Y. (2010) *Globalisation and Higher Education in the Arab Gulf States*. Oxford: Symposium Books.

Giddens, A. (1990) *The Consequences of Modernity*. Cambridge: Polity Press.

Halpin, D. & Troyna B. (1995) The Politics of Education Policy Borrowing, *Comparative Education*, 31(3), 303-310.

Hopkins, A.G. (2002) *Globalization in World History*. London: Verso.

Mahshi, K. (2002) *Developing Education in Palestine: a continuing challenge*. Paris: UNESCO. http://www.unesco.org/education/news_en/131101_palestine.shtml (accessed 22 April 2011).

Maintz, J. (2004) *Agencies for International Cooperation in Technical and Vocational Education and Training: a guide to sources of information*. Bonn: UNESCO-UNEVOC International Centre.

MAS (The Palestine Economic Policy Research Institute) (2011) *Reducing Aid Dependency in the Palestinian Territory*. Economic Feature. http://www.portlandtrust.org/sites/default/files/peb/special_economic_feature_may__2011.pdf

Mazawi, A.E. (2000) The Reconstruction of Palestinian Education: between history, policy politics and policymaking, *Journal of Education Policy*, 15, 371-375.

Ministry of Education and Higher Education (MoEHE) (2000) *Five-Year Education Development Plan, 2000-2005*. Ramallah: MoEHE.

Ministry of Education and Higher Education (MoEHE) (2008) *Education Development Strategic Plan 2008-2012: towards quality education for development*. Ramallah: MoEHE.

More, A.L. (2008). *International Assistance to the Palestinians after Oslo: political guilt, wasted money*. Abingdon: Routledge.

More, A.L. (2010) *International Assistance to the Palestinians after Oslo: political guilt, wasted money*. Oxford: Routledge.

Mundy, K. & Murphy, L. (2000) Transnational Advocacy, Global Civil Society? Emerging Evidence from the Field of Education, *Comparative Education Review*, 45(1), 85-126.

Nicolai, S. (2007) *Fragmented Foundations: education and chronic crisis in the Occupied Palestinian Territory*. Paris: International Institute for Educational Planning & Save the Children UK.

Ochs, K. & Phillips, D. (2002) Comparative Studies and 'Cross-National Attraction' in Education: a typology for the analysis of English interest in educational policy and provision in Germany, *Educational Studies*, 28, 325-339.

Ozga, J. & Lingard, B. (2007) Globalisation, Education Policy and Politics, in B. Lingard & J. Ozga (Eds) *The Routledge Falmer Reader in Education Policy and Politics*, pp. 65-82. London: Routledge.

Palestinian National Authority PNA (2008) *Palestinian Reform and Development Plan*. Ramallah: Palestinian National Authority.

Palestinian National Authority (PNA) (2009) *Palestine: ending the occupation, establishing the state*. Ramallah: Palestinian National Authority.

Palestinian National Authority (PNA) (2010) *Building Palestine: achievements and challenges*. Ramallah: Palestinian National Authority.

Phillips, D. (1989) Neither a Borrower Nor a Lender Be? The Problems of Cross-national Attraction in Education. *Comparative Education*, 25(3), 267-274.

Phillips, D. (2004) Toward a Theory of Policy Attraction in Education, in: G. Steiner-Khamsi (Ed.) *Lessons from Elsewhere: the politics of educational borrowing and lending*. New York: Teachers College Press.

Phillips, D. & Ochs, K. (2004) Researching Policy Borrowing: some methodological challenges in comparative education, *British Educational Research Journal*, 30(6), 773-784.

Popkewitz, T.S. (2004) Foreword, in G. Steiner-Khamsi (Ed) *The Global Politics of Educational Borrowing and Lending*. New York: Teachers College Press.

Rawolle, S. & Lingard, B. (2008) The Sociology of Pierre Bourdieu and Researching Education Policy, *Journal of Education Policy*, 23(6), 729-741.

Rizvi, F., Engel, L., Nandyala, A. & Sparks, J. (2005). *Globalization and Recent Shifts in Educational Policy in the Asia Pacific: an overview of some critical issues*. Bangkok: UNESCO Asia Pacific Regional Bureau for Education.

Robertson, D.B. & Waltman, J.L. (1992) The Politics of Policy Borrowing, *Oxford Studies in Comparative Education*, 2(2), 25-55.

Robertson, S., Novelli, M., Dale, R., Tikly, L., Dachi, H. & Alphonce, N. (2007) *Globalisation, Education and Development: ideas, actors and dynamics*. Department for International Development (DFID). http://www.dfid.gov.uk/documents/publications/global-education-dev-68.pdf (accessed 20 March 2011).

Sayigh, Y. (2007) Inducing a Failed State in Palestine, *Survival: Global Politics and Strategy*, 49(3), 7-39.

Scholte, J.A. (2002) *What is Globalisation? The Definitional Issue – Again.* Warwick: Centre for the Study of Globalisation and Regionalisation, University of Warwick.

Sen, A. (2002a) *Development as Freedom.* Oxford: Oxford University Press.

Sen, A. (2002b) How to Judge Globalism, *The American Prospect*, 13, 28-36.

Sommers, M. (2004) *Co-ordinating Education during Emergencies and Reconstruction: challenges and responsibilities.* Paris: UNESCO-IIEP.

Steiner-Khamsi, G. (Ed.) 2004 *The Global Politics of Educational Borrowing and Lending.* New York: Teachers College Press.

Stiglitz, E. Joseph. 2002. *Globalization and Its Discontents.* New York: W.W. Norton.

Taylor, S. & Henry, M. (2007) Globalization and Educational Policymaking: a case study, in B. Lingard & J. Ozga (Eds) *The RoutledgeFalmer Reader in Education Policy and Politics.* London: Routledge.

Tilly, C. (2004) Past, Present, and Future Globalizations, in G. Steiner-Khamsi (Ed.) *The Global Politics of Educational Borrowing and Lending.* New York: Teachers College Press.

UNESCO (2000) *The Dakar Framework for Action.* Paris: UNESCO.

United Nations (UN) (2003) *The Question of Palestine & United Nations.* United Nations Department of Public Information. http://www.un.org/Depts/dpi/palestine/ (accessed 23 April 2011).

Waldow, F. (2009) Undeclared Imports: silent borrowing in educational policy-making and research in Sweden, *Comparative Education*, 45(4), 477-494.

World Bank (2002) *Constructing Knowledge Societies: new challenges for tertiary education.* Washington, DC: World Bank.

World Bank (2005) *Reshaping the Future: education and post-conflict reconstruction.* Washington, DC: World Bank.

CHAPTER FOUR

Qatar's Independent Schools: education for a new (or bygone?) era

BROOKE BARNOWE-MEYER

Introduction

Qatar's K–12 education system has undergone a series of remarkable transformations in the past half-century, none so dramatic as the introduction of so-called 'independent schools' in 2004. Publically financed, privately operated independent schools have ushered in a new era of education reform in Qatar, one focused on school autonomy, accountability, variety and choice, as well as instructional creativity and curricular innovation. Independent school advocates – including a powerful international magistracy from the United States, the United Kingdom, New Zealand and Germany – have suggested that market-style mechanisms of choice and competition have made struggling schools more flexible, innovative and diverse, freeing Qatari educators from bureaucratic regulation and the monopolistic inefficiency of a highly centralised public system. The magistracy has failed, however, to acknowledge the baroque roots of the independent school model, one explicitly borrowed from the United States despite a troubled history of failed schools, poor student achievement, and scant evidence of innovation in curriculum or instruction. This chapter will briefly explore the legacy of the original 'independent schools' – US charter schools – and analyse the profound impact this legacy carries in Qatar. It is argued that as the nation rapidly transitions its remaining public schools to independent institutions, an over-reliance on free market principles and magisterial 'expertise' appear to have limited Qatar's true potential for educational growth, innovation and reform.

1. Qatar at a Glance

The State of Qatar is one of the smallest nations in the Gulf region, occupying an 11,427-square kilometre peninsula in the Persian Gulf (see Figure 1). The Qatari people, numbering approximately 350,000, are a small minority in a total national population of 1.6 to 1.8 million (Anderson et al, 2010; Qatar Statistics Authority [QSA], 2012). Recent demographic figures estimate that 28% of the population is Arab (15% Qatari), 24% Indian and 16% Nepali (United States Department of State, 2012). The remaining population consists of Filipino, Pakistani and Sri Lankan nationals, in addition to a small number of persons of other, mainly Western European, ethnic origins (Gonzalez et al, 2008; United States Department of State, 2012). The vast majority of Qatari nationals adhere to Wahhabi Islam – a traditionalist Sunni sect originating in neighbouring Saudi Arabia – although small segments of the population are self-identified members of other Sunni or Shi'ite sects (Gonzalez et al, 2008). Arabic is the official and most widely spoken language in Qatar, although English has increasingly emerged as the preferred medium of communication in the nation's private business sector (Gonzalez et al, 2008). Nearly 50% of the Qatari population – approximately 800,000 people – reside in the coastal metropolis of Doha, the nation's capital city and vibrant commercial centre (QSA, 2012).

At the beginning of the twentieth century, Qatar's settled population of 27,000 occupied a small settlement of coastal villages dependent on fishing, pearl diving and camel breeding for subsistence (Gonzalez et al, 2008). The discovery of oil in 1939, however, dramatically transformed Qatar's prospects for growth and future economic prosperity. The active exploration and development of the peninsula's oil resources following the Second World War produced a spike in economic activity and population growth in Qatar throughout the 1950s and 1960s. The oil boom of the 1970s doubled the nation's population as non-national workers flocked to Qatar in pursuit of new employment opportunities (Gonzalez et al, 2008). By the late 1970s, nearly 750,000 residents – 60% expatriates – had permanently settled in Qatar (Brewer et al, 2006). Declining oil reserves slowed both population and economic growth in the 1980s and early 1990s, prompting Qatari leaders to pursue an ambitious economic diversification plan. A number of public enterprises were privatised or semi-privatised, and several policies were adopted to establish a more 'business-friendly' regulatory climate (Gonzalez et al, 2008, p. 37). Output was increased in the nation's petrochemical, steel and fertiliser industries, and efforts made to expand its fledgling tourism and hospitality sector. Exploitation of the nation's vast natural gas reserves – the third largest in the world – also began in earnest in the early 1990s.

These efforts, and others, resulted in extraordinary economic growth [1] (Gonzalez et al, 2008). Qatar responded to its rapidly expanding economy and its relatively small population base by turning to non-national workers to meet its complex labour-market needs throughout the latter decades of the twentieth century (Gonzalez et al, 2008). Today, non-Qataris comprise over 80% of the nation's working-age population (Gonzalez et al, 2008). Of the approximately 12% of Qataris in the economically active population, over 90% are employed in the government sector and in state-owned enterprises (Gonzalez et al, 2008). In contrast, almost all private-sector workers – nearly 99% – are non-nationals (Gonzalez et al, 2008). Most Qataris have historically perceived the public sector as a more attractive employment option, citing greater total compensation, benefits and job security, shorter working hours, and a more prestigious public reputation (Gonzalez et al, 2008). Many private-sector employers, however, note a preference for non-nationals, claiming Qataris lack both the practical skills and language proficiency demanded within the nation's rapidly growing non-government sector (Gonzalez et al, 2008).

To ensure the nation's economic sustainability, the Qatari government has pursued a variety of policies to enhance the human capital of its nationals (Gonzalez et al, 2008). Although Qatar has adopted less strident nationalisation policies than many of its Gulf Cooperation Council (GCC) neighbours, so-called Qatarisation plans have become an increasingly popular alternative to educational interventions and training programmes (Donn & Al Manthri, 2010). In June 2000, Qatari leaders introduced a five-year Strategic Qatarization Plan establishing a 50% target for Qatari participation in the nation's thriving energy and industry sector. In partnership with Qatar Petroleum and other leading industry monoliths, the government offered both public and private businesses incentives to recruit and hire more national workers (Anderson et al, 2010). Although the number of Qataris in the sector increased threefold from 2000 to 2010, the overall 50% threshold target remains but a distant goal (Qatar Petroleum, 2011).

Despite Qatarisation efforts, overall Qatari labour-force participation remains low. Female nationals are much less likely than their male counterparts to be represented within the workforce. Only 50% of Qatari women work outside the home, 85% in the nation's gender-segregated education sector (Anderson et al, 2010). Nearly one-fifth of all working Qataris are employed within both the K-12 and higher-education sectors (Gonzalez et al, 2008); as noted by Gonzalez et al (2008, p. 48), however, 'there are not enough teaching jobs for qualified teachers who seek such positions', limiting the employment opportunities available to both Qatari and expatriate women.

2. Education in Qatar

It is within the nation's K-12 sector that Qatari leaders have increasingly placed their hopes for the nation's successful transition from a carbon-based to knowledge-based economy. Through its educational institutions, Qatari leaders have committed to expanding and enhancing the nation's stock of human capital, to building 'strong, solid citizens who are informed and engaged and who understand how to function in a global economy' (Supreme Education Council, 2010). The past decade has paid witness to an extraordinary educational transition in Qatar, from an arguably cumbersome and impotent public system to a market-driven, public–private institutional partnership based on principles of autonomy, accountability, variety and choice.

Several initiatives intended to reform the failing system were introduced in the late 1990s. A number of so-called 'complex schools' – those in which students progressed through academically and pedagogically connected primary, preparatory and secondary schools for the full duration of their studies – were launched on a limited basis in 1999 (Brewer et al, 2006). Featuring English-language instruction and a curriculum heavily focused on science, complex schools were designed to allow partial independence from the Ministry of Education (MoE), granting teachers and administrative personnel 'significantly more operational and instructional freedom than their colleagues in traditional schools' (Brewer et al, 2006, p. 5). A small number of vocational schools were also introduced, providing an option (for secondary-school-aged boys only) to study a trade rather than pursue the Ministry's more rigorous academic curriculum.

In October 2001, a nine-member interdisciplinary team of RAND researchers with reportedly 'wide expertise in education research and policy analysis' began on-site investigations of Qatari schools (Brewer et al, 2006, p. 5). The team had four initial review goals: (1) to understand and describe the existing system; (2) to identify problems within the system; (3) to recommend alternative reform options; and (4) to devise a plan to implement the chosen option(s) (Brewer et al, 2007). Data was gathered from approximately 15 institutions (boys' and girls' schools at primary, preparatory and secondary level, managed by both Ministry personnel and private entities) through school and classroom observations, focus groups, interviews and document analysis (Brewer et al, 2006). At the time of the RAND study, Qatar's K-12 education system served approximately 100,000 students, two-thirds of whom attended schools that were financed and operated by the Ministry of Education (RAND-Qatar Policy Institute, 2007).

Within a mere four months of the study's initiation, RAND issued a comprehensive account of its findings, documenting Qatar's education system in the bleakest of terms. The Ministry was found to engage in little communication with parents, employers, or any of the nation's colleges, vocational institutes or universities (RAND-Qatar Policy Institute, 2007). School administrators had limited authority and few resources, and repeatedly expressed frustration with their inability to influence Ministry policies or procedures (RAND-Qatar Policy Institute, 2007). The Ministry's top-down authority extended to curriculum development and implementation as well, as both teachers and administrators perceived the single, nationally mandated curriculum as rigid, outdated and resistant to reform. Restrictions were placed upon the instructional autonomy and creativity of teachers, and few had access to opportunities for professional development or advancement. No accountability for student performance existed at either the school or system level, and a significant portion of Qatari students – nearly half – failed secondary-school exit examinations. Schools themselves were found in a shocking state of decay and disrepair; classrooms and school buildings were often overcrowded, dilapidated and in desperate need of expansion and refurbishment.

Based on its analysis, RAND staff and national leaders worked cooperatively to develop a remedial plan 'informed by evidence on education reform around the world, yet suited to the Qatari situation' (Brewer et al, 2006, p. 9). RAND noted the 'fundamental need [for] clear curriculum standards oriented towards the desired outcomes of schooling', and in January 2002 presented the nation's leaders with three vastly different systemic reform models: a Modified Centralised Model; a Charter School Model; and a Voucher Model.

In May 2002, His Highness Sheikh Hamad Khalifa al-Thani announced the adoption of the second reform option – refined and renamed the 'Independent School Model', as it could more easily be translated into Arabic – while also expressing a long-term preference for a voucher system (Brewer et al, 2006; Constant et al, 2010). The Qatari emir also announced the development of national, standardised student assessments aligned with 'internationally-benchmarked curriculum standards' (Brewer et al, 2006, p. i).

Although RAND deftly represented the 'Independent School Model' as uniquely responsive to Qatar's educational needs and challenges, the very same reform configuration had in fact, by 2002, been introduced and implemented in more than 35 US states. RAND and other magistracy actors have repeatedly portrayed the American charter-school model as educational 'best practice'.

3. Charter Schools: a baroque arsenal

Although frequently hailed as 'the potential antidote to all that is pathological in weak public schools' (Frankenberg & Lee, 2003, p. 3), in fact there is scant evidence to suggest that charter schools are indeed educational 'best practice'.

> Unfortunately, despite claims by charter advocates, there is no systematic research or data that show that charter schools perform better than public schools. Since charter schools embody wildly different educational approaches and since charter and public schools obtain their enrollment in very different ways, evaluations and comparisons between the two require very careful analysis. At a minimum, it is certainly safe to say that there is little convincing evidence for the superiority of charter schools over public schools in the same areas. In fact, some of the studies suggest that charter schools are, on average, even weaker. (Frankenberg & Lee, 2003, p. 3)

Rather than representing the best in educational practice, the charter school model in the United States – and by association, the independent-school model in Qatar – more aptly serve as stark examples of Donn and Al Manthri's (2010, p. 153) 'baroque arsenal': educational goods, services and models of practice 'discussed, designed, and generated years before their delivery', marketed and sold to states across the globe in spite of lingering questions regarding their potential for true reform. Indeed, although described as being 'informed by evidence on education reform around the world' (Brewer et al, 2006, p. 9), it appears little to no mention was made to Qatari leaders of the model's profound failures in its country of origin.

Ample evidence existed prior to the organisation's arrival in Qatar suggesting that charter schools were, at best, faltering both operationally and academically, and at worst, built on faulty theoretical foundations threatening to undermine the educational attainment of thousands of US students. In the hands of RAND and its many magisterial partners, however, the charter-school model was earnestly lauded in Qatar. Emboldened by Qatar's enthusiasm for reform and by its own domestic commercial advocacy of charter schools, RAND embarked on an ambitious plan to export the charter model to Qatar.

Despite the flawed theoretical foundations and baroque legacy of charter schools in the United States, Qatar enthusiastically pressed forward with the adoption of the independent-school model in 2002. The model was a vast departure for Qatar and indeed the entire region, as no other Gulf state had attempted to create an education system 'based on an internationally benchmarked curriculum, global best practice and Islamic values in a technologically emerging society' (Anderson et al, 2010, p. 236). The Qatari model – entitled 'Education for a New Era' – was based on four key principles developed by RAND experts in consultation with national leaders:

- *Autonomy.* Within the new decentralised system, independent schools would operate autonomously, subject only to terms and conditions specified in a time-limited contract. Individual school

operators, rather than a central governing body, would determine all policies regarding admissions, programmatic options, staffing and classroom pedagogy.
- *Accountability.* Although autonomous, independent schools would be held accountable to the government through numerous mechanisms and measures of compliance (RAND-Qatar Policy Institute, 2007). Schools would be subject to regular conformance audits from a small central governing body. The results of year-end student assessments would also be made publically available at the school level, allowing parents to choose institutions with preferred educational approaches and achievement levels.
- *Variety.* Diverse schooling and programmatic options would be encouraged within the new system, as individual independent schools would be given the freedom to specify and promote a unique educational philosophy and operational agenda (Brewer et al, 2006).
- *Choice.* Provided with updated information on school characteristics and performance outcomes, parents would be permitted to choose institutions most ideally suited to their child(ren)'s academic needs and interests. Independent schools would be tuition-free and open to all Qatari children as well as those of expatriate government employees.

Although variety in schooling options was a key principle of the reform, independent schools were expected to follow a set of national-curriculum standards in four core subject areas – Arabic, English, science and mathematics – considered by RAND and Qatari leaders as most critical for the nation's future social and economic growth (Brewer et al, 2006). Other subjects would not conform to a set of specific standards, although schools were free to offer additional academic options at their discretion (Brewer et al, 2006). Two types of curriculum standards – content-based and performance-based – would be articulated by educational 'experts' in the early stages of reform implementation; individual schools, however, would have 'wide latitude' in designing appropriate curricula and academic programmes to meet the pre-defined criteria (Brewer et al, 2006, p. 16).

4. The Independent-School Model: organisational structure

In addition to its central role in articulating the reform's key principles, RAND also designed a detailed implementation plan specifying the organisational structure of the new K-12 system. The plan called for the development of four new government institutions – three permanent and one temporary – to aid in restructuring the power and authority vested within the Qatari system (RAND-Qatar Policy Institute, 2007).

Three permanent institutions – the Supreme Education Council, the Education Institute and the Evaluation Institute – were designed to provide the vital infrastructure necessary to support the new independent schools as the reform progressed. Established by Emiri decree in November 2002, the Supreme Education Council (SEC) was responsible for total oversight of reform development and implementation. The Education Institute was responsible for overseeing the development and maturation of the new independent schools, selecting school operators, negotiating and monitoring school contracts as well as allocating financial resources, establishing rigorous curriculum standards and providing professional development programmes for teachers and school administrators (RAND-Qatar Policy Institute, 2007). The Evaluation Institute was responsible for monitoring performance in all Qatari schools – independent, Ministry and private – through standardised student assessments, surveys of students, teachers, parents and principals, and operation of a national education data system (Brewer et al, 2006; RAND-Qatar Policy Institute, 2007). The Evaluation Institute was also to develop and publish annual school 'report cards', providing parents with information on school quality as well as focusing attention on areas most in need of improvement (Constant et al, 2010).

An additional temporary body – the Implementation Team – was assembled in October 2002 to assist in the development of the three permanent institutions while also performing 'oversight, coordination, and advisory functions during the transition to the new system' (RAND-Qatar Policy Institute, 2007, p. 2). The Implementation Team was also intended to 'serve as a forum for resolving differences', particularly between members of the Qatari leadership, RAND and members of various international organisations recruited in the reform effort for their reported experience and educational 'expertise' (Brewer et al, 2007, pp. 17-18).

Rather than a total abolishment of the Ministry system, the RAND plan called for a parallel system to function 'operationally and physically separate from the MoE' (Brewer et al, 2006, p. 16; RAND-Qatar Policy Institute, 2007). The new institutions were intended 'to be less reliant than the Ministry on rules and hierarchy', 'to employ a relatively small number of staff', and encouraged to 'support collaboration, teamwork, individual creativity, initiative, and personal accountability' (Brewer et al, 2006, p. 7). Although Ministry staff and Ministry-operated schools were to remain largely unaffected during the early years of the reform effort, MoE institutions were expected to take part in national standardised student assessments and produce performance 'report cards' in accordance with SEC mandates (RAND-Qatar Policy Institute, 2007).

5. Evaluating 'Education for a New Era' in Qatar

To evaluate the progress of the reform in its early years, RAND conducted case studies of 16 Qatari schools – 12 independent institutions (including four schools from each of Generations I, II and III) and four Ministry institutions – over a period of two years from 2005 to 2007 (Constant et al, 2010). The study results reveal both positive indicators of improvement and tremendous challenges in implementation. As a result of the K-12 reform, RAND claims that many of Qatar's children 'are now in more learner-centered classrooms with improved facilities where better-prepared and better-trained teachers guide them in accordance with internationally benchmarked standards' (Rand-Qatar Policy Institute, 2007, p. 4). Coordination challenges, fundamental design flaws and an institutional coup, however, were found to slow and hinder reform efforts:

> One ongoing, key challenge was that of maintaining everyone's focus on the interrelated changes to the whole system, especially as the number of staff and contractors expanded. The reform's design recognized this challenge, calling for the SEC and Implementation Team to be responsible for these larger considerations. The SEC (at an overall level) and the Implementation Team (at a working level) coordinated tasks, monitored progress, and identified the need for mid-course corrections. (Brewer et al, 2007, p. 15)

Within a mere six months of the Implementation Team's establishment, however, the SEC dissolved the body and absorbed its functions, noting the 'reform's rapid pace and large size ... [had] rendered the task of handling the numerous aspects of coordination difficult and overly time-consuming' (Brewer et al, 2007, p. 9). With its dissolution, 'an important and useful mechanism for keeping the many reform programs aligned with the original vision was lost' (Brewer et al, 2007, p. 15). In lieu of the team's coordination and assistance, Institute directors were expected to bring major issues to the SEC, and to work with foreign contractors with 'outside technical expertise if Qatari experts were not available' (Brewer et al, 2006, p. 17; Brewer et al, 2007).

The majority of implementation challenges, however, were in fact attributed to the pool of international consultants and 'experts' – the so-called magistracy – to whom Qatari leaders repeatedly turned throughout reform design and implementation. Given Qatar's small population and lack of relevant domestic expertise, Institute leadership relied heavily upon both RAND personnel and international contractors to make key decisions in the early stages of the reform (Brewer et al, 2006; Brewer et al, 2007; RAND-Qatar Policy Institute, 2007). While RAND enthusiastically touts the valuable knowledge and experience contributed by international experts, they acknowledge that their work styles frequently conflicted with those of their Qatari colleagues (Brewer et al, 2006). Such conflicts at times produced 'friction and inefficiency', particularly in adopting design principles 'largely unknown' in Qatar (Brewer et al, 2006, p. 24). Rather than recommending that international contractors adapt to indigenous work styles and social mores, RAND has repeatedly suggested that effective reform implementation depends upon the willingness and ability of *Qataris* 'to learn and get comfortable with new patterns of behavior' (Brewer et al, 2006, p. 24). With regard to its own role in implementation challenges, RAND merely notes that its dual responsibility of assisting in the implementation itself while also monitoring its quality 'added to the complexity' (Brewer et al, 2007, p. 18).

The impact of the reform on a number of specific education challenges in Qatar – including curriculum development, classroom pedagogy, professional development, parental involvement and student achievement, as well as school autonomy, accountability and choice – has also been decidedly mixed. Although some progress has been made in each aspect of the system, profound challenges remain. The following section draws upon the findings of RAND – and others – to evaluate Education for a New Era through its various goals and manifestations.

Curriculum Development

Prior to the launch of the reform in 2002, the Qatari Ministry of Education dominated all aspects of curriculum development and implementation. The single, nationally mandated curriculum was perceived by teachers and school administrators as rigid, outdated and resistant to reform, as well as following an inflexible implementation schedule that 'permitted no alteration to suit student differences or student progress' (Constant et al, 2010, p. 452; see also Brewer et al, 2006). In contrast, the reform called for all decisions regarding textbooks, pedagogical approaches, instructional strategies and lesson plans to be made not by a centralised government body, but by independent schoolteachers and administrators (Zellman et al, 2009). This design was intended to permit teachers greater autonomy and flexibility in the classroom, thereby increasing student motivation and enhancing student achievement:

> The expectation behind the design was that Independent school teachers would be motivated to align lessons with the curriculum standards to ensure that their students acquired the requisite knowledge and skills and therefore performed well on national assessments. (Zellman et al, 2009, p. 71)

Independent schoolteachers in RAND focus groups indeed reported greater levels of autonomy in the classroom than did their Ministry school colleagues (Zellman et al, 2009). Such autonomy, they noted, 'allowed them to be more flexible in their instructional approaches and to incorporate a greater number of practical applications in their lessons' (Zellman et al, 2009, p. 59). Many teachers, however, complained that the curriculum standards were 'too abstract' and 'offered too little guidance for school administrators and teachers attempting to develop discipline-specific criteria' (Zellman et al, 2009, p. 60). Teachers reported they had not been properly trained to select or develop curricula, and indeed felt 'overwhelmed' (Zellman et al, 2009, p. 57), 'overburdened' (p. 58) and 'unqualified' to do so (p. 57). Although some of these feelings diminished as the year progressed, others expressed continued resentment and frustration at the amount of time and energy expended to develop curricula and materials during non-school hours (Zellman et al, 2009).

In response to comments regarding the abstract nature of the standards, the Education Institute contracted the Center for British Teachers (CfBT) 'to provide standards implementation support' (Zellman et al, 2009, p. 61). The organisation, which had developed the original standards in 2004, provided 'guidance on scheduling and sequencing of instruction consistent with or in support of the standards' (Zellman et al, 2009, p. 61). It also suggested a 50-day extension of the Ministry school year – then 130 days – and a teaching day of approximately 5.5 hours (Zellman et al, 2009). The Institute also established a resource centre in which teachers could seek advice on instructional materials from subject-matter and development specialists (Zellman et al, 2009). Each independent school was also matched with an international school support organisation (SSO), although teachers and administrators noted that consultancy staff were often unavailable, in addition to their other duties, to assist with curriculum development.

Classroom Pedagogy

Before substantive reform measures were introduced in 2004, Qatari classrooms were often sites of standardised instruction, pedagogical monotony and student apathy. Ministry teachers rarely experimented with alternative instructional tools and techniques, and seldom required students to think critically or creatively:

> The predominant method of delivering instruction in Ministry classrooms was in whole groups, with the teacher standing in front of the class and lecturing, answering student questions, or calling on students to recite or answer questions. Students were almost never asked to analyze or synthesize any facts or material; most of the cognitive work was limited to demonstrating knowledge through recall of information. (Zellman et al, 2009, 75)

The reform, however, aimed to 'significantly change the classroom learning environment' in Qatar's schools (Zellman et al, 2011, p. 57). In contrast to the didactic approach employed by Ministry institutions, the reform called for independent schools to 'expand the pedagogical options available to teachers' and to establish a culture within each school characterised by flexibility, experimentation and sensitivity to students' interests, needs and progress (Zellman et al, 2011, p. 75). Teachers were encouraged to experiment both with new technologies – including computers, calculators and audio-visual equipment – and with new instructional groupings – including small groups and one-one-instruction (Zellman et al, 2011). They were also encouraged to enhance so-called 'higher-order thinking' in their students, and to promote practical research skills such as critical reasoning, sceptical analysis, synthesis and evaluation (Zellman et al, 2011).

According to RAND researchers, independent-school teachers were indeed significantly more likely than their Ministry colleagues to experiment with new pedagogical tools and techniques (Zellman et al, 2009; Constant et al, 2010; Zellman et al 2011). Teachers in independent schools were more likely to utilise non-traditional instructional methods and technologies, and less likely 'to rely on textbooks to deliver their lessons' (Zellman et al, 2009, p. 83). Independent-school teachers were also more likely to use one-on-one and small groupings, to work with individual students and to encourage interaction between students in class (Zellman et al, 2009). They encouraged students to develop their own problem-solving strategies with greater frequency than Ministry teachers, and were more likely to engage their students in discussions of ideas and concepts using a variety of visual aids and illustrations (Constant et al, 2010). Independent-school teachers also placed significantly higher cognitive demands on their students, 'asking them to demonstrate comprehension and application of new material, and to synthesize and evaluate knowledge' in new ways (Zellman et al, 2011, p. 57).

Despite these promising results, RAND found a notable scarcity of pedagogical innovations in both Ministry and independent schools. Whole-group activity 'continued to be the most frequent instructional format' (Zellman et al, 2009, p. 77) in both types of institutions, and teachers struggled to adjust their sermonic styles to reform expectations. In more than 80% of the classrooms surveyed, lessons and exercises continued to demand only 'observation' and 'recall' (Zellman et al, 2009; Constant et al, 2010); demands for higher-order thinking 'were still relatively limited', and students were not generally prompted 'to think analytically or to synthesize or evaluate facts or ideas' (Zellman et al, 2009, p. 86).

Professional Development

During the 2001 RAND review, Ministry teachers expressed a strong desire to assume greater responsibility and a more active role in the learning process (Brewer et al, 2006). Those surveyed, however, noted few opportunities for professional development and advancement within the Ministry system (Brewer et al, 2006). The reform was determined, however, to 'encourage a culture of teaching professionalism' in Qatar, one in which teachers were recognized for their skills and knowledge, rewarded for their ability to enhance student motivation and student learning, and urged to explore new instructional methods, approaches to assessment, uses of technology and strategies for curriculum planning and implementation (Zellman et al, 2009, p. 28).

RAND researchers found that independent-school teachers – both Qatari and non-Qatari – received a great deal more in-school professional development training than their Ministry school colleagues (Brewer et al, 2006). Although both Ministry and independent-school teachers were offered the opportunity to participate in development workshops, teachers in independent institutions were far more likely to report receiving the types of professional development activities 'consistent with the reform's expectations' (Zellman et al, 2009, p. 53). Independent-school teachers did report, however, feeling 'overwhelmed and burned out' by the sheer number of activities required (Zellman et al, 2009, p. 50). They also expressed concern with the reform's emphasis on English-language proficiency, noting that efforts to improve teachers' fluency – particularly in mathematics and science courses – had become the dominant professional development concern in many independent Qatari schools (Zellman et al, 2009):

> [A] number of Arabic teachers felt that they needed more opportunities for content-focused professional development in the subject of Arabic and, particularly, extra training on how to implement the Arabic standards. In one case, an Independent school had not provided training of this kind from its own professional development budget because, the teachers there contended, the top priority was to raise the English competence of both teachers and students.
> (Zellman et al, 2009, p. 89)

In 2011 the Office of Academic Research at Qatar University published the results of a study further evaluating the impact of professional-development training on teachers in Qatar's schools. The study by Nasser and Romanowski (2011) found that one-third of the 40 teachers surveyed felt the professional-development activities offered by their schools were 'useful' (p. 162). The majority of teachers, however, echoed the concerns voiced by RAND study participants, expressing disappointment and frustration with the content and organisation of development activities.

They described the workshops as 'haphazard', lacking 'logical flow or continuity' (p. 162) and 'removed from the realities of classroom practice' (p. 165). Many teachers believed they were 'generally coerced' (p. 166) into workshops and had been 'forced to conform to a set of expectations alien to their own needs' (p. 165).

Teacher Satisfaction

In its study results, RAND touts the benefits of the reform for Qatari teachers, describing those in independent schools as having 'redefined' their role as educators (Brewer et al, 2006, p. 23). Seeing themselves for the first time as 'facilitators of learning, rather than as the 'teaching machines' that many felt themselves to be' in Ministry institutions (Brewer et al, 2006, p. 23), RAND asserted that independent-school teachers derived a number of 'intangible benefits' from their work (Zellman et al, 2009, p. 37). Independent-school teachers in RAND focus groups indeed expressed positive feelings about higher levels of autonomy and freedom in the classroom, as well as the ability to recognize and respond to individual learning needs (Zellman et al, 2009).

These remarks, however, were overwhelmed by a litany of complaints from Qatari educators. The majority of teachers in RAND focus groups repeatedly expressed a preference for teaching in Ministry schools, citing the increased workload and need to develop curriculum and materials as major deterrents to employment in an independent school (Zellman et al, 2011). Although teachers in RAND focus groups acknowledged that independent schools paid higher salaries to compensate for the greater workload and longer hours, most noted these benefits did not offset the significant disadvantages (Zellman et al, 2011). Both Qatari and non-Qatari teachers also expressed concerns about job security, noting that 'despite good performance, they might lose their job at any minute simply on the whim of [an] independent school operator' (Zellman et al, 2011, p. 38):

> For Qatari teachers, the notion of working under contracts subject to annual renewal is a vast departure from the guaranteed lifetime employment offered by the Ministry. Independent school contracts violate the historical right to a guaranteed permanent job that prevails in Qatar's government sector. (Zellman et al, 2011, p. 38)

Parental Involvement and Concerns

Prior to the reform, there was little expectation – and indeed, little evidence – that Qatari parents sought increased involvement in their child(ren)'s education (Constant et al, 2010). Although the 2001 RAND review noted that parents 'appeared open to the idea of new schooling options' (Brewer et al, 2007, 2), they also reported extremely low levels of engagement with both the Ministry and their child(ren)'s school (Brewer et al, 2006). In RAND focus groups conducted following the reform's initiation, however, parents with children in independent schools reported higher levels of involvement in and greater satisfaction with their child's school than did parents of children in Ministry institutions (Zellman et al, 2011). Independent-school parents were also more likely to have attended a school event and to have formed or participated in a parent association, advisory board or workshop (Brewer et al, 2006; Zellman et al, 2009; Constant et al, 2010). In addition to greater involvement in school activities and operations, independent-school parents reported significantly higher levels of communication with their child(ren)'s school, and were more likely to report having received regular updates on their child(ren)'s academic performance (Zellman et al, 2009).

Although feedback from independent-school parents was generally positive, parental concerns and complaints also featured prominently in RAND's focus group sessions. Parents expressed alarm, particularly in the early years of reform implementation, that operators were 'skimping on the purchase of materials to increase their profits', a worry compounded by the absence of textbooks – 'the hallmark of a Ministry education' – in most independent-school classrooms (Zellman et al, 2011, p. 58). Parents also expressed a 'widespread belief that insufficient attention was being paid to the Islamic, Arab, and Qatari identity of students' (Zellman et al, 2009, p. 115), and concern that English was taking precedence over Arabic in many independent-school curricula (Zellman et al, 2011).

The SEC and Education Institute quickly responded to parents' profit-seeking and textbook complaints. The SEC announced that all privately incorporated, for-profit independent schools would promptly convert to non-profit status in March 2006 (Constant et al, 2010, p. 458). In 2007 the Education Institute developed a list of 'acceptable materials' – those for which approximately 70% of content covered curriculum standards – and mandated that independent schools select a primary textbook from this list (Zellman et al, 2009). Parental concerns regarding the prominence of English in the curriculum remained largely unaddressed until January 2012, however, when the SEC issued a decree establishing Arabic as the official language of instruction in several key departments – including law, business administration and international affairs – at Qatar University (Haroon, 2012). In response to the dramatic changes at the nation's largest institution of higher learning, a number of independent schools have also reverted to mathematics and science instruction in Arabic. Official alterations to the curriculum standards, however, have not yet been made.

Student Satisfaction and Achievement

In contrast to their parents and teachers, students enrolled in independent schools expressed relatively few complaints with the new system. Independent-school students in RAND focus groups were considerably more likely than their Ministry school peers to report being interested in and proud of their school (Zellman et al, 2009). Students in independent schools were more likely to report being satisfied with school activities, and substantially more likely to agree 'that their school was preparing them to obtain a good job' (Zellman et al, 2009, p. 102). Teachers in independent institutions were also more likely to report that their students were motivated to learn inside and outside the classroom (Zellman et al, 2009).

Standardised examination results in 2005 and 2006 indicate that independent-school students outperformed their Ministry school peers in all four tested subject areas (Zellman et al, 2011). These findings, however, mask significant challenges and shortfalls within the new system. Although independent-school students indeed scored higher than Ministry students in all subject areas when assessed in Arabic, they tended to receive comparatively lower scores in mathematics and science when tested in English (Zellman et al, 2011). Only when RAND controlled for numerous factors having an impact on student achievement – including differences in students' prior scores, language of assessment, parents' education level, as well as teachers' education level and years of experience – did independent-school students perform better overall than their Ministry school peers (Zellman et al, 2009). However, results for students in both school types were low. In 2006, no students in a Ministry or private Arabic school, and less than 1% of students in an independent school, met the standards for mathematics and science (Zellman et al, 2009). Only 3% of students in Ministry and private Arabic schools met the Arabic standards, and only 1% met those in English (Zellman et al, 2009). Independent-school students performed only slightly better, with 6% meeting standards in Arabic and 7% in English. The poor relative performance of Ministry students is perhaps not surprising, however, given the exclusive emphasis on reform and standards implementation within independent schools:

> Independent schools, compared with Ministry schools, paid higher teacher salaries, provided more training and mentoring to teachers, and implemented student-centered pedagogical approaches with greater frequency. Independent schools were expected to align their curricula to the national standards as part of the reform effort and had made strong efforts to do so. Ministry schools did not have the autonomy to revise their curricula to directly address the national standards. (Zellman et al, 2009, p. 127)

Although independent-school students have continued to perform better than their Ministry peers on national assessments, their overall performance remains low. In 2009, only 4% of independent-school students performed at desired proficiency levels across all four tested subject areas (Constant et al, 2010).

School Autonomy

Within the newly decentralised system, independent schools are intended to function autonomously, subject only to limited terms and conditions specified in an operational contract. Decision-making authority is to rest, theoretically, 'with those closest to the work itself' – school operators, administrators and teachers (Brewer et al, 2006, p. 14). Education for a New Era has indeed afforded independent-school operators greater autonomy in pedagogical practice and resource allocation (Zellman et al, 2009). RAND also notes the greater freedom afforded to independent-school operators 'to recruit teachers who are best able to meet the needs of their schools and to offer salaries commensurate with experience and skills' (Zellman et al, 2009, pp. 28–29).

The nation's unique labour-market conditions and cultural values, however, have posed serious recruitment and retention challenges to independent-school operators. Both religious doctrine and Qatari social standards require that children over the age of 11 be instructed by teachers of the same gender. Male Qataris, however, generally 'prefer other occupations' (Zellman et al, 2011, p. 59) and 'do not consider teaching an attractive career'. As a result, boys' schools rely heavily on expatriate educators; in 2006, approximately 93% of male secondary teachers in independent institutions were expatriates (Zellman et al, 2011). Although Qatari women once favoured teaching as a career, preferring the 'relatively short hours and gender-segregated workplace' (Zellman et al, 2011, p. 59), RAND reports a declining interest in the occupation over the last decade. As other career opportunities have opened to women and more have explored alternative fields in higher education, the number of Qatari women in independent schools has fallen sharply.

In May 2005, in an effort to encourage school operators to hire more Qataris and to interest more nationals in applying for teaching positions, the SEC established minimum salary requirements and minimum recruitment targets for Qataris in independent schools (Zellman et al, 2009). In March 2006 the SEC issued a further directive requiring independent schools – some then operating as privately incorporated, for-profit businesses – to convert to non-profit institutions 'with a single Qatari operator who was qualified to be and would serve as the school's principal' (Zellman et al, 2011, p. 60; see also Constant et al, 2010). The policy was a vast departure from the original Qatari law requiring a minimum of two people – only one of whom must be Qatari – to apply for and operate an independent school (Constant et al, 2010). In addition to expanding its Qatarisation requirements, in September 2007 the Qatari government also announced a 40% increase in the base salary of nationals employed in the Civil Service – including teachers – as well as a substantial increase in the monthly minimum salary of Qatari university graduates (Zellman et al, 2009; Constant et al, 2010).

These labour-market conditions and the policy responses to them, however, have both 'reduced operator autonomy and limited variety in operators' backgrounds' (Zellman et al, 2011, p. 59). Although minimum percentage targets for Qatari teachers 'have not [yet] been enforced strictly as quotas' (Zellman et al, 2011, p. 59), independent-school operators expressed a belief that 'the burden of finding qualified Qatari teachers unfairly fell on their shoulders' (Zellman et al, 2009, p. 34). Alterations to operational guidelines have also been viewed as problematic. Although intended to increase the number of Qataris in management positions and to prevent 'non-specialists' from overseeing government-funded institutions, their effect was to force 'non-Qataris and those who came from outside the Ministry system to leave their positions as school operators' (Zellman et al, 2011, p. 60). In addition to reducing diversity among both operators and schools, the new policy had a pernicious effect on reform implementation, as described by Constant et al (2010, p. 458):

> As a result [of the new guidelines], about half of Generation I and II operators exited the system and about half of the planned Generation III schools were not able to open [as intended].

Changes in financial policies and funding guidelines have also had a profound impact on operator autonomy and school innovation. The sudden elimination of special project grants in 2005-6, and of start-up funds for new schools in 2007-8, substantially altered the ability of schools to develop and offer the types of innovative academic programmes envisioned by the reform. School administrators reported in RAND focus groups that frequent policy changes had 'fostered a sense of instability'; many reported increasing reluctance to attempt bold innovations, particularly those involving an element of financial risk (Constant et al, 2010, p. 459).

School Accountability and Choice

Independent schools, as a key principle of the reform design, were intended to be held accountable to the government and to parents through a variety of conformance and compliance measures. Schools were to be subjected to regular financial audits; in addition, the results of the annual Qatar Comprehensive Educational Assessment (QCEA) student assessments were also to be made publically available at the school level, allowing parents to choose institutions with preferred educational approaches and achievement levels. Independent schools, like their US charter counterparts, were intended 'to combine market pressure through parental choice with public accountability through public oversight' (Rotherham, 2005, p. 46).

Demand for spaces in high-quality government schools far exceeds supply, however, as many independent schools have long waiting lists for enrolment (Zellman et al, 2011). The number of children in an independent-school classroom is limited to 25, reducing the capacity of independent institutions to accept and enrol new pupils. Without significant increases in school supply, a key reform accountability mechanism – parental choice – cannot fully operate (Zellman et al, 2011). As a result, 'market forces are not imposing accountability on school operators as the reform design intended' (Zellman et al, 2011, p. 60). As the SEC has issued policy directives in response to public complaints – including those eliminating profitable institutions and establishing Qatarisation targets – so too have they reduced operator autonomy and variety in the system:

> Policymakers have increasingly resorted to regulatory approaches both to address public concerns and to hold schools accountable. But use of regulatory accountability methods without a clear mechanism to encourage performance improvement risks a return to the practices of the former Ministry. (Zellman et al, 2011, p. 60)

The SEC recently responded to capacity shortages by raising the maximum number of classroom pupils from 25 to 30, and by announcing the introduction of new 'high-quality schooling options' [2] (Zellman et al, 2011, p. 59). Although RAND declares these initiatives 'promising', it acknowledges that schooling capacity must expand significantly 'to have a noticeable effect on demand for high-quality school places' (Zellman et al, 2011, p. 59).

6. Conclusion

Qatar's K-12 education system has indeed transformed dramatically since the introduction of the first independent schools in 2004. RAND, while acknowledging many of the challenges confronting 'Education for a New Era' in its early years, today enthusiastically lauds the nation's new system, actively promoting the adoption of a similar reform model in other GCC states (RAND-Qatar Policy Institute, 2007). Little reference is made in either the organisation's published reports or public rhetoric, however, to the past and present shortcomings of the charter-school model in the United States. Ample evidence suggests that America's experiment in taxpayer-financed, market-driven educational provision is, at best, a struggling work-in-progress, and at worst, an abject failure for thousands of the nation's students. Rather than adopting the best in international institutional and curricular arrangements, Qatar may indeed be sidled with an outdated and intensely baroque system antithetical to the nation's hopes and potential for true reform.

Notes

[1] Real gross domestic product (GDP) grew at an average of 10% annually from the mid- to late-1990s, well above the average 3.5% growth rate observed in other GCC states (Gonzalez et al, 2008). Per capita GDP doubled from an average of US$14,000 in 1990 to more than US$28,000 in the year 2000 (Gonzalez et al, 2008; UNData, 2012); by 2009, individual incomes had reached nearly US$70,000 (UNData, 2012).

[2] In 2008-9, the SEC introduced a voucher system, permitting parents to enrol their child(ren) in any Qatari private school using government-issued tuition vouchers. The SEC has also sponsored several branch campuses of elite international private schools.

References

Anderson, M.K., Alnaimi, T.N. & Alhajri, S.H. (2010) National Student Research Fairs as Evidence for Progress in Qatar's Education for a New Era, *Improving Schools*, 13, 235-248.

Brewer, D.J., Augustine, C.H., Zellman, G.L., Ryan, G., Goldman, C.A., Stasz, C. et al (2007) *Education for a New Era: design and implementation of K-12 education reform in Qatar*. Executive Summary. Santa Monica, CA: RAND Corporation.

Brewer, D.J., Goldman, C.A., Augustine, C.H., Zellman, G.L., Ryan, G., Stasz, C. et al (2006) *An Introduction to Qatar's Primary and Secondary Education Reform*. Working Paper [WR-399-SEC] prepared for the Supreme Education Council. Doha: RAND Education.

Constant, L., Goldman, C.A., Zellman, G.L., Augustine, C.H., Galama, T., Gonzalez, G. et al (2010) Promoting Quality and Variety through Public Financing of Privately Operated Schools in Qatar, *Journal of School Choice*, 4, 450-473.

Donn, G. & Al Manthri, Y. (2010) *Globalisation and Higher Education in the Arab Gulf States*. Oxford: Symposium Books.

Frankenberg, E. & Lee, C. (2003) *Charter Schools and Race: a lost opportunity for integrated education*. Cambridge, MA: The Civil Rights Project at Harvard University.

Gonzalez, G., Karoly, L.A., Constant, L., Salem, H. & Goldman, C.A. (2008) *Facing Human Capital Challenges of the 21st Century: education and labor market initiatives in Lebanon, Oman, Qatar, and the United Arab Emirates.* Doha: RAND-Qatar Policy Institute.

Haroon, A. (2012) Elation, Worries on the Campus. *The Peninsula*, 28 January. http://www.thepeninsulaqatar.com/qatar/181277-elation-worries-on-the-campus.html (accessed 6 July 2012).

Nasser, R. & Romanowski, M. (2011) Teacher Perceptions of Professional Development in the Context of National Educational Reform: the case of Qatar, *International Journal of Training & Development*, 15 (2), 158-168.

Qatar Petroleum (2011) Press Release for the 11th Annual Qatarization Review Meeting. http://www.qatarization.com.qa/Qatarization/Qatarization.nsf/en_Pages/en_News_NewsLibrary (accessed 6 July 2012).

Qatar Statistics Authority (QSA) (2012) Population Structure. http://www.qsa.gov.qa/eng/PopulationStructure.htm (accessed 6 July 2012).

RAND-Qatar Policy Institute (2007) *A New System for K–12 Education in Qatar.* Research Brief. Doha: Rand-Qatar Policy Institute.

Rotherham, A. (2005) The Pros & Cons of Charter School Closures, in R.J. Lake & P.T. Hill (Eds) *Hopes, Fears, & Reality: a balanced look at American charter schools in 2005.* Seattle, WA: National Charter School Research Project at the University of Washington.

Supreme Education Council (SEC) (2010) *Education for a New Era: 2009 annual report.* Doha: SEC.

UN Data (2012) Qatar. http://data.un.org/CountryProfile.aspx?crName=QATAR (accessed 6 July 2012).

United States Department of State (2012) Background Note: Qatar. http://www.state.gov/r/pa/ei/bgn/5437.htm (accessed 6 July 2012).

Zellman, G.L., Ryan, G.W., Karam, R., Constant, L., Salem, H., Gonzalez, G. et al (2009) *Implementation of the K-12 Education Reform in Qatar's Schools.* Santa Monica, CA: The RAND Corporation.

Zellman, G.L., Constant, L. & Goldman, C.A. (2011) *K-12 Education Reform in Qatar.* Santa Monica, CA: The RAND Corporation.

CHAPTER FIVE

Higher Education in Qatar: does a US medical school break the baroque arsenal?

TANYA KANE

Weill Cornell Medical College in Qatar (WCMC-Q) is one of a myriad of educational transplants proliferating from the Gulf to Singapore to South Africa. Within the context of the Gulf alone, there is competition with other globally recognised and prestigious university programmes in the Emirates and Saudi Arabia. Education City is Qatar's flagship campus created by the Qatar Foundation for Education, Science and Community Development's (QF), which can be viewed as vying with other Gulf States to become the regional 'educational hub'.

This chapter examines the transfer of a US pedagogical model to the Arabian Gulf against the wider context of the globalisation of higher education. In observing the local reception of what is presumed to be a universal medical education and its partial but by no means total translation into local terms, this case study explores whether WCMC-Q constitutes what has been referred to in previous chapters as 'a baroque arsenal' and is based on anthropological fieldwork that was conducted between 2006-8.[1] The degree was designed in New York City and subsequently transferred to Doha; thus the ethics, materials, methods and practices are far removed from their original context. WCMC's medical degree is Western professional training geared towards the demands of the US health-care system. Through its production of US-style doctors in a non-US setting, the transnational medical school serves as a niche through which to explore the tensions and new forms of knowledge that arise in global models of tertiary education.

The global educational landscape has been transformed due to technical improvements which now enable non-conventional academic institutions to access the resources and pedagogy of world-renowned centres of learning, remotely. Consequently, we are beginning to see the emergence of new academic providers and a greater mobility of educational programmes. Western models of education are thereby being disseminated around the globe and are fast becoming the preferred educational commodity for developing nations.

In this sense, globalisation has fundamentally altered the conditions surrounding the delivery of education, effectively homogenising pedagogical strategies and streamlining education policy and reform. While education exchange has been going on for centuries (i.e., via the movement of faculty and students, the borrowing of curricular documents), this current wave of globalisation is different as it incorporates new roles, markets, agents, tools, rationales and policies (Donn & Al Manthri, 2010, p. 27). Within the context of higher education, the term 'denationalisation' is used to describe 'the process whereby developmental logics, frames, and practices, are increasingly associated with what is happening at a larger (beyond the nation) scale' (Olds, 2010). With the advent of denationalisation, education-policy makers are responding to new challenges, which include meeting the demands of growing knowledge economies (Knight, 2006), as well as recognising the implications of emergent international curricula and academic institutions (Resnik, 2008).

Amidst these transformations, governments throughout the world are being forced to evaluate how well indigenous systems of education are preparing their students for participation in an academia which, as a result of globalisation, is increasingly centralised and, to a large extent, Westernised. Such assessments are leading to reforms devised specifically to address the inadequacies of extant educational systems. Keen to advance the domestic provision of education, there is an increasing trend in the Arab Gulf States to import exogenous policies and educational programmes in an effort to rectify identified shortcomings.

Based on their affluence, the Gulf States are not normally categorised as developing nations; however, it can be argued that their education systems are still at an emergent stage. As the global education sector expands, developing nations are beginning to rely on educational imports from developed countries in 'the centre' or 'core'. Rich as they are, the Gulf nations are in a position to purchase education programmes from abroad. As a result:

> new organisational forms in higher education – 'accreditation', 'quality assurance', qualifications frameworks – transform the regional-local education systems of the Gulf and replace them with structures, systems and processes which are located elsewhere. (Donn & Al Manthri 2010, p. 24)

Despite their success in recruiting high-profile Western institutions, however, the Arab Gulf States are still generally considered to be part of the educational 'periphery' on the basis that they lack developed knowledge-based economies and embedded research culture, and because they rely on imported products such as materials, services and expertise from the centre.

Donn and Al Manthri (2010) are among the first to examine the impact that the importation of education programmes has on the Arab Gulf states that rely on this strategy. They claim that the consumption of a 'baroque arsenal' of pedagogical products from the West allows the producers to benefit on two accounts: the money they receive for their outmoded/second-hand programmes is then reinvested and generates new knowledge that can be sold on again; and that this borrowing undermines capacity building and impedes production of an indigenous knowledge economy. Further, they contend that countries of the periphery will continue to be such as long as this borrowing scenario continues.

This is an interesting argument and one addressed in this chapter. On the basis of a research-based project in Qatar, attention is drawn to the possibilities of nuancing relationships between countries of the core and the periphery. It will be proposed that the example of Weill Cornell Medical College in Qatar may provide an example beyond 'the baroque arsenal'.

Changing Objectives of Higher Education

Just as universities are prone to marketisation strategies, so too are broader education policies. We are beginning to see the increasing alignment of education supply and employment demand with overhauls framed by neoliberal rhetoric propounding the merits of job creation, increasing standards, competitiveness and human-capacity building. Governments are starting to incorporate market policies into domestic education agendas in a bid to remain (or in the case of Qatar, *become*) competitive in an increasingly connected world (Whitty et al, 1998). Altbach provides a brief synopsis of the changing face of education:

> A revolution is taking place in education. Education is increasingly becoming an internationally traded commodity. No longer is it seen primarily as a set of skills, attitudes and values required for citizenship and effective participation in modern society. Rather, it is increasingly seen as a commodity to be purchased by a consumer in order to build a 'skill set' to be used in the market place or a product to be bought and sold by multinational corporations, academic institutions that have transmogrified themselves into businesses, and other providers. (2002, p. 2)

The market philosophy of neoliberalism – which emphasises the functional value of education in terms of future employment – is a salient feature of education in the developed world. Nowadays, many Western universities (both public and private) are run like businesses, complete with administrators charged with managing and delivering prescribed, measurable outcomes (Gewirtz, 2002). These shifts, coupled with funding cuts to the education sector, have forced academic institutions in the core not only to vie for students domestically, but also to explore new consumer markets where their pedagogical wares might be taken up, resulting in the commodification and massification of tertiary education (Neave & Van Vught 1991; Poovey 2001; van der Wende 2003; Morey 2004). Treating education (1) as a commodity, and (2) as job training rather than an enrichment of the human mind with inherent (as opposed to economic or societal) value, is generally considered a neoliberal perspective, and one fostered by the imperatives of global capitalism. How far this plays out in one country of the Gulf is the subject of the next section.

Qatar: a case study

Qatar has transitioned from a tribal and nomadic society to a modern state over the course of a few decades. Fuelled by hydrocarbon proceeds, the 1950s and 1960s marked a period of unprecedented prosperity and social development, as well as an influx of immigration for the former pearl-diving nation. Flanked by Saudi Arabia and Iran, the small peninsular state of Qatar is noted for its strategic position in terms of world politics, its oil and gas reserves and its autocratic but benevolent leadership. Qatar has a population of 1.7 million (QSA, 2011), the majority of whom live in the capital city Doha, the locus of Qatar's power (i.e., the financial centre and seat of government).

Qatar's confirmed gas reserves rank third largest in the world (Economist Intelligence Unit, 2004, p. 18). Owing to its current status as the largest exporter of liquid natural gas, Qatar boasts one of the world's highest per capita incomes and an economy that has grown exponentially over recent years. This, coupled with the consistently strong performance of oil and gas prices over the past decade has resulted in handsome profits for the small Gulf nation. The current leadership adopts an enlightened approach to their current wealth and has sought to diversify its economy in order to prepare for a time when their hydrocarbon resources are no longer a guarantee to prosperity. As part of this approach, Qatar's leadership spends vast sums of the nation's petroleum wealth in an effort to create a knowledge-based economy. Similarly, the Qatari state has sought to invest its current resources in public infrastructure geared to improve education, health care and commercial ventures. Qatar is also beginning to invest heavily in research and development as a means of promoting future economic development.

With an indigenous population estimated as being between 250,000 to 350,000, Qatari nationals barely represent a quarter of the resident population. The small pool of working-age citizens has forced the nation to rely extensively on professionals from Western countries to achieve national projects driven by neoliberal logic. The demands of Qatar's fast-evolving high-tech society have outpaced the nation's capacity to produce a domestic workforce equipped with the appropriate skills and professional expertise required to establish locally based enterprises. Nor does the nation possess the necessary institutional infrastructure to train the indigenous population. The affluent state can, however, afford to purchase services from elsewhere as required but the powers that be recognise that such short-term solutions 'will not build the local expertise the country needs to reach a state of sustainability' (QF, 2007). In order to remedy this situation and limit their future dependency on foreigners the leadership is setting up joint ventures and academic partnerships that 'will in time recruit and train increasing numbers of talented Qataris, and in this way the skills will transfer to the local population' (QF, 2007). In essence, the state is using social engineering to modernise the country and safeguard a sustainable and productive future for its citizens through investment in education.

Qatar's Educational Landscape

That higher education is gradually becoming synonymous with occupational training is evidence of the role that the rapidly changing labour market is having on educational reform. In the case of Qatar, the government is attempting to recalibrate specific sectors of society and to broaden its range of commercial endeavours through the introduction of new technologies, infrastructure improvement, expansion of the service sector and diversification into non-oil industries. Education makes up a key component of this diversification strategy, entailing heavy investment in skills-training programmes and tertiary-education provision to better prepare nationals for employment in the new private-sector industries. Skills acquisition is now regarded as a necessary condition of economic development and reflects how educational goals have been redefined in relation to the demands of the economy. Within the context of neoliberalism, a well-educated population is a valuable labour resource. The provision of appropriate training/education is aimed at ensuring that each individual is performing to his/her highest potential and in this way contributes to the diversification and sustainability of the economy. With education at the core of the Qatari leadership's desire to build a sustainable future and to help the nation compete in the world market, it has been imperative for the nation to improve its provision of education, especially at the tertiary level.

Committed to developing its education sector, the State of Qatar allocates approximately one fifth of government spending to education (19.6%), representing 3.3% of gross domestic product (GDP) (UNESCO, 2008). In 2001, the Qatari leadership commissioned the RAND Corporation to assess the country's elementary- and secondary-education system (K–12) and to submit recommendations for the design and implementation of a new standard of education system designed to address the changing demands of the nation. The RAND report revealed that the Qatari education system was 'rigid, outmoded, and resistant to reform' and underscored the need for stronger performing primary- and secondary- education systems in order to support the nation's new economic and social developments (Brewer et al, 2007, p. xvii). To this end, RAND introduced an Independent School Model based on a curriculum structured by standards, assessments, professional development and the use of data as performance indicators. This standards-based system enveloped the principles of autonomy, accountability, variety and parental choice. These reforms have resulted in the use of internationally benchmarked standards, the creation of learner-centred classrooms, facility upgrades, a restructuring of the power and authority structures of the education system, and a more comprehensive system of teacher training.

At the tertiary level, the Qatari leadership is attempting to position itself in the global education landscape by launching itself as a regional knowledge hub. In its drive to become an advanced knowledge-based society, the government is attempting to build human capacity by educating its citizenry to the highest standards. These objectives are being realised through the founding of the Qatar Foundation, the establishment of Education City and the recruitment of world-renowned universities. In addition to positioning Qatar as a regional and international centre for educational excellence, QF's support of advanced research also aims to establish the foundation as a centre of excellence in research.

Qatar Foundation (QF) and Education City

Qatar Foundation was founded by Emiri Decree in 1995 by His Highness Sheikh Hamad bin Khalifa Al-Thani and is chaired by his consort, Her Highness Sheikha Moza bint Nasser. QF is an independent, non-profit organisation guided by the principle that its people are the nation's greatest natural resource. The organisation's vision and motivations are explicit: 'To develop people's abilities through investments in human capital, innovative technology, state of the art facilities and partnerships with elite organizations, thus raising the competency of people and the quality of life' (QF, 2007). QF is ultimately responsible for overseeing the implementation of the QF mission and taking new initiatives forward. Funding comes directly from the Qatari government.

QF is directly responsible for the governance of Education City and is not subject to any government ministry or department.[2]

Education City, a 1000-hectare campus allocated by the state, is the primary locus of QF activities. Education City is home to the Middle Eastern campus of Weill Cornell Medical College and a number of other premier universities, each having been selected because of their educational niches. It also contains a science and technology park, which operates as a free zone within which a number of blue-chip companies and world-class research facilities are encouraged to establish without the normal restrictions imposed by the Qatari foreign investment legislation. It is a distinctive educational enclave that supports a matrix of social, political, economic and technological conditions conducive to recruiting international universities and foreign expertise. It is a self-contained and self-sufficient techno-hub that functions as an independent entity on the outskirts of Doha. Education City is a site where extraterritorial expertise interfaces with local stakeholders (e.g., Qatar Petroleum, Hamad Medical Corporation) in the exchange and creation of new knowledge. The clustering of institutions in a localised educational and technological zone 'connects the state, as venture capitalist, with foreign research institutions and global companies, creating a network that fosters interactions, risk-taking and innovations among expatriate and local knowledge workers' (Ong, 2005, p. 340). As QF is entering its second decade and many of the planned institutions and facilities are now in place, QF's research mission is beginning to come to the fore.

WCMC-Q

According to the QF President, when its Board of Management first conceived of the idea of Education City, it conducted a markets-need analysis wherein they identified a need for a medical school, an engineering school and a business school. The results of this assessment indicated that setting up a medical school should be their first priority. With its vision of modernising and implementing international standards in health-care provision, QF was keen to recruit the 'best of the best' and looked West on the basis that as yet, none of the regional universities 'has been able to communicate on the international scene' (QF President, personal communication, Sept. 2008). QF's selection criteria were explicit: it would reject any ventures that simply proposed setting up an adjunct satellite institution; and it was only willing to recruit an institution that guaranteed to offer a medical education of the same calibre and was thus willing to confer the *same* degree as that offered in the United States. QF's insistence on educational equivalence was coupled with the expectation that any prospective institutional partnership would also contribute to an embedded domestic research programme intended to generate indigenous knowledge.

Established at the request of QF and in partnership with Cornell University in 2002, WCMC-Q is an institutional clone of the US medical school. Set out in the Memorandum of Understanding, the Cornell Board retains the 'freedom to train medical students the way [they] do in New York' (Interview, WCMC-Q Dean 2008), and thus exerts the same autonomy and governance in Qatar that it has in the United States. WCMC-Q offers a combined six-year pre-medical and medical programme where the Medical Program 'replicates the curriculum, quality and standards' of that in America and shares its tripartite commitment to education, research and patient care (college website). Like their US peers, WCMC-Q students sit US medical-licensing board examinations throughout the duration of their training. The two programmes are educationally equivalent and the same MD degree is awarded on both campuses. In May 2008, Cornell became the first US university to confer its medical degree overseas.

Too often 'global' academic ventures become disconnected satellite campuses functioning independently from the original programme. The early success of WCMC-Q can, however, be attributed to the strong links existing between the two campuses. WCMC-Q is conceived of as an extension of the NY campus rather than an adjunct; this is essential to ensure the standards and integrity of the Cornell brand. The Doha campus is connected to the 'mothership' not only through teaching and administration, but also through transnational scholarship (e.g., Grand Rounds via video-streaming) and collaborative scientific research (e.g., Qatar National Research Fund endowments). Throughout their medical training, Qatar-based students are encouraged to undertake research and internships at the NY campus (and vice versa). It is certainly the case that this integrated partnership has taken time to develop and is the result of a reflective administration, one that is willing to examine itself critically and which confronts problems as they arise and continually strives to improve.

How the Programme Works

The desire to deliver the same degree programme has required the enterprising college both to extend the remit of its NY faculty, as well as compete in the global marketplace for a limited supply pool of academic and technical talent. The initial absence of a comprehensive in situ faculty in Qatar forced Cornell to think creatively not only about how to mobilise and stretch the teaching capacity of its NY faculty, but also how it utilised cutting-edge technology to circumvent the shortage of expertise whilst delivering the same calibre of medical training to the small cohorts in the distant locale. Effective transmission of the degree to two physically disparate sites led the college to devise an innovative and interactive pedagogical model that managed working relationships across time and space.

In the initial years, the medical curriculum at WCMC-Q was strategically delivered by a team of medical-faculty members who were resident in Qatar (referred to administratively as 'on-site faculty', or OSFs), as well as remote lectures broadcast from NY featuring subject experts. At that time up to 70% of the lectures were recorded and video-streamed from the NY campus. Thus, the original lecture was delivered first to the NY cohort at which time it was recorded and subsequently broadcast seven thousand miles away in a lecture hall in Doha. That the majority of lectures originated in and were conveyed to a live NY audience had interesting implications for the content, assumptions and language employed. Cornell's distinctive institutional arrangement involved a combination of specific presences and absences in the delivery of its programme, each mode affording a different degree of intersubjectivity.[3]

Circumventing Absence

There were a number of structural realities that accounted for some of the medical instruction not being delivered 'in person'. Foremost amongst these reasons were issues related to medical-faculty recruitment, including: the cost of maintaining resident faculty members abroad; the reluctance on the part of faculty to leave well-established research laboratories in the metropole; the absence of an active academic research and publishing community in Qatar;[4] the perceived negative impact on career progression; clinical commitments to patients; financial reasons related to private practices and pharmaceutical endorsements; unwillingness to uproot families; and apprehension concerning safety in the Arab world in a post-9/11 environment. To circumvent the absence of a sizeable faculty in Doha, it was necessary for Cornell to create virtual communities in order to make the remote NY teaching staff 'present' at the new branch campus.

The distinctive configuration of absences and presences shaped the educational programme and resulted in the emergence of an innovative pedagogical form. A number of intentional and unintentional consequences arose between the two campuses as the exogenous medical education package was transferred from the metropole to the desert. The transnational programme was not simply a process involving the exportation of 'universal' knowledge from the US core to the periphery, but also involved reciprocal influence, the co-production of knowledge and a system that generated a process of feedback in the opposite direction.

The Doha campus interacts extensively with WCMC in New York for its day-to-day functioning, thus state-of-the-art technologies feature prominently in the transnational educational model operating at WCMC-Q. The educational arrangement requires both material and virtual proximity in order to facilitate knowledge transfers and to support the full spectrum of educational encounters associated with the professional training. The assemblage of technological infrastructure at WCMC-Q is uniquely aggregated in order to transcend the physical constraints of distance and time as well as to aid in the sharing of pedagogical resources. Information and communications technology is what allows the dual-sited campus to share one library, one faculty, a single curriculum and to form one virtual community bound together under a shared Cornellian identity.

Success of the transplanted curriculum was highly dependent on a multimodal network of workers situated at both sites who coordinated the physical transfer of pedagogical materials (e.g., textbooks, scientific apparatus, cadavers) and the development and use of interactive technologies (e.g., lecture streaming; virtual microscopy; an e-library; electronic transmission of course materials and exams). The main structural differences lay in the way in which each institutional setting assembled actors, materials and information within their respective realms. The new branch of the medical school was itself an assemblage of technologies, institutions (e.g., Cornell, QF, NY Presbyterian Hospital and Hamad Medical Corporation) and infrastructures (e.g., United States Medical Licensing Examination, Arab Board Examinations): a compilation of mechanisms put together in a neoteric transnational spatio-temporal recasting of tertiary education.

As yet, the implications associated with different types of pedagogical presences and absences inherent in distance education remain under-theorised. Through electronically mediated technologies, a person can achieve a pseudo-presence enabling him/her to transcend his/her real position and to engage in real time with actors in a different social space. The institutional interactions that occurred between the Cornell campuses provided useful exemplars of different modes of co-presence of academics who congregated physically (face-to-face) or virtually (face-to-screen) to facilitate knowledge sharing in real time or via recorded lectures. The rationales behind the selection of particular modes of transmission for specific types of information transfers was illuminating, indicative as they were of what kinds of bonds programme administrators deemed to be both necessary and effective in medical training at a distance.

In some teaching scenarios co-presence was deemed unnecessary for the actual transfer of scientific knowledge and abandoned altogether (i.e., delivered via video-streamed lectures [VSL]),[5] whereas co-location was the preferred mode of interaction when demonstrative teaching was involved. Acquisition of tangible skills such as physical examinations and interfacing with patients demanded close observation of professionals in action. The sensitive and uncertain nature of these interpersonal encounters render them more susceptible to unforeseen complications, thus physical co-location ensured that an expert was on hand to provide help and support.

Knowledge in a Different Context

The crossborder institutional model used at Cornell serves as a good example of geographically dispersed people being brought into close contact with each other via knowledge exchange and the sharing of pedagogical artefacts. Sourced and imprinted in the United States, the circulation of culturally laden institutional forms and teaching tools permit the Qatar-based students 'to participate in the imagined realities of other cultures ... eroding the "natural" connection or isomorphism between culture and place' (Inda & Rosaldo 2002, p. 11). Thus, the deterritorialisation of the educational form results in the actor having to apprehend and mediate seemingly foreign concepts, ideas and practices as well as indigenous ones, under the gaze of his/her local community.

Indeed, despite acquiring a 'universal' skill set and being trained in the American medical tradition, divergences in clinical practice also mirrored cultural particularities of the Qatari social and medical environment. The 'American way' of doing things did not always translate or conform to cultural mores and standard practice within the Gulf setting. The medical school recognised that its autonomy-based ethics course reflected US notions of individualism and anticipated that issues such as informed consent and patient autonomy might be at odds with local values in the more collectivist Gulf setting. According to the professor charged with writing and delivering the specially designed medical ethics curriculum at WCMC-Q, the uncertainties surrounding the universal validity of the Western model were compounded by the fact that the courses had to simultaneously:

> cultivate the knowledge, skills, and attitudes to prepare [their] students to address ethical dilemmas in clinical practice from their own cultural perspectives and also from a North American perspective. And while asking students to consider ethics from a Western perspective ... [having] to avoid the impression that [they] were attempting to engage in indoctrination. (Rodriguez del Pozo & Fins, 2005, p. 136)

Cultural nuances shape medical ethics so Arab students' interpretations of certain principles occasionally differed from those endorsed at WCMC-Q.

The case study of WCMC-Q student doctors operating in the clinical terrain reflects the influence of the local environment on the global in that it afforded an opportunity to see how the informants imposed their own cultural dispositions on clinical practice and interpreted what they were taught at Cornell in accordance with their own cultural codes. In particular, it was the ethics and codes of conduct that became 'Qatarized' in Doha, shaped as they were by Arab mores and values, demonstrating that 'not all aspects of biomedicine become equally hybridized when they [are] diffused from the core areas of development to the peripheries' (Finkler, 2004, p. 2048). Thus, ethical, infrastructural and procedural components warrant negotiation in the Qatari context.

Western Medical Practice in Qatari Clinics

For students at WCMC-Q, medical knowledge is disseminated in two main venues: the US medical school where they are taught the science of medicine and Hamad Medical Corporation (HMC), the Arabic teaching hospital where they initially learn how to be doctors.[6] Prior to the arrival of Cornell, HMC was not a teaching hospital and therefore had not been recognised by the Joint Commission International (JCI), an international arm of the Joint Commission that accredits health-care institutions. This meant that in the beginning Cornell could not offer all the constituent parts of its medical curriculum in Qatar and students had to go to New York for some of their training. HMC and Cornell have worked together closely in an attempt to upgrade the status of the pre-existing Qatari hospitals, most of which were awarded JCI accreditation at varying points in 2006. Specifically, this involved the cosmetic overhaul of medical facilities and a concerted effort to improve the quality of health-care services at HMC through the implementation of a series of structural and procedural changes as per the recommendations of JCI.

Biomedicine is the predominant form of health care available in Qatar. The proliferation of medical instruments (e.g., stethoscopes, blood-pressure cuffs, ECGs, defibrillators); a common medical vernacular; and the widespread availability of branded pharmaceuticals are testament to the globalisation and homogenisation of medicine. This means that biomedicine in Doha largely resembles that found in NY. Upon closer examination, however, medicine in Qatar is distinctive owing to its incorporation of Arabic and Islamic elements into its practice. Finding themselves at the nexus of US training and indigenous medical facilities in their quest to become professional doctors, WCMC-Q students were sometimes forced to negotiate opposing institutional agendas based on their own cultural understandings. Like many of their HMC mentors, students reared in the Gulf were able to draw from an esoteric cultural palette that was accessible on account of being members of the same cultural and/or religious communities (e.g., shared Islamic beliefs and cultural practices). Having grown up in Qatar or the Arab world, many of the young physicians-in-training related to the manner in which biomedicine was practised in HMC health-care facilities and initially empathised with patients' expectations, even when modes of practice deviated from those taught at Cornell.

Cornell has been working in conjunction with the Qatari health-service providers in order to upgrade the provision of health care, but a university's sphere of influence is limited. As most clinical training occurred on HMC premises, WCMC-Q students occasionally reported encounters with doctors who exhibited discordant values and utilised techniques different from those demonstrated at the medical college. Many of the practitioners working in HMC completed their medical training in the Arab world and they have assumed the professional norms and incorporated the procedural skills of their own role models into their medical practice.

In clinical contexts, universities can neither vet all the practitioners students encounter, nor can academic institutions control alternative modes of practice that its students invariably observe, which have the potential to 'undermine the learning objectives of the formal curriculum' (Jaye et al, 2006, p. 148). Continuity of US medical values and ways of doing things were sometimes hampered because they were not always consistently modelled or reinforced in the clinical setting. According to some WCMC-Q students, continuity of practice was not achieved until they were immersed in the NY clinical setting during the latter stages of their training. For instance, the prescriptive form of taking complete patient histories taught at Cornell was radically curtailed in the Qatari setting:

> When second year medical students were furnished with a course handout outlining questions pertaining to sexual behaviour that they were expected to pose during patient interviews, the Qatari students sitting beside me were mortified on the basis that such queries were not culturally sensitive. Thrusting the paper under my nose and jabbing her finger at specific questions one of the abaya-clad girls said, 'These questions are inappropriate. To ask them would make the patient think that you [the student-physician] are crazy. 'Are you married? Do you have a child? Are you a virgin?' The order of the questions is ridiculous!' She went on to explain that if the answer to the question about marriage is negative, it would be unsuitable to continue with this line of questioning, highlighting the unequivocal expectation that an unmarried Muslim female would doubtless still be a virgin. A cursory look at the sheet did include examples of some culturally askew questions including: 'Do you have sex with men,

women or both?'; 'In general, are you satisfied with your sexual relationship?'; 'Are you using a method of STD protection?'; 'How many partners have you had in your lifetime?' Outraged as they were, the students had failed to notice that the course handout did highlight the need to 'individualize the questions for each patient' and the 'importance of understanding and respecting cultural, social, ethnic and religious issues'.

Whilst Islamic values certainly informed medical-student conduct, there was no compelling evidence of a specifically Islamic or Arabic imprint on the scientific facets of the imported curriculum, suggesting that biomedical science is for the most part both mobile and replicable. While the science 'in itself' posed no problems even to the most devout Muslim students, in the case of medical training there can be no 'science in itself'; it is all about practice, and practice always takes place in a context. As knowledge moves from the 'classroom to the bedside' – and especially in a scenario when it is transferred to an entirely different culture – the *application* of science can create dilemmas and this is where the ethical challenges of pedagogical borrowing or 'internationalisation' arise.

Producers, Not Mere Consumers of Knowledge

Although Education City does not yet contribute significant outward flows of exports to the benefit of other economies, QF has every intention of achieving this in the future through the synergy of its current academic collaborations (e.g., Qatar National Research Fund; Sidra/Cornell affiliation). Qatar's Science and Technology Park has been specifically incorporated into the grounds of Education City to function as an incubator for commercially viable ideas developed at universities like Cornell and is supported by a massive financial endowment. Rivalling the United States, the State of Qatar has pledged 2.8% of its GDP to research and development. This funding is made available through QF via grants awarded by the Qatar National Research Fund (QNRF) through which successful peer-reviewed proposals can be awarded between US$20,000– US$350,000 per annum (QF, 2007). Her Highness underscores the importance of scientific innovation and research in her statement: 'I firmly believe that the optimal investment of our resources should not turn us into consumers of knowledge. It should rather encourage us, as well, to produce knowledge' (QF, 2007). The QF network of institutions is designed to contribute to the exchange of scientific knowledge locally, regionally and globally. Not content with being a passive receiver of goods, the leadership of Qatar is determined to generate and export new knowledge, reversing epistemic flows from the periphery to the centre.

QF's President cited Cornell's impressive research track record as one of the premier reasons the US institution was recruited to Education City (personal communication 21 September 2008). This contrasts with Donn and Al Manthri's (2010) concerns about importing a 'baroque arsenal' of educational products, joint projects between Cornell's NY and Doha campuses are beginning to produce new scientific knowledge, procedures and potential medical treatments. The research conducted at WCMC-Q's Biomedical Research Program (BMRP) is geared specifically to improving the public health of the nation and the region. Plans also include the establishment of a central sample repository that will be available to research clinicians. Cornell's involvement in Qatar has vast scope for collaborative medical and scientific research with unprecedented access to new patient populations in a largely understudied part of the world. By focusing on genomics, microscopy, proteomics, computational biology, biostatistics and indigenous flora and fauna, Cornell is taking advantage of its Middle Eastern research base to make scientific advances in these areas.

In line with WCMC-Q's Vision 2010-2015 Strategic Plan and its objective of establishing the institution as a centre of excellence in biomedical research, Cornell's BMRP is an important step towards the development of embedded research in Qatar. Through its core labs, which provide 'centralized functionalities and platforms that are not realistically achievable in individual laboratories', WCMC-Q's research facilities provide unprecedented support infrastructure for biomedical researchers and scientists from around the region (WCMC-Q, 2011). In its initial stages, the BMRP already employs almost 100 individuals and includes a number of training programmes designed to develop sustainable human capacity building in science and research. For instance, the WCMC-Q Training Program for Qatari Nationals and The Research Specialists and Clinical Coordinators Program have been implemented to support graduates of local and regional universities.[7] These training schemes represent an important means of transferring technical knowledge and expertise to the national population. As the new research platform expands and becomes more embedded in Qatar, scientific discoveries and the production of locally generated data pertaining to illnesses such as diabetes, obesity and metabolic diseases have the potential to be filtered back to the source (through peer-reviewed journals) and contribute to scientific knowledge.

According to Butler (2006), there are relatively few scientific publications generated in countries belonging to the Organization of the Islamic Conference. To date, the Arab region is second only to sub-Saharan Africa in its low output of scientists, academic research and scientific publications (Fergany, 2006, p. 33). Cornell's recruitment represents a concerted effort to redress the region's poor scientific track record. Within the sphere of academia, particularly in scientific disciplines, publications in international, peer-reviewed publications 'secures privilege' and prestige (Barnett, 2005, p. 787). During the 2010/11 academic year, WCMC-Q medical faculty published 55 papers in Western refereed journals including: *The Lancet, Nature, Proceedings of the National Academy of Sciences* and *Science* (WCMC-Q, 2011).[8] In addition, WCMC-Q recently hosted its first international research conference which attracted over 600 clinicians from around the globe. This patronage and indigenising of science marks a dramatic shift from passive consumption to active production of scientific knowledge and suggests that the medical college is helping the peripheral nation of Qatar to move towards the centre. It is also a challenge to the hitherto unquestioned hegemony of the West in the production and definition of authoritative knowledge. Thus, the co-production of knowledge generated in Education City marks a departure from neighbouring countries that simply purchase and utilise epistemic packages from the core.

Conclusion

Bourdieu (1984) contends that tertiary education cannot be studied in isolation, but rather must be examined within a broader social sphere. Context must be considered. This point is all the more pertinent in an era of globalisation when an increasing number of academic institutions are transplanting their academic programmes to foreign environments where structural factors unique to each social milieu have an impact on the educational experience. Western pedagogical programmes being imported to the Gulf States do not necessarily embrace Islamic values and the predominant Arabic ethos. This is particularly true of WCMC-Q where students are effectively enrolled in a hybrid programme, that is, Cornell's medical training is designed for a US setting but experienced largely in an Arab/Islamic culture. Further, questions pertaining to the universality of these pedagogical models must be raised. That biomedical practices and institutions originating in the metropole can be copied exactly and be replicated seamlessly elsewhere can no longer be presumed. Based on the WCMC-Q scenarios presented above it is clear that some facets of the curriculum contravened normative cultural values and medical practices in the Gulf setting.

It is significant, however, that the Qatari leadership did not recruit a well-established regional medical school, of which there are several (e.g., Egypt, Lebanon, Saudi Arabia), but rather deliberately opted to import one from 'the core'. Although a regional medical college would offer a professional training more in keeping with core Qatari values and culture as well as obviate the need to attain JCI accreditation, the US programme was perceived to be superior both in terms of its quality of training and its capacity to develop a domestic research platform which could communicate at an international level.

Education City stands at the intersection of two sets of interests, needing to be at one with the globalised world while aspiring to stand apart from it. The assemblage of institutions compiled within the specially designated educational zone clearly illustrates a paradoxical case of importing the alien to fortify the native. Put simply, Qatar is adapting to preserve its future integrity. By tapping into global academic circuits and utilising educational programmes from abroad, the Qatari elite is seeking primarily to strengthen and sustain its domestic situation.

The Qatari leadership is applying a selective form of neoliberal logic and an enterprising mode of Islamic governmentality in Education City to train new kinds of Qatari subjects. In the neoliberal era of globalised higher education, universities are expected to produce commercially oriented individuals, actors who are groomed to work in the global workplace and participate in knowledge economies. However, the Qatari state is not aiming to produce neoliberal subjects trained for employment in global knowledge-driven economies. Rather, citizens are being presented with opportunities to equip themselves with specific skills in order to participate in the development of a *domestic* knowledge-based economy. Even though the education procured at the foreign universities trains Qataris to perform in world arenas, a number of measures have been implemented to keep Qatari values afloat and to nourish a local set of principles of development (e.g., Qatarisation, a sponsorship system, zoning strategies). Unlikely as it seems, based on the small numbers of nationals currently graduating from the programme, the idea behind WCMC-Q as far as the sponsors are concerned is first and foremost to train Qatari doctors. Eventually, this will help nationalise the health-care sector by reducing its dependency on foreign expertise and assert, for the first time, domestic control of the system. Some students and faculty predict that Cornell is producing a small elite stratum of Western-trained medical elite who will assume the top-ranking administrative positions and leadership roles in hospitals and the Ministry of Health. If this is indeed the case, that students graduating from the US curriculum are destined to be the leaders, this points to an emerging hierarchical culture in which who and what counts as a legitimate medical training is narrowly defined.

As the trend to borrow non-indigenous training packages continues, it remains more important than ever to understand how these imports function on the ground. While some scholars caution that consumption of foreign educational packages ultimately stifles domestic knowledge production and reduces a nation's capacity to compete in the future (Bubtana 2007; Donn & Al Manthri 2010), it is contended that the transnational educational partnership between QF and Cornell is breaking the baroque-arsenal mould and provides an alternative model for the region.

In Qatar's case, the strategy of recruiting internationally renowned universities such as Cornell is intended to create a solid foundation upon which future education and research will be set. Pedagogical borrowing is a means of expediting immediate development projects geared to facilitate the medium and long-term goals of expanding and modernising public utilities, services and infrastructure as well as firmly establishing Qatar as a knowledge-based society and regional educational hub. With money to spend on research and development, initially relying on imported epistemic products, professional practices and institutional frameworks circumvents the problem of Qatar not having a tradition of medical pedagogy on which to build. The transplanting of a top Western medical school into Qatar sets the nation on a trajectory that is similar to that seen in the academic core. Although, like all transplants, there is an element of artificiality to this venture (and the accompanying risk of rejection), the Qatari model appears to provide an alternative to the model whereby outmoded practices and products from the centre are passed on to peripheral states. The Qatari model is more akin to a co-venture and, as a result, the recipients are better equipped to upgrade and maintain the standard of their medical profession and in a better position to embark on its own research agenda. It is an elaborate process that will take time to become fully operational and firmly embedded in its new context. While this may take years, Qatar has sufficient funding and commitment to support the regenerative process.

The Qatari leadership's insistence on partnerships and the granting of the same degrees helps to prevent procurement of a baroque arsenal. These requirements demand active engagement with the local community ensuring that foreign academic providers both invest in and integrate their institutions into the Qatari landscape through collaborations with local stakeholders.

WCMC-Q is producing doctors who will not only raise the standards of health care through the provision of state-of-the-art patient care to the people of Qatar, but also contribute to advances in medicine as it opens up new scientific confluences through biomedical research geared to address the region's health-care challenges. Whether a reliance on foreign educational providers for immediate capacity building is shortsighted or not remains to be seen. What is evident at this stage is an educational reciprocity between Cornell and Qatar wherein both parties are influencing and learning valuable lessons from each other as they partner to establish a premier academic medical and research centre in the desert.

Notes

[1] The fieldwork coincided with the inception of the transnational medical college. This timing afforded opportunities to witness many critical events and historic moments in the evolution of the nascent institution. My informants report that much has changed in the intervening period as the Qatari campus now exerts more local ownership over the programme.

[2] As much of Education City's initial development was done on an ad hoc basis, there is little in the way of archival evidence in the form of policy and funding documents, organisational charts or strategic plans (although a plethora of documents are produced later on). The absence of these artefacts of institutional life documenting their initial intention and execution of the project are indicative both of the autonomy afforded to QF and the lack of transparency required of its leadership. When the World Bank was asked by the Planning Council of Qatar and QF to help them conduct a knowledge-economy assessment of the nation and to help formulate a knowledge-based economy vision in 2007 (a full seven years after WCMC first commenced negotiations with QF) it noted that: 'Qatar [was] already implementing a number of knowledge economy measures and projects but many of these projects were initiated without an overall coherent long-term vision developed with inputs from key stakeholders' (World Bank, 2007, p. 2).

[3] The subjective involvement between participants in which shared cognition and consensus of meanings function as resources that help actors to interpret aspects of social and cultural interaction (Crossley, 1996).

[4] Qatar launched the nation's first international publishing house, Bloomsbury Qatar Foundation Publishing, in 2010.

[5] A designated OSF who is responsible for the material at the Qatari campus attends most VSLs. This position does not exist on the New York campus. The breadth of information in each module (e.g., Brain and Mind, Human Structure and Function) is such that the OSF cannot reasonably be expected to have the required level of expertise in every area of the subject and for this reason the OSF relies on the expertise of faculty members located at the New York campus. On occasion, the OSF acts as a cultural broker helping to clarify any points that are not obvious (e.g., pausing lectures to clarify the meaning of words or to provide explanations of culturally bounded concepts).

[6] Students have the option of undertaking electives and subinternships in US hospitals during the latter stages of their training.

[7] These initiatives are part of a collaboration with QF's Qatar Science Leadership Program.

[8] This statistic does not include the international publications of the WCMC-Q Premedical Faculty.

References

Altbach, P. (2002) Knowledge and Education as International Commodities: the collapse of the common good. *Journal of International Higher Education,* 28, 19-36.

Barnett, R. (2005) Recapturing the Universal in the University, *Educational Philosophy and Theory,* 37 (6), 785-797.

Bourdieu, P. (1984) *Homo Academicus.* Stanford: Stanford University Press.

Brewer, J.B., Augustine, C.H., Zellman, G.L., Ryan, G., Goldman, C.A., Stasz, C. et al (2007) *Education for a New Era: design and implementation of K–12 education reform in Qatar.* Santa Monica, CA: RAND-Qatar Policy Institute.

Bubtana, A. (2007) WTO/GATS: possible implications for Arab higher education and research. Paper presented to UNESCO's Second Research Seminar for the Arab States, 'The Impact of Globalisation on Higher Education and Research in the Arab States', Rabat, 24-25 May.

Butler, D. (2006) The Data Gap, *Nature,* 444 (2): 26-27.

Crossley, N. (1996) *Intersubjectivity: the fabric of social becoming.* Thousand Oaks, CA: Sage.

Donn, G. & Al Manthri, Y. (2010) *Globalisation and Higher Education in the Arab Gulf states.* Oxford: Symposium Books.

Economist Intelligence Unit (2004) *Country Profile 2004 – Qatar.* London: The Economic Intelligence Unit.

Fergany, N. (2006) Islam and Science: steps towards reform, *Nature* 444 (2 Nov.), 33-34.
http://www.nature.com/nature/journal/v444/n7115/full/444033a.html (accessed 13 April 2010).

Finkler, K. (2004) Biomedicine Globalized and Localized: Western medical practices in an outpatient clinic of a Mexican hospital, *Social Science and Medicine,* 59(10), 2037-2051.

Gewirtz, A. (2002) *The Managerial School: post-welfarism and social justice in education.* London: Routledge.

Inda, J. & Rosaldo, R. (2002) *The Anthropology of Globalization: a reader.* Malden, MA: Blackwell.

Jaye, C., Egan, T. & Parker, S. (2006) 'Do as I say, not as I do': medical education and Foucault's normalizing technologies of self, *Anthropology and Medicine,* 13(2), 141-155.

Knight, J. (2006) 'Higher Education in the Trade Context of GATS', in Internationalisation in Higher Education: European Responses to the Global Perspective (EAIE). Paper presented to UNESCO's Regional Scientific Committee for the Arab States, Al-Ain, UAE, 6-7 June.

Morey, A. (2004) Globalization and the Emergence of For-Profit Higher Education, *Higher Education* 48, 131-150.

Neave, G. & van Vught, F. (Eds) (1991) *Prometheus Bound: the changing relationship between government and higher education in Western Europe.* Oxford: Pergamon Press.

Olds, K. (2010) Are We Witnessing the Denationalization of the Higher Education Media? GlobalHigherEd, 14 July. http://globalhighered.wordpress.com/2010/07/14/are-we-witnessing-the-denationalization/ (accessed 20 August 2010).

Ong, A. (2005) Ecologies of Expertise: assembling flows, in A. Ong & S. Collier (Eds) *Global Assemblages: technology, politics and ethics as anthropological* Problems. Oxford: Blackwell.

Poovey, M. (2001) The Twenty-First-Century University and the Market: what price economic viability? *Differences,* 12(1), 1-16.

QF (2007) Qatar Foundation Homepage. http://www.qf.org.qa/output/page84.asp (accessed 14 February 2011).

QSA (2011) Total Population. Qatar Statistics Authority Website http://www.qsa.gov.qa/eng/index.htm (accessed 1 February 2011).

Resnick, J. (2008) *The Production of Educational Knowledge in the Global Era.* Rotterdam: Sense Publishers.

Rodriguez del Pozo, P. & Fins, M. (2005) The Globalization of Education in Medical Ethics and Humanities: evolving pedagogy at Weill Cornell Medical College in Qatar, *Academic Medicine,* 80(2), 135-140.

UNESCO (2008) Resources for Education. UNESCO Institute for Statistics Brief Education in Qatar. http://stats.uis.unesco.org/unesco/TableViewer/document.aspx?ReportId=121andIF_Language=engandBR_Country=6340 (accessed 5 July 2010).

Van der Wende, M.C. (2003) Globalisation and Access to Higher Education. *Journal of Studies in International Education,* 7(2), 193-206.

WCMC-Q (2011) *Annual Report 2011.* Doha: WCMC-Q.

Whitty, G., Power, S. & Halpin, D. (1998) *Devolution and Choice in Education: the school, the state and the market.* Buckingham: Open University Press.

World Bank (2007) Qatar Knowledge Economy Project. Turning Qatar into a Competitive Knowledge-Based Economy: knowledge economy assessment of Qatar. World Bank. http://siteresources.worldbank.org/KFDLP/Resources/QatarKnowledge Economy Assessment.pdf (accessed 15 December 2010).

CHAPTER SIX

The School Education System in the Sultanate of Oman

SANA AL BALUSHI & DAVID GRIFFITHS

Introduction

This chapter concentrates on the school-education system in the Sultanate of Oman, although the process that the educational provision has gone through in the Sultanate is similar in many ways to that experienced by neighbouring Gulf Cooperation Council (GCC) countries. All the GCC countries have witnessed considerable progress in recent decades in raising literacy and enrolment rates. On the other hand, international reports have consistently warned that educational outcomes in the Arab region in general, and in the Gulf in particular, lag behind those of other regions in the world. Participation in international benchmarked student assessments has confirmed the comparatively low levels of learning achievement standards of GCC students.

Globalisation and technological changes have made human-capital development increasingly important for a nation's economic progress. The 2003 *Arab Human Development Report* cites lack of knowledge capital as the main long-term problem faced by the Arab world, stating that the knowledge gap, not the income gap, 'determines the prospects of countries in today's world economy' (UNDP, 2003). The World Bank (2008) report *The Road Not Travelled: education reform in the Middle East and North Africa*, looked at investment in education in the region over the past four decades in order to determine how much of this investment has been translated into higher economic growth. The report claimed that, compared to East Asia and Latin America, the high levels of investment in education in the region have not been accompanied by higher economic growth or gains in productivity. One of the major reasons for this, the report claimed, has been an insufficient emphasis on providing a 'quality' education service in the region.

In the face of this evidence, the response of many of the GCC countries has been to embark on a comprehensive reform of their education systems aimed at improving student outcomes. A lack of internal expertise has meant that the GCC countries have, to a large extent, been reliant upon outside agencies to assist them with both increasing access to education and with improving the quality of the education being provided. These outside agencies have exerted both 'hard' policy influences (e.g. funding and project support) and 'soft' policy influences (e.g. promoting ideas such as education for all, efficiency, effectiveness, standardisation of teaching and learning, decentralisation, privatisation and lifelong learning) on the development of education in the GCC countries. The assumption is that all education systems that function effectively and produce high-quality learning should share the same values and operational principles and that local differences regarding their stage of development and culture are of little relevance. Although the GCC countries have responded to these agencies in different ways and in different degrees, all have accepted the need to introduce externally designed solutions to solve their local problems.

While not mutually exclusive, two distinct stages in the development of the school-education system in Oman can be determined. The first stage was between 1970 and the mid-1990s, when the principal aim was to expand educational provision to all parts of the country and to all sections of society. The second stage can be dated from the mid-1990s onwards, when the attention shifted towards introducing reforms to improve qualitatively the school-education system.

A series of 'tidal waves' of international influences have impacted on both of these development stages. The first was the 'borrowing' phase in which, in the 1970s, the curriculum and textbooks used in Oman were lifted in their entirety from neighbouring Arab countries. From 1980 to the mid-1990s, experts from neighbouring Arab countries – mainly from Egypt and Jordan – were brought in to write a curriculum specifically for Oman, although the majority of the material continued to be derived from the curriculum in the home countries of the experts. In the second 'developing' phase, from the mid-1990s to 2010, experts were brought in, mainly from North America and the United Kingdom, to train Omani personnel to write and develop curriculum and assessment materials. The third 'collaborating' phase, which has just begun, involves a bottom-up approach in which the expertise of those working in the field will be used to further develop the system (Figure 1).

Our main focus in this chapter is to examine on the impact of these 'tidal waves' of international influence in the context of the reform of the teaching profession in Oman between 1970 and the present time. Before concentrating on that, we would like to put the education system in Oman into context by briefly describing the significant progress the country has made in raising literacy and enrolment rates in the short period since 1970.

```
┌─────────────────────────┐     ┌──────────────────────────────────────────┐
│        Stage 1          │     │              Stage 2                     │
│  Quantitative Expansion │     │       Qualitative Improvement            │
│       (1970–95)         │     │          (1995–present)                  │
│           ↓             │     │         ↙            ↘                   │
│    "Borrowing Phase"    │     │  "Developing Phase"  "Collaborating Phase"│
└─────────────────────────┘     └──────────────────────────────────────────┘
```

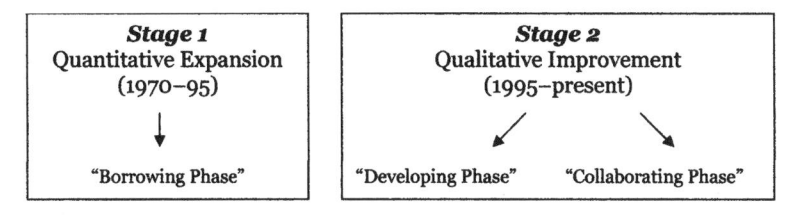

Figure 1. Stages in the development of education in the Sultanate of Oman.

Education For All

First launched in 1990 at the World Conference in Jomtiem, the Education for All (EFA) initiative (UNESCO, 1990) was further developed in the Dakar Framework of 2000 as six major goals with specific targets to be achieved by 2015 (UNESCO, 2000). As a signatory to the Dakar Framework, Oman agreed to dedicate itself to meeting its commitments towards achieving these goals. Work on this began immediately following the ascension of His Majesty Sultan Qaboos in 1970, so, in a sense, Oman had been striving towards education for all for 20 years prior to the official launching of EFA.

The vision of the Sultan was to see Oman emerge from its long period of isolationism by re-entering the global arena and to use its natural and human resources to develop a modern economy. The problem was that at that time there were only three schools in the whole country, with a mere 900 students (all male and all at the primary level). Figures from UNESCO indicate that in that year, nearly 66% of Oman's adults were illiterate. The virtual absence of a school-education system was hardly a sound basis for realising His Majesty's vision.

One of his government's first commitments was to develop a public-education system that would reach all parts of the country and would include all sections of society. To achieve this, the government established a Ministry of Education which was responsible for *all* educational matters in the Sultanate, including literacy and adult-education programmes and those concerning higher education. (In 1995 the responsibility for higher education was passed to the newly created Ministry of Higher Education).

It was agreed from the outset that 12 years of government schooling should be offered free of charge to all Omani children. The education system was called 'General Education' and was organised into three stages: elementary (grade levels 1-6); preparatory (grade levels 7-9); and secondary (grade levels 10-12). At the end of all these three stages, successful students were awarded with a certificate; the effect of certificating all three stages was that significant numbers of students left the system at the end of elementary, i.e. grade 6, and again at the end of preparatory, i.e. grade 9, to join the labour market. At that time, this suited the needs of the country's young and fast-developing economy for a literate but essentially low-skilled workforce.

The lack of a public-education tradition in Oman meant that the first task for the newly created Ministry of Education was to conduct a campaign to raise people's awareness of the importance of universal formal education for their present and future wellbeing. Compulsory school attendance was not enacted into law, and this remains the case today, but the government encouraged attendance by providing free education for all who wanted it and free textbooks for all classes. Where distance required it, free transport was provided from home to school and boarding facilities were provided for students who lived in rural areas. In addition, both the government and the private sector offered assistance to children from low-income families, such as providing school uniforms and free meals.

Once the demand for education had been aroused in the population, the Ministry had to meet the major challenge of providing the required infrastructure and staffing levels. The government committed itself to a prodigious investment for building schools although, at the beginning, schools were also opened in rented premises, in specially constructed non-permanent buildings and even in tents.

By 1971 the number of schools had increased to 42 and the student population to over 15,000. Education for preparatory level students (grades 7-9) was introduced in 1972 and for secondary level (grades 10-12) in 1973. In a period of only 20 years, the education system in the country was catering for more than 300,000 students in 780 schools and with a teaching force of over 15,000; by 2010 there were over 522,000 students in 1040 schools (Figures 2 and 3). Despite the very late start, and despite the lack of compulsion, education participation levels in Oman are now equal to or above other countries in the Middle East and North Africa (MENA).

In 1970, the three schools that existed in the Sultanate did not offer any places for girls, and 88.3% of women in the country were illiterate. By the end of 1970, 1136 girls were receiving education, all at the elementary level. By the end of 1974, girls were enrolled at all three levels: elementary, preparatory and secondary. The percentage of female school students has increased from 12.7% in 1971-72 to over 49% in 2008/2009, when the number of girls attending school totalled over 265,000 (Oman Ministry of Education, 2009, 2011). The achievement of almost universal education for girls has been one of the Sultanate's great success stories in the last few decades.

SCHOOL EDUCATION SYSTEM IN OMAN

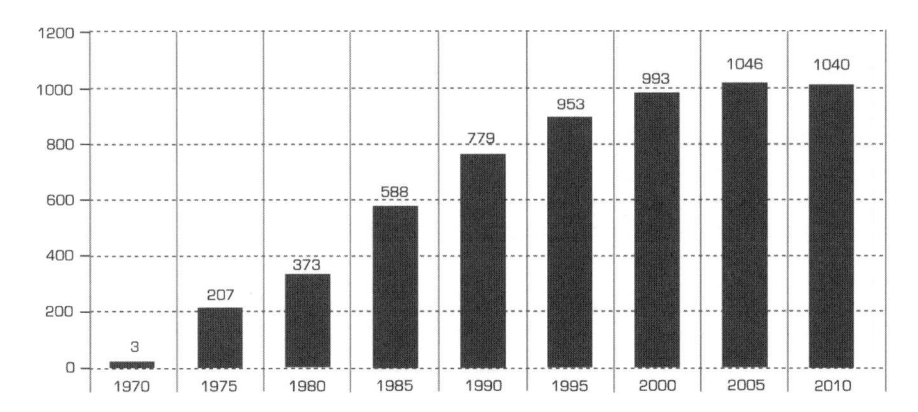

Figure 2. Number of schools in Oman, 1970-2010.
Source: Department of Statistics, Ministry of Education,
Sultanate of Oman (2006).

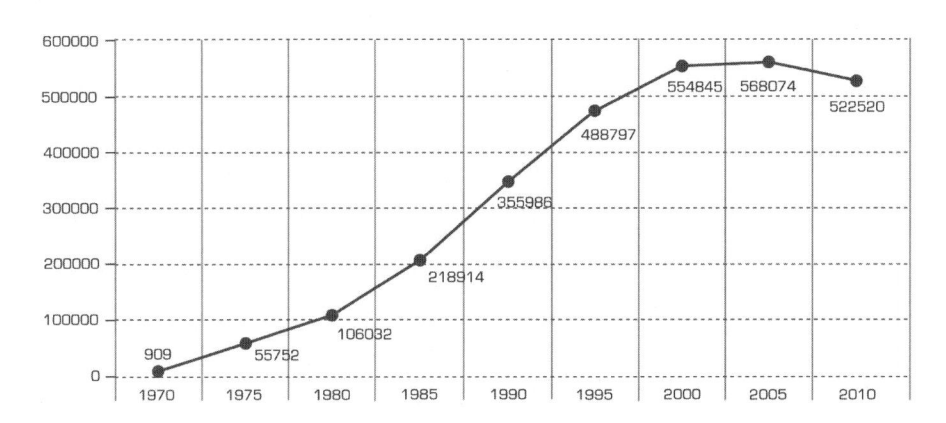

Figure 3. Number of students in Oman, 1970-2010.
Source: Department of Statistics, Ministry of Education,
Sultanate of Oman (2006).

The Teaching Profession during the Quantitative Expansion Period

In 1970 there were only 30 teachers in the country, all of whom were male. To satisfy the need to obtain large numbers of teachers to help increase access to education as quickly as possible, an extensive overseas teacher-recruitment drive was carried out. Teachers were recruited from fellow Arab countries such as Egypt, Jordan and Tunisia and, for teachers of the English Language, from Britain, Sudan and countries in the Indian sub-continent.

It was also necessary to recruit many teachers with low qualifications into the system. Omani citizens who had completed their secondary education abroad and, to begin with, those who had completed their elementary education inside Oman were also recruited as teachers (as more teachers were recruited, the minimum qualification requirement was raised to completion of preparatory education and then to completion of secondary education). In 1972, nearly 50% of the teachers employed in Oman's schools held qualifications of a lower level than the equivalent of a General Certificate of Secondary Education (GCSE) and a mere 8% possessed a university degree.

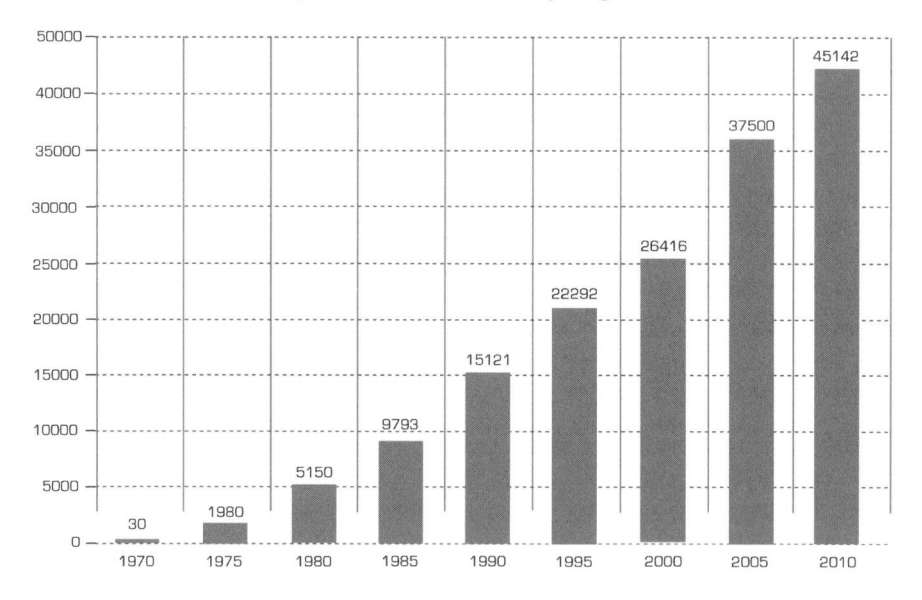

Figure 4. Number of teachers in Oman, 1970-2010.
Source: Department of Statistics, Ministry of Education,
Sultanate of Oman (2006).

The scale and pace of the teacher-recruitment drive can be seen in Figure 4. Throughout the 1970s, over 90% of teachers were expatriates. In 1975, two Teacher Training Institutes were established, one for males and one for females, and this allowed many more Omani teachers to be trained and recruited. This also enabled the minimum qualification requirements for teaching to be raised, first to a one-year certificate and then to a two-year diploma following graduation from grade 12. These institutes were almost exclusively staffed by expatriates, mainly from other Arab countries such as Egypt, Jordan and Sudan and this meant that the educational values, beliefs, teaching and learning methodologies and assessment practices prevalent in these countries were imparted to the new Omani teaching force. The effects of this on the attitudes and professional practice of teachers in Omani schools are still being felt today.

By 1990, the Ministry was employing more than 4360 Omani teachers, although this still represented less than 29% of the total teaching force. However, a policy for the Omanisation of the Sultanate's economy had been introduced in the Third National Development Plan (1980-85), and this committed the Ministry to gradually replacing its expatriate teachers with Omani nationals. The pace made by the Ministry in this regard can be seen by the fact that by 2000, the number of Omani teachers had risen to nearly 17,750, representing more than 67% of the total teaching force, and to over 40,250, more than 89% of the teaching force, by 2010 (Table i).

Year	Teachers			School Administrators		
	Total	Omani	Omanisation (%)	Total	Omani	Omanisation (%)
1980	5,150	423	8.2	696	183	26.3
1990	15,121	4,361	28.8	1,080	703	65.1
2000	26,416	17,743	67.2	2,472	2,299	93.0
2010	45,142	40,274	89.2	8,685	8,648	99.6

Table I. Omanisation of Ministry of Education staff, 1980-2010.
Source: Oman Ministry of Education (2011).

In the early years, curricula and textbooks were brought in from other Arab countries. The courses were heavily content-laden, teacher-centred and emphasised rote learning. Assessment was conducted entirely through high-stakes end-of-year examinations, which almost exclusively tested memorisation, and which all students were required to pass in order to progress to the next grade level. The main concern for assessment at the end of grade 12 was to provide a test of minimum competence for entry to university.

By the late 1970s, with the assistance of curriculum experts from neighbouring countries, the Ministry began to develop its own curriculum, subject syllabi, textbooks and teacher guides. Following the establishment of the Arab Gulf Cooperation Council (GCC) in 1981, the Education Bureau of the GCC coordinated educational policies and unified the curriculum framework in all member states, i.e. United Arab Emirates, Bahrain, Kuwait, Saudi Arabia, Oman and Qatar. However, the emphasis on a teacher-centred, content-driven approach and tested by high-stakes examinations assessing lower-order skills remained the same.

Traditional teacher-centred teaching approaches were the dominant practice in the countries that supplied most of Oman's teaching force, curriculum writers and teacher trainers, and so it is of little surprise that these were the approaches adopted in Oman. It could be argued that a traditional pedagogical approach to teaching and learning was dictated by very large class sizes which in Oman, even as late as the mid-1990s, often contained between 40 and 50 students. Moreover, such an approach is easier to defend when the over-riding educational priority is to eradicate illiteracy, which it was in Oman in the early years. However, by the mid-1990s the significant increase in the number of enrolments in schools, with most students progressing to secondary level, meant that universal formal education had, to all intents and purposes, been achieved.

During most of this period, the main priority for the Ministry of Education was to increase the quantity of provision and access to its services as quickly as possible. Now, however, new priorities were beginning to emerge.

The Call for Reform

Impressive as the expansion of educational provision had been, by the mid-1990s a number of developments provided compelling arguments for carrying out a thorough reform of the Sultanate's education system. The first of these involved Oman's participation in the UNESCO/UNICEF (1997) sponsored studies on reaching the goals of Education for All, entitled 'Monitoring Learning Achievement (MLA)'. The results from these studies revealed lower than expected student-achievement levels in Oman. Deficiencies in the existing school system had also been highlighted in a World Bank study, which described primary education in many of Oman's schools as taking place in inadequate school facilities that required double-shifting of students, and were taught by inadequately trained teachers and supported with minimal instruction resources.

Impetus for reform also came from the United Nations international conference on education, held in Jomtien in 1990, which recognised that the quality of education provided was a prime determinant for the achievement of the Education for All goals. The need for countries to place increased emphasis on the qualitative dimension of education was stressed even more strongly in the Dakar Framework for Action in 2000. Goal Two of the Framework commits countries to the provision of primary education 'of good quality', and Goal Six includes commitments to improve all aspects of educational quality so that everyone can achieve better learning outcomes, 'especially in literacy, numeracy and essential life skills'.

Moreover, the government's determination that the country should be a productive participant in the globalised economy brought further pressure for change. In 1995, a conference on *The Vision for Oman's Economy – Oman: 2020* was launched to flesh out a strategy for achieving economic balance and sustainable development in the country (Oman Ministry of National Economy, 1995). Proceeds from the production and sale of oil and gas had allowed the government to develop the country's infrastructure. However, compared to its Gulf neighbours such as Kuwait, Qatar and the United Arab Emirates, Oman has much smaller resources and a more pressing need to diversify its economy in order to promote future sustainability.

The Vision 2020 conference concluded that emerging global and national economies require workers who are technologically literate, can engage in analytical thinking, are skilled communicators and are professionally flexible. Oman's future prosperity and economic growth would, therefore, depend on how effectively the education system could provide young Omani citizens with the knowledge and skills they need to participate in the changing economy and job market.

International organisations such as the World Bank, the United Nations and the Organisation for Economic Cooperation and Development (OECD) were telling developing nations such as Oman that the need now was to supply graduates to work in the so-called emerging 'knowledge economy', in which knowledge resources such as know-how and expertise were more critical than other economic resources such as physical capital and natural resources. This meant that a new approach to education, which recognised and catered for the differing abilities and aspirations of all students, was now required.

Reforming Education

The Ministry of Education responded to this challenge by embarking on a number of major reform initiatives aimed at achieving comprehensive qualitative improvements across the entire school system. The most ambitious of these has been the Basic Education (Oman Ministry of Education, 1998) programme. Basic Education, which will eventually replace the General Education system, was developed by the ministry in cooperation with the Canadian company Educational Consultancy Services (ECS). It runs from grades 1 to 10, and is divided into two stages: Cycle One (grades 1-4) and Cycle Two (grades 5-10). This programme was first introduced in 1998 in 17 schools and by 2010, the number of schools involved had grown to over 800, which amounts to nearly 86% of all grade 1-10 schools.

The guiding principle behind the design of the new Basic Education curriculum was to include relevant knowledge and skills-based content that would help prepare young Omanis for life and work under the new conditions created by the global economy and encourage them to engage in life-long learning. Globalisation places a higher economic value on particular types of knowledge and skills and, in recognition of this, the Ministry followed practice in countries throughout the world in developing new subject areas, such as information technology and life skills. In addition, it was agreed that Omani students required a stronger background in mathematics and science, and greater proficiency in both Arabic, their mother tongue, and in English, the language of the global economy. One consequence of these changes was that the focus on a traditional 'liberal arts' education which also serves society's broader, long-term goals has diminished.

The Ministry encouraged a shift away from teacher-centred learning to student-centred learning. Teachers were informed that they are expected to deploy strategies to develop skills and attitudes that encourage autonomous and cooperative learning, critical thinking, problem solving, research and investigative techniques, creativeness and innovation. As will be explained later, however, there is a gap between the Ministry's expectations and the realities of practice in the classrooms.

Prior to the introduction of Basic Education, the common practice in Oman had been to measure students' learning by means of examinations only. Important decisions, such as letting students progress to the next grade or, at the end of grade 12, selecting them for a place at college or university, were taken solely on the basis of how well they performed on the day of the examination. A study of the grade 12 examinations carried out by the Scottish Qualifications Authority (SQA) in 1996 found that the questions almost exclusively tested rote learning and memorisation. With the assistance of SQA, the Ministry established working groups for all the academic subjects. These working groups, which comprised of teachers and supervisors, were trained on how to construct test items that assessed higher-order thinking skills. The test items produced by the working groups were incorporated into the Basic Education assessment system.

The working groups were also instructed on how to devise new specifications at all grade levels in order to introduce a wider range of assessment instruments. Continuous assessment was given greater prominence on the grounds that this would not only help to provide a more accurate picture of a student's attainments and needs, but would also achieve a better match between assessment and what has been taught and learned in the classroom, thereby giving greater validity to the assessment system. Teachers are now expected to assess the performance of students in a variety of ways, such as short written or oral tests, quizzes, performance-assessment tasks, projects, portfolio work and student self-assessments. In an attempt to increase the reliability of the continuous assessment, moderation procedures for the checking of the marks awarded by teachers was introduced.

If reform is to be sustained it is important that processes for ensuring that improvement is continued over the longer term are put in place. The SQA assessment project is a good example of an initiative set up with the intention of sustaining the reform by increasing capacity within the Ministry. It is unfortunate, therefore, that the Ministry disbanded the working groups shortly after the project ended and, as a result, the expertise built up in specification and item writing was not properly utilised. Moreover, despite the introduction of moderation procedures, the move towards continuous assessment underestimated the pressures teachers are under, particularly those living and teaching in small communities, to inflate the marks of their students.

In 2000 the Ministry started to plan for the reform of grades 11 and 12 in order to synchronise them with the Basic Education reform. The Centre for British Teachers (CfBT) (2001) was commissioned to offer recommendations leading to the creation of a new curriculum, instruction and assessment models for grades 11 and 12, and a plan for development and implementation. The Ministry followed this up with an extensive consultation exercise before introducing the new Post-Basic Education system at the beginning of the 2007/2008 school year (Oman Ministry of Education, 2008). The curriculum is organised on a 'core plus electives' model and students are given an element of choice even in the core subject areas. A range of courses relevant to the varying abilities, interests and aspirations of students has been developed. This provides students with opportunities for specialisation, e.g. in science, IT, social studies, as well as for selecting general interest-type courses. The curricular model emphasises the learning of key skills, or fundamental competencies, which will enable students to operate effectively in a wide range of contexts.

Standards-based education reform became popular in the West in the 1990s. It became the education orthodoxy that the quality of education can best be improved by setting high performance standards for teaching and learning and then measuring whether these standards have been met. In the name of accountability and transparency, students, teachers and schools in countries throughout the world were increasingly being measured and tested. Student assessment became a global business and countries with developing education systems were exhorted to bite the new 'magic bullet'.

In response to this, the Ministry piloted national tests in science and mathematics during the 2005/2006 academic year and is developing plans to make national tests at grades 4, 7 and 10 in selected key subjects a permanent feature of the evaluation system. The Ministry has, however, resisted the temptation to follow the practice in many countries of using the data from the tests for accountability purposes, such as compiling league tables to compare schools or introducing reward-sanctions structures for teachers and schools. Oman also participated in the 2007 and 2011 Trends in International Mathematics and Science Studies (TIMSS) and is presently preparing to participate in the next cycle of Progress in Reading Literacy Study (PIRLS), an international comparative study of the reading literacy of grade 4 students.

In addition, the Ministry is developing a framework of standards that will signpost the ways in which the professional capacity of teachers should grow progressively across their career. These standards are likely to be an important development in helping to clarify roles and evaluate staff performance as well as in determining appropriate staff development programmes. The intention is that this will be the first step in the development of a comprehensive standards framework that will include curriculum and performance standards.

The Teaching Profession during the Period of Qualitative Improvement

International research has consistently shown that home background and teaching quality are the two most significant influences on student-learning achievement. The OECD study in 2005, entitled 'Teachers Matter' concluded that:

> Of those variables which are potentially open to policy influence, factors to do with teachers and teaching are the most important influences on student learning ... improving the efficiency and equity of schooling depends, in large measure, on ensuring that competent people want to work as teachers, that their teaching is of a high quality, and that all students have access to high quality teaching.

The successful implementation of the Ministry's reform initiatives was, therefore, largely dependent on the quality of the response from its teaching staff.

Taken together, the reforms introduced in Oman since the mid-1990s represent a significant change in emphasis and constitute a major challenge for teachers. Their experience was based on a recently established education system dominated by a traditional teacher-centred approach. Now, the role asked of teachers is much more complex and demanding. They are expected to apply new classroom management techniques to enable them to move away from whole-class teaching rewarding rote learning, towards student-centred methods emphasising group work and individualised approaches which promote inquiry learning and display evidence of analytical and higher-order skills. They are expected to differentiate the curriculum in order to reduce barriers and increase student participation as well as to introduce appropriate classroom techniques to enable them to manage differentiated learning. They are expected to acquire knowledge and skills in assessment to enable them to identify what their students know and can do, and what steps they need to take to improve their learning.

In order to encourage teachers to use student-centred techniques, class sizes were reduced significantly; in grades 1-4 of Basic Education a maximum class size of 30 students was stipulated. An in-service programme to update teachers on both the substance of the new curriculum and on its means of delivery was put in place.

As mentioned earlier, during the 1970s and 1980s, the need for rapid expansion meant that many teachers with low qualifications were recruited into the system. By 2008, over 83% of teachers in Oman held a Bachelor of Education (BEd) degree or higher (Table II).

	Omani	Expat
Post-General Certificate Diploma	6,934	232
University degree	29,649	4,269
Post-Graduate Diploma	1,670	80
Master	140	167
Doctorate	5	3

Table II. Teachers by qualification, 2008/9.
Source: Oman Ministry of Education (2009)

In cooperation with the University of Leeds in the United Kingdom, the Ministry of Education carried out a major initiative to enable Omani English-language teachers to upgrade their diploma qualifications to a Bachelor of Arts (BA) in Teaching English to Speakers of Other Languages (TESOL). The Project began in 1998 and the first BA degrees were awarded in 2003 to 285 students. By the time the final batch of students received their degrees in the middle of 2010, more than 820 had been awarded a BA degree. The best TESOL students received the opportunity to study for an MA at the University of Leeds and by the end of the project there were 40 MA graduates with a further five students receiving funding from the project to study for a PhD.

Similarly, the Ministry is taking steps to ensure that teachers in subjects other than English can upgrade their two-year teaching diplomas to a BA. It is cooperating with the Ministry of Higher Education and Sultan Qaboos University (SQU) to enable teachers and administrators to continue their studies at higher-education institutes. Between 2001 and 2005, 743 teachers graduated from SQU with a BA. In addition, teachers and other Ministry staff are being given the opportunity to complete their Masters' degrees at higher-education institutions either inside or outside Oman.

Research has shown a positive relationship between student performance and measurable teacher characteristics, such as teaching qualifications, academic ability and subject knowledge, although to a lesser extent than might be expected (OECD, 2005). Other important factors include: motivation; creativity; ability to convey ideas in a clear and convincing manner; creation of effective learning environments for different types of students; and the ability to work effectively with colleagues and parents (OECD, 2005). The Ministry has stated that it expects its teachers to change their classroom approaches, and while there are examples of excellent practice there is also evidence that many teachers have experienced difficulties in making the hoped-for transition.

In many ways the Ministry should, perhaps, have been unsurprised by this outcome. For one thing, the Ministry of Education has no responsibility for pre-service teacher training; the College of Education at Sultan Qaboos University (SQU), private institutions in Oman and institutions abroad are the sources of newly qualified teachers. An international review of teacher education reported that while most professions conduct much of their training in real-life settings (e.g. doctors and nurses in hospitals, lawyers in courtrooms), relatively little teacher training takes place in the teachers' own classrooms (McKinsey and Company, 2007). This is certainly the case in Oman; in SQU, teaching practice accounts for approximately 6% of the total credits for the course. Student teachers have teaching practice for one day per week in the seventh semester and for two days per week in their final (eighth) semester. Teaching practice is not offered during the first three years of the course. It is hardly surprising, therefore, that many newly qualified teachers report that they experience problems in aspects of teaching such as classroom management and in accommodating individual student differences.

The past experience of teachers – as school students and as students in higher education – was of a teacher-centred didactic approach to teaching and learning. The Ministry did provide in-service training on child-centred approaches, much of it bought in from outside agencies, but these were usually one-off programmes lasting from 3 to 15 days, developed independently of the teachers' practice contexts and which did not involve real and sustained engagement on tasks leading to an identifiable impact on learning. There is increasingly strong evidence that one-off training events such as these have limited lasting impact and, in Oman, many teachers seem to have dismissed the new strategies as either unrealistic or inappropriate. Those who did attempt to change their teaching practices often ran into difficulties; several studies have shown that teachers often feel deskilled when they first attempt to change their classroom practices and that without ongoing support and encouragement they are likely to revert back to their previous practices (e.g. Black et al, 2003).

The educational reforms put in place in Oman were mainly externally devised, although they were for the most part modified to the Omani situation. The involvement of teachers in this process was minimal, but it was expected that they would enthusiastically implement and support the reform process. It recently became clear, however, that the Ministry has, to a large extent, failed to persuade teachers of the desirability of many of its reforms, including the move to student-centred learning. Following the protests that swept through the Arab region in 2011, teachers in Oman requested the Ministry to implement various changes. Some of these requests related to improvements in teachers' conditions of service, but others demanded a move back to the education system that existed before the start of the reform process.

Encouraging Collaborative Practice

When Oman embarked on its reform programme in the mid-1990s, outside agencies were saying that the adoption of certain 'global education standards' were a prerequisite for systems to perform in an internationally competitive way. Countries were being told to introduce learning standards for students, teaching standards for teachers and assessment and curriculum standards for educators and that this should be backed up by rigorous accountability mechanisms (Mullis et al, 2008). The view was that making students, teachers and schools compete will improve the quality of education, in the same way as competition encourages companies to thrive in market economies. This view is increasingly becoming questioned. Experience from highly standardised and accountable school systems suggests that this can lead to the de-professionalisation of teachers' work, a shift in emphasis from teaching and learning for understanding to being successful in high-stake tests and a narrowing of the curriculum through 'teaching to the test'.

Increasingly, countries are beginning to question the view that educational reform can be achieved only through externally designed solutions. Research on education reforms suggests that a major condition for sustainable improvement is the building of capacity within countries to develop reforms that meet local needs and conditions. A recent international review of improving school systems commented that in successful school systems 'peer-led creativity and innovation inside schools becomes the core driver for raising performance' (McKinsey and Company, 2010). Collaborative practice, whereby teachers work together to develop effective instructional practices, shift the drive for change away from the centre to the schools and helps to ensure that system improvement is self-sustaining.

For this to happen, teachers must be able to engage directly and willingly with the change process. They need to be agents of change not, as they have tended to be up until now, passive or reluctant receivers of externally imposed prescription. For the most part, the teaching force in Oman continues to lack the skills and, in particular, the self-confidence to conduct such 'peer-led creativity and innovation'. Considerable work is required before effective collaborative practice can become a reality. Teachers need to be helped by providing them with time and resources to learn, plan and reflect together about their work in school. Professional communities to enable teachers and principals to engage in collaborative work need to be established.

In an effort to create the internal capacity to improve the quality of teaching, the ministry in cooperation with the University of Cambridge began piloting its International Diploma for Teachers and Trainers (CIDTT) in 2010-11. The CIDTT Diploma is a practical classroom based training programme which aims to equip teachers with the skills, knowledge and understanding required for effective classroom practice, particularly with regard to student-centred and formative assessment techniques. The Ministry's intention is to put two senior teachers in every school in the country through the CIDTT programme. These senior teachers will then be responsible for training and supporting teachers in their schools to change their classroom practices through engagement in self evaluation, reflection and inquiry.

There has been a devolvement of responsibility for the supervision of teachers from the regional supervisor to the senior teacher, whose role has been enhanced. The senior teacher is expected to determine the difficulties and problems facing teachers during the teaching process and the implementation of the curriculum and to then find solutions and devise programmes to improve teachers' performance. This initiative represents a move away from the generally centralised nature of the supervision system to one where the senior teacher can make decisions within his or her school. As a result, senior teachers are in a unique position to influence and change teaching practices in their schools. It is hoped that the CIDTT school-based training programme will be relevant to the needs of teachers and will help to promote local communities of practice with access to ongoing Ministry support.

The Ministry is also attempting to develop capacity within schools to enable them to be self-critical, to be able to identify their strengths and weaknesses and to take responsibility for their own development. In 1998 the Office for Standards in Education, the English agency responsible for school inspections, delivered a report with recommendations on how to plan and carry out school reviews (Ofsted, 1998). Using this as a starting point, the Ministry developed its own proposals for the introduction of a school self-evaluation system, complemented by external evaluation. The focus of school self-evaluation is on classroom practice, i.e. student learning. Only 15 schools participated in the performance evaluation project in 2002/3, but by the beginning of the 2010/11 school year, all schools in the country were doing evaluations.

Conclusion

When His Majesty Sultan Qaboos ascended to the throne in 1970, the country was starting from what was virtually a clean slate in terms of schools and educational provision. Yet, within a period of only 30 years, Oman was well on the road to fulfilling its commitment to providing

Education for All. A report from the World Bank in 2001 described the development of Oman's education system in the decades 1970-2000 as 'massive', 'unprecedented' and 'unparalleled by any other country'.

When the country was concerned with increasing access to education during its 'borrowing' phase, curriculum, teachers and experts were imported from neighbouring Arab countries. This allowed access to education to increase very rapidly in a short period of time, although it also helped to institutionalise a culture of providing a content-heavy curriculum emphasising rote learning and an assessment system dominated by high-stakes examinations.

The Ministry of Education realised that it could not afford to limit its attention to issues of access and enrolment, infrastructure and central administration. All its efforts would go to waste if attention were not also devoted to the improvement of quality. Waste, because important resources would be invested without being translated into learning outcomes and because children, the adults of the future, would have gone through school without acquiring the skills they need to operate in an increasingly complex world.

When the priority turned to improving quality during the 'developing' phase, the expertise of international agencies and companies, mainly from the United Kingdom and North America, was used. It was hoped that the new Basic and Post-Basic Education systems would help to create a culture of high standards. However, Oman's participation in international studies such as the Trends in International Mathematics and Science Study (TIMSS) have indicated that improving student-learning outcomes remains a key challenge for the Ministry; while the performance levels of students in Oman compare favourably with students in other GCC countries, they fall short of students in Western and Asian countries (Mullins et al, 2008).

Apart from factors such as socio-economic status and home background, student learning is most strongly influenced by what and how teachers teach. The Ministry devoted a considerable financial outlay on encouraging teachers to upgrade their qualifications and in providing an in-service programme promoting the use of student-centred learning. The Ministry has found, however, that while determining appropriate interventions to improve teacher quality is relatively straightforward, it is far more difficult to ensure that they produce the desired outcome or that improvement can be sustained over the longer term. The training of teachers by personnel from both Ministry and outside agencies during this phase focused on specific one-off sessions using pre-packaged materials in an attempt to recreate the mastery of new teaching strategies. To sustain change, however, requires teachers to go well beyond this.

The decision to move to a new third 'collaborating' phase is an attempt to put the processes in place that will sustain change so that improvement is continued over the longer term. The standardisation of teaching and learning was, for a long time, being promoted as the only way to achieve sustained improvement. Now, countries wanting to develop their education systems are increasingly looking towards establishing professional learning communities of teachers and schools. Improvements in the quality of students' learning, it is felt, can best be brought about through building the capacity of teachers to think about their teaching. They have to be given time and resources to learn, plan, experiment and reflect together about their work in school. They need to begin to take responsibility for their own professional development, to build their pedagogical expertise, and to evaluate the impact of their actions on the quality of their students' learning.

As the education system seeks to become more responsive to the needs of learners, higher-learning institutions and the labour market, more flexibility will be required. Mechanisms to promote lifelong learning that allow learners to change track and to return to formal learning after work need to be established. Developments in communications technology will provide scope for quite different approaches to offering access to learning. They will also pose increasing challenges to conventional schooling, with much greater diversity in how schools organise themselves. It is hard to predict what these changes will mean but it is clear that increasingly teachers will need to be flexible, bold and creative and, just as importantly, promote these qualities in their students. The challenge for the Ministry of Education is to ensure that teachers receive the levels of support and encouragement they require in order to build their professional capacity.

References

Black. P., Harrison. C., Lee. C., Marshall, B. & William, D. (2003) *Assessment for Learning: putting it into practice*. London: Open University Press.

Centre for British Teachers (2001) *Report from the Consultancy Study on the Reform of Years 11 and 12*. Muscat: Ministry of Education.

Education Consulting Services (1995) *Reform and Development of General Education in the Sultanate of Oman*. Muscat: Ministry of Education.

McKinsey & Company (2007) *How the World's Best School Systems Come out on Top*. mckinseyonsociety.com/downloads/reports/Education/Worlds_School_Systems

McKinsey & Company (2010) *How the World's Most Improved School Systems Keep Getting Better*. mckinseyonsociety.com/downloads/reports/Education/How-the-Worlds-Most-Improved-School-Systems

Mullis, I.V.S., Martin, M.O., Foy, P., Olson, J.F., Preuschoff, C., Erberber, E. et al (2008) *TIMSS 2007 International Mathematics Report: findings from IEA's Trends in International Mathematics and Science Study at the Fourth and*

Eighth Grades. Chestnut Hill, MA: TIMSS & PIRLS International Study Center, Lynch School of Education, Boston College.

Office for Standards in Education (Ofsted) (1998) *Reviewing the Work of Schools*. Muscat: Ministry of Education.

Oman Ministry of Education (1998) *Basic Education in the Sultanate of Oman: the theoretical framework*. Muscat: Ministry of Education.

Oman Ministry of Education (2006) *From Access to Success: Education for All (EFA) in the Sultanate of Oman 1970-2005*. Muscat: Ministry of Education.

Oman Ministry of Education (2008) *Post-Basic Education Programme, Grades 11 and 12*. Muscat: Ministry of Education.

Oman Ministry of Education (2009) *Educational Statistics Yearbook (2008/2009)*. Muscat: Educational Statistics Department, Ministry of Education.

Oman Ministry of Education (2011) *Educational Statistics Yearbook (2010/2011)*. Muscat: Educational Statistics Department, Ministry of Education.

Oman Ministry of Education & UNESCO (1997) *Monitoring of Learning Achievement Project: assessment of learning achievement of grade 4 students in Oman*. Muscat: Ministry of Education.

Oman Ministry of National Economy (1995) *2020 Vision for Oman's Economy: towards a better economic future*. Muscat: Oman Ministry of National Economy.

Organisation for Economic Cooperation and Development (OECD) (2005) *Teachers Matter: attracting, developing and retaining effective teachers*. Paris: OECD.

Scottish Qualifications Authority (1996) *Report on a Visit to the Sultanate of Oman*. Edinburgh: Scottish Qualifications Authority.

United Nations Development Programme (2003) *Arab Human Development Report: building a knowledge society*. New York: UNDP, Regional Bureau for Arab States.

United Nations Educational, Scientific and Cultural Organization (UNESCO) (1990) *World Declaration on Education for All, Jomtien*. Paris: UNESCO.

UNESCO (2000) *The Dakar Framework for Action: Education for All. Meeting Our Collective Commitments*. Paris: UNESCO.

World Bank (2008) *The Road Not Travelled: education reform in the Middle East and Africa*. Washington, DC: MENA Development Report.

International Influences on Adult Literacy and Basic Education in Turkey

ÖZLEM YAZLIK[1]

Introduction

Adult literacy and basic education (ALBE) is a major developmental task in Turkey: a nation-state established out of the remains of the Ottoman Empire in 1923. A number of scholars have observed that, historically, illiteracy has been defined as a 'problem' in Turkey (Bilir 2005; Yıldız, 2006; Sayılan, 2009).[2] It has also been noted that state initiatives to expand literacy and schooling and placing hopes in them for nation formation and social and economic progress started in the late nineteenth century (Alkan, 2000; Fortna, 2011). Building on and expanding these earlier efforts, there have been many literacy campaigns and activities undertaken by the Turkish government following the activities of the 'Nation Schools' in the early years of the Republic, more recently including the Campaign for Supporting National Education started in 2001, the campaign bearing the slogan 'Turkey is Literate' initiated in early 2008, and finally the latest literacy campaign launched in September 2008 with the slogan 'Mother-Daughter to School' (Ünlühisarcıklı, 2009).

Most estimates put the literacy rate in the young Republic in the 1920s at or under 10%; these literate citizens were able to read and write in the Arabo-Persian alphabet which was in use before the adoption of the Latin alphabet in 1928 (Fortna, 2011).[3] The adoption of the Latin alphabet for Turkish, which consists of 29 letters (21 consonants and eight vowels), meant all citizens of the new nation-state became illiterate: they did not know the new Turkish/Latin alphabet (Duman & Williamson, 1996). The adoption of the Latin alphabet was regarded to be useful for introducing an effective medium for writing Turkish and playing an important role in the rise of literacy (Lewis, 1999). However, a number of critics pointed out that the adoption of the Latin alphabet severed the continuity across texts and generations, rendering the texts written in the Arabo-Persian alphabet inaccessible to people born after 1928 (Parla, 2008; Fortna, 2011). The same critics noted that the Turkish language came to be seen as a signifier of the Turkish national identity, territorial unity of the nation-state and modernity.

Literacy education, therefore, played a central role in the efforts of the new nation-state to create a sense of national unity around a common language and new alphabet, as well as in tackling what was seen as backwardness and ignorance among rural populations (Ünlühisarcıklı, 2008; Taşçı-Günlü, 2008). Taşçı-Günlü noted that the literacy materials used in the major literacy campaigns between 1928 and 2001 invited people to learn to read and write in order to be 'modern', using bluntly didactic messages and representing illiterate or semi-literate persons as otherwise 'incomplete and ignorant' (2008, p. 192). In fact, 'modernisation' was equated with the contents and practices of modern material culture and scientific progress associated with the Western world. However, in contrast to Taşçı-Günlü's focus on the brusque messages of modernisation and nationalism in the content of the literacy campaigns, especially in the earlier ones, a number of critiques (Kirazoğlu, 2003; Sayılan & Yıldız, 2009) found it important to acknowledge the positive characteristics of the literacy activities between 1928 and 1950 such as mobilisation of extensive financial and community resources and the promotion of active citizenship in both rural and urban areas.

The period between 1950 and 1980 has been described as an era of rapid social changes by Sayılan and Yıldız (2009). They drew attention to the expansion of capitalist markets in Turkey and how these led to a shift in the government vision of education. Education was no longer seen as requiring mobilisation of collective action and extensive financial resources; it became merely one of the various public services that the government put at the disposal of individuals and attracted less state funding. Sayılan and Yıldız observed further that starting with the planned development period after 1960, illiteracy was defined as a problem of social and economic development. A number of scholars noted that international influences were introduced into the field of literacy with the UNESCO-promoted Functional Literacy Programme carried out between 1972-74, with its strong vocational rationale and emphasis on development (Yıldız, 2006; Taşçı-Günlü, 2008; Sayılan & Yıldız, 2009).

These international influences have encouraged a strong vocational emphasis on social and economic development. Indeed, this link between literacy and development reflects the post-Second World War directives from the United Nations as well as from Western political elites (Escobar, 1995). These, it can be argued, have impacted profoundly upon various Turkish Government approaches to literacy. As Escobar noted, recognition of literacy as a global 'problem, especially in the Third

World', emerged in the 1950s. And since that time, Western influences have maintained an updated version of what 'literacy' is, why it is important and how countries can achieve it.

This chapter addresses these concerns. It draws attention to the current Turkish approaches to literacy and to ALBE especially. It delineates developments in the field of literacy, especially New Literacy Studies, and contrasts this understanding with the more economistic and functional approach. In light of these contrasting influences and following Hamilton et al (2001, p. 24), the chapter highlights the values and goals assigned to ALBE in the following government policy documents: *Adult Literacy and Basic Education Programme* (MoNE, 2005a), *Adult Literacy and Basic Education Programme (1. and 2. Level)* (MoNE, 2007), *Basic Education in Turkey: background report* (MoNE, 2005b), *Ninth Development Plan: 2007-13* (SPO, 2006), *Policy Document: Women and Education* (GDSW, 2008), and *Lifelong Learning Strategy Paper and 2009-2013 Lifelong Learning Action Plan* (MoNE, 2009). There follows an examination of the role of international influences on the curriculum reform of 2005 and the involvement of non-governmental organisations (NGOs) in the delivery of literacy programmes. The chapter ends with a discussion that provides an account of how far the recent government understanding of literacy is the result of interventions by international organisations and what this means for the future of ALBE in Turkey.

1. Definitions of Literacy

The central idea underpinning the current policy of literacy and education continues to be the link between literacy and development. Literacy is defined as a motor of social and economic development, with the latter being emphasised. The government policy context is dominated by the assumption that levels of literacy and education are 'the most significant impetus of socio-economic development' (GDSW 2008, p. 5). Underlying this approach is a functional view of literacy, as promoted by UNESCO since the 1960s (UNESCO, 2004). Although recent UNESCO policy documents display a shift towards socio-cultural and more critical approaches to literacy, they contain conflicting portrayals of literacy, since in them literacy is also described in functional terms related to the labour market and individual economic productivity (Wickens & Sandlin, 2007).[4]

It appears that views of literacy that emphasise a need to increase employment and earnings are the ones now dominating the Turkish policy context. In its Ninth Development Plan 2007-2013, literacy and numeracy were identified as 'preconditions for lifelong learning' by 'increasing the employment skills of individuals in line with the requirements of a changing and developing economy and labour market'

(SPO, 2006, p. 98). Furthermore, this document identified the European Union (EU) and the Organisation for Economic Cooperation and Development (OECD) as setting the standards for conceptualising literacy in Turkey. It is noted: 'In order for literacy not to be minimised to solely alphabetic knowledge, literacy as a concept shall be handled under EU and OECD standards and shall be defined in this context' (SPO, 2006, annex).

As many writers have noted, traditional definitions of literacy, with their economistic and individualised approaches to lifelong learning and their emphasis on employment-related technical skills (Hamilton et al, 2001; Martin, 2003; Crowther, 2004; Tett, 2005), form the backbone of the Turkish policy context. This understanding of literacy requires a classroom-based approach to learning and assumes a similarity in learning styles and purposes across different texts and contexts.[5]

To ensure this standardisation, ALBE courses in Turkey are offered under the monitoring and inspection of the Ministry of National Education (MoNE). Their curricula were reorganised in line with the Primary School Curriculum Reform in 2005 as part of the full membership negotiations with the European Union (Esen, 2007; Çayır, 2009). The adult-education curricula document emphasised the aim of teaching adults 'functional' literacy skills and 'the concept of lifelong learning' (MoNE, 2007, p. 2). This newly emerging official lifelong-learning discourse in turn is marked by an emphasis on individual learning and increasing people's economic skills and employability (SPO, 2006; MoNE, 2009).

This rather narrow focus is a pity as recent international influences on ALBE courses in Turkey have a strong potential to influence the scope and purpose of ALBE activities, which can include much more than the narrow focus on employment-related goals (Hamilton et al, 2001). In contrast to skill-based and economistic approaches to literacy, socio-cultural and more critical approaches to literacy offer more: they recognise and respect people's various non-economic motivations to participate in adult-literacy classes such as the wish to feel and be seen as 'educated' (Robinson-Pant, 2000; Bartlett, 2007; Riemer, 2008), the wish to transform literacy classes into safe public spaces to reflect on gendered power relations in the community (Attwood et al, 2004; Khandekar, 2004; Millican, 2004), or the intention to use and improve a mother tongue when it is one of the country's unofficial languages (Trudell & Klaas, 2010). Next, I explore the insights from New Literacy Studies which have a socio-cultural approach to literacy, situating the meaning and uses of literacy in its social context and pointing to the links between literacy and power (Barton & Hamilton, 1998; Street, 2001). These insights help in understanding Turkish Government approaches to literacy. They are also useful in developing adult-literacy and basic-education programmes which build on people's existing uses and valuations of literacy and cultural knowledge.

2. New Literacy Studies

The field of New Literacy Studies has challenged the skills-based model of literacy which sees literacy's main importance as a means of economic participation in society and as a set of technical skills to be learned and used the same way in various social contexts, standardising it through the use of prescribed texts, tests and unified outcomes (Hamilton et al, 2001; Taylor, 2008; Myhill, 2009). Research carried out within New Literacy Studies has been informed by traditions of ethnography and is based on the view that people have different literacies in different domains of life such as home, workplace, school and community settings; literacy practices are purposeful and vary according to the demands of life and people's various motivations to make changes in their lives (Heath, 1983; Street, 1984; Barton, 1994; Barton & Hamilton, 1998).[6] Furthermore, New Literacy Studies have emphasised the link between literacy and power, revealing how 'powerful literacies' (Crowther et al, 2001) associated with such formal domains as law, education and the workplace are embedded in interpersonal and structural power hierarchies and their socially prestigious types of knowledge and identities (Papen, 2002).

Research carried out in this tradition has emphasised the practices of alternative literacy programmes which have built on people's existing literacy practices in the home and community rather than seeing them as inadequate for literacy development. They encouraged people to problematise their understanding of educational failure and challenged assumptions regarding the homogeneity of language forms (Auerbach, 1989; Addison, 2001; Tett, 2005). Lyn Tett (2005) provided an excellent description of such a family-literacy programme in Scotland where parents were helped to recognise and work on the numerous literacy practices they used in their everyday lives, gave presentations on their negative and positive experiences of schooling, collected texts from different genres (bills, newspapers, cereal packets) and worked on them to realise different forms and purposes of writing, as well as creating stories for their children reflecting their lives. I draw upon this research in order to understand and explain the concepts and recent developments in the ALBE policy documents in Turkey.

3. From Policies: four key questions

There are two levels of adult-literacy and basic-education courses in Turkey offered under the monitoring and inspection of the Ministry of National Education (MoNE). The objectives of Level 1 courses include teaching adults how to read and write, teaching basic mathematics and the knowledge and skills deemed necessary in daily life (MoNE, 2007). This course is considered equivalent to the third grade of the eight-year compulsory education system in Turkey, and is planned as 90 class hours (Ünlühisarcıklı, 2009). In addition to state-funded People's Education Centers (PECs), to deliver the Level 1 literacy course MoNE cooperates with three NGOs: the Rotary Club, the Association for Supporting Contemporary Life and the Mother-Child Education Foundation (Nohl & Sayılan, 2004). The state PECs, with their extended network, attract about 14 times as many participants to the Level 1 courses as these three NGOs together: in 2002, for example, 189,494 as opposed to 14,516 (Nohl & Sayılan, 2004).

Level 2 literacy courses are offered by PECs and state-primary-school teachers appointed by MoNE (Ünlühisarcıklı, 2009). The courses aim to educate adults towards a primary-school education which is the equivalent of the fourth and fifth years of the eight-year compulsory basic education and consists of 180 class hours organised around four different courses: Turkish (75 hours), Mathematics (45 hours), Social Studies (30 hours) and Science and Technology (30 hours) (MoNe, 2007). The curricula of the adult-literacy programmes were based on the new Primary School Curriculum in 2005 which was developed as part of the full membership negotiations with the EU (Esen, 2007; Çayır, 2009). Such international influences on ALBE in Turkey are likely to influence the scope and purpose of ALBE activities, which are discussed in policy documents in varying degrees of explicitness (Hamilton et al, 2001). Next, I highlight the recent government thinking on ALBE that is evident in the policy documents by addressing four key questions.

(i) What is the concept of literacy in recent policy documents?

As already shown, the government policy context is dominated by the functional definition of literacy that assumes that levels of literacy and education are 'the most significant impetus of socio-economic development' (GDSW, 2008, p. 5). This skills-based understanding frames literacy as a discrete, employment-related technical skill to be learned in literacy classrooms and used in the same way across different texts and contexts; this is also the dominant view in EU and OECD thinking in the area of adult literacy and basic education (Hamilton et al, 2001). ALBE policy documents focus on the use of standard Turkish as well as on the transfer of the formal elementary-education curriculum into ALBE courses, assigning a higher social status to a particular dialect and official school knowledge in contrast to people's existing social and cultural knowledge.

(ii) How are learners and teachers positioned by the policies?

The policy documents treat potential participants in ALBE courses as an undifferentiated group of people with deficiencies: The *Adult Literacy and Basic Education Programme (1. and 2. Level)* (MoNE, 2007) for instance refers to the goal of programme as 'rectifying adults' reading, writing and basic education deficiencies', aiming in general at 'people who do not know how to read and write' (preface). Although there is reference to target groups such as 'the illiterate, primarily residing in rural areas and who are disadvantaged (the old, women, and handicapped etc.)' (MoNE, 2009, annex 4.1), the main effect is a homogenising one that projects a mass of people that needs the encouragement of the state to participate in educational activities.

Basic Education in Turkey: Background Report (MoNe, 2005b) and *Ninth Development Plan: 2007-2013* (SPO, 2006) have a deficit view of adult learners that ignores or undervalues their life experiences and the capabilities and skills that are embedded in these. *Ninth Development Plan: 2007-2013* represents rural migrants as unskilled workers: 'Those who migrate to urban areas as a result of the structural change in agriculture are deprived of a regular income and experience social adaptation problems because they have low levels of education and are unskilled workers' (para. 254). *Basic Education in Turkey: Background Report* identifies one of the goals of non-formal education as 'to organise short, medium and long term course programmes for those who do not have any skills or competencies, especially the unqualified female workforce' (MoNE 2005b, p. 41). These documents are striking in that they characterise adults with no assumed skills for urban jobs as possessing no skills or competencies at all.

Teachers of ALBE programmes are mentioned only in the curricula documents *Adult Literacy and Basic Education Programme* (MoNe, 2005a) and *Adult Literacy and Basic Education Programme (1. and 2. Level)* (MoNE, 2007). These documents define the role of teachers as facilitators of student-centred teaching and adapters of pre-determined learning activities in government-commissioned textbooks. In these documents teachers do not appear as powerful actors with rights and capabilities who are involved in the process of curricular change and who can affect key decisions shaping the educational system. The overwhelming majority of ALBE courses at the People Education Centers are offered only by primary-school teachers appointed by MoNE, who are not trained specially for adult-literacy work (Ünlühisarcıklı, 2009). Thus it is striking that nowhere in the policy documents are the needs of teachers for professional development in the field of adult literacy and education addressed.

*(iii) What kind of learning activities
are programmes expected to engage in?*

Although there are three NGOs offering Level 1 literacy courses, since PECs have the most students for Level 1 and since Level 2 can only be taught by state primary-school teachers, most learners are taught in PECs or primary-school classrooms in groups of 10 to 20 students – although MoNE regulations state that literacy courses can be offered to any number of students, unlike other courses for which there is a requirement of a minimum of 12 students (MoNE, 2011a).

The curricula of the Level 1 and Level 2 adult-literacy and basic-education programmes were reorganised in line with the Primary School Curriculum Reform in 2005. The curriculum reform was considered by many as a welcome shift from a behaviourist approach that emphasised memorisation and recitation of facts without any analysis and questioning to a more constructivist pedagogy that promoted an active learner engaged in obtaining information and constructing knowledge through critical thinking and inquiry (Curriculum Review Commission, 2005; Batuhan, 2007; Koç et al, 2007; İşler & Çakıroğlu, 2009; Şahin, 2010). Whilst welcoming the new curricula as a progressive change, these researchers noted that the successful implementation of the curricula was hampered by the lack of teacher training and relevant educational technologies and material resources in most schools. İşler & Çakıroğlu (2009) and Şahin (2010) noted further that as long as national selection and placement tests were in place, teachers would find it necessary to teach to the exams to ensure student success in national exams. This was an important point, supported with empirical evidence from the study of Altınyelken (2010) in eight schools in Ankara.

In the case of adult-literacy courses, it is unclear to what extent the changes in the curricula influenced the teaching and learning in these courses. Some studies on adult literacy carried out after 2005 noted that in some literacy classes the teachers supported or replaced the textbooks prepared within the new curricular changes with teaching materials they themselves bought or developed (Güngör, 2006; İnce, 2008; Ünlühisarcıklı, 2009). Despite a highly centralised curriculum, all the teachers in these studies were reported to have left out parts of the curriculum they found too difficult for their students, regarding the duration of the programme as too short for a curriculum they considered overloaded. Such modification of the centralised curriculum by individual teachers in line with the needs of their participants, bypassing as it does to a certain extent the centralised approach of the official policy documents, is a welcome characteristic of the programmes. This responsive and responsible understanding of teaching should be built on in order to work toward literacy courses that involve adults in the decisions affecting their own learning to a greater extent.

Within the current policy context, both Level 1 and Level 2 ALBE courses take place through face-to-face contact with the teacher and other participants. Adults need a Level 2 certificate in order to enrol in open primary education conducted through distance-education methods: TV and radio broadcasting, access to course notes via the Internet and the distribution of textbooks to learners (MoNE, 2011b). The policy documents emphasise the need to develop distance-education methods and on-line learning (MoNE, 2005b; SPO, 2006; MoNE, 2009), but it is unclear to what extent the recent emphasis on the use of information technologies will influence the provision of Level 1 and Level 2 ALBE teaching.

(iv) What outcomes are literacy programmes and learners expected to achieve?

The policy documents use current illiteracy rates and levels of participation in formal education to justify the need for increased literacy and participation rates in ALBE (MoNE, 2007, p.2; GDSW, 2008, p. 34; MoNE, 2009, p. 17). These increased rates are emphasised for their assumed importance in employability and economic growth. The latest literacy campaign launched in September 2008 by the wife of the current Prime Minister with the slogan 'Mother-Daughter to School' for example set itself the target of teaching reading and writing to three million adults in four years (Ana-Kız Okuldayız, 2011). However, emphasising the number of participants and literacy rates as the major outcome of literacy programmes does little to support important social and emotional outcomes of adult-literacy courses such as increased social status and decision-making power in the family and community, and the increased sense of self-worth and self-confidence. Moreover, new literacy practices learned through participation, such as creative writing, letter writing and signing one's own name, all give participants a new voice and authority in the community (Robinson-Pant 2000; Kendrick & Hissani, 2007). Positive outcomes such as these can result from the simple fact of participation in the course, which is seen as a symbolic return to formal schooling (Friedrich, 2000; Millican, 2004; Walter, 2004, Riemer, 2008).

4. Curriculum Reform: international pressures

The field of education and adult literacy has been identified as being under attack from neoliberal policies of marketisation and privatisation of education starting in the 1980s (Ercan, 1998; Gök, 2004; Sayılan & Yıldız, 2009). These critiques point out that since the country lacks a solid structural foundation for compulsory elementary education, neoliberal policies have led to more pronounced class, regional and gender-based inequalities in access to education and literacy in Turkey.

In connection with decreasing government commitment to providing quality education to all, Sayılan and Yıldız (2009) and Sayılan (2009) have pointed out that the involvement of NGOs in the provision of adult literacy in Turkey is a development that is in line with calls by UNESCO (at the World Conference on 'Education for All' in Jomtien in 1990) to NGOs and civil-society organisations for their support in adult-literacy projects. It can be suggested that the growing NGO involvement in the provision of adult literacy in Turkey is part of a global trend which has been described as a defining characteristic of the decade following the Jomtien conference (Müller, 2000). This point is confirmed by the fact that the three NGOs in Turkey that provide adult literacy education– the Rotary Club, the Association for Supporting Contemporary Life, and the Mother-Child Education Foundation – started their adult literacy activities in the 1990s. Whilst Sayılan and Yıldız (2009) and Sayılan (2009) acknowledged the dynamism of NGOs in mobilising adults to attend literacy programmes, they pointed out that NGO activities should not be seen as a substitute for programmes that should be funded by the government as part of its legal responsibility to make the right to literacy and education a reality (Constitution of Turkish Republic, Art. 42).

International directives are also apparent when one examines the curricula of the Level 1 and Level 2 adult literacy and basic programmes. Sayılan (2009) noted that in parallel with the Primary School Curriculum Reform, the new adult-literacy curricula advocated student-centred learning and active participation of adults in the decisions influencing their learning within the framework of a constructivist approach. However, she pointed out that the learning activities in the textbooks were still teacher-centred and did not prioritise critical awareness of and action about adults' self-identified life concerns. Sayılan also noted that the introduction of 'life skills' as a learning topic in the new curriculum reflected a global trend that started with the UNESCO World Conference on 'Education for All' in Jomtien in 1990. Indeed, recent UNESCO policy documents represented life skills as a major part of adult literacy education (UNESCO, 2000, 2003, 2006) and noted that different countries have different interpretations of life skills ranging from a focus on basic reading and writing skills and health knowledge to problem solving in everyday life. In the Turkish context, the curricula and textbooks' focus on entrepreneurship, team work, problem solving and information and communication technologies can be seen as complementing the traditional functionalist view of literacy as the key to economic development and individual economic productivity (Sayılan 2009).

Conclusion

The dominant assumption in the ALBE policy documents in Turkey is that there is only one literacy: schooled literacy. This set of technical skills, it is thought, can be taught sequentially in a similar way through school classrooms or adult literacy courses and it can be applied across variant texts, contexts and cultures (Barton, 1994; Crowther & Tett, 2001). This assumption is characteristic of the skills-based model of literacy which sees literacy as a discrete, employment-related skill; this is also the dominant view in the European Union (EU) and OECD (Organisation for Economic Cooperation and Development) thinking on literacy (Hamilton et al, 2001). The skills-based model of literacy is closely related to the traditional functional definition of literacy with its focus on social and economic development through increased employment and earnings which still appears in recent UNESCO documents, along with socio-cultural and more critical understandings of literacy (Wickens & Sandlin, 2007). Furthermore, recent ALBE curricula and textbooks include life skills as a learning topic, reflecting the global trend that started with the UNESCO World Conference on 'Education for All' in Jomtien in 1990 (Sayılan, 2009). The choice of economistic skills such as entrepreneurship, team work, and information and communication technologies among life skills in the ALBE curricula (Sayılan, 2009) seems to be in line with the economistic, skills-based thinking of literacy in the policy documents.

It is important to challenge this model with insights from New Literacy Studies that explore and validate people's real-life knowledge and literacy practices, which involve a lot more than employment-related uses of literacy. Moreover, these insights help us raise questions about future developments in the adult literacy policy context in Turkey. Fortunately, in the ALBE system as actually applied in many classrooms teachers can use their professional judgment and agency to leave out parts of the curriculum that they find to be too difficult for a particular group of adult learners (Güngör, 2006; İnce, 2008; Ünlühisarcıklı, 2009). They are also responsible for assessing the academic success of the course participants, as opposed to measuring achievement by standardised national tests. Under the influence of international thinking on adult literacy, the Turkish government may be encouraged to introduce quantified performance criteria and standardised tests for the existing Level 1 and Level 2 Literacy Courses. Given the argument of the foregoing analysis, this would be a retrogressive step. So too would be any move on the part of the government to replace face-to-face teaching at Public Education Centers (PEC) partly or fully with distance-education methods. Further emphasis on NGO-led projects could also be detrimental to ALBE as this would result, inevitably, in an effort to cut the funding of already poorly financed and equipped PECs.

It will become important for the government and other key players (local, national and international) to ensure the delivery of ALBE textbooks that are prepared with adults and their real-life literacy practices and concerns in mind. This is much more appropriate to adult learning than to continue with the current situation of the transfer of the formal primary-school curriculum – intended, after all, for children – into ALBE textbooks. Throughout this chapter, it has been argued that this process ignores the basic principles of adult education. Additionally, it assigns a higher status to standard Turkish and textbook knowledge.

The recent policy context in Turkey suggests that adult educators need to work together to address these recent developments so that we can create courses that validate people's existing cultural knowledge and literacy practices and help them identify and act on their self-defined life concerns. Through this approach, doors are opened to more personal, critical and respectful possibilities of literacy. We can also ensure that international definitions of 'literacy' and 'adult literacy' are contextualised not only by the needs of international organisations and their views of skills and labour markets, but also by the aspirations of adult learners themselves in Turkey.

Notes

[1] This chapter is based on a paper presented at the fifth conference of the ESREA research network 'Between Global and Local: Adult Learning and Development in 2011', Boğaziçi University, Istanbul.

[2] The information available on literacy in Turkey is mostly in the form of statistical data based on census surveys. Thus the official illiteracy rate, which labels people as either literate or illiterate depending on self-declaration, was 2.7% among men and 11.9% among women in 2010 among the population over 15 years of age (TUIK, 2011).

[3] The adoption of the Latin alphabet was part of the Turkish language reform which aimed to purge Turkish of Arabic and Persian words and grammatical features, and thus decrease the gap between the language of ordinary citizens who spoke with mostly Turkish words and the language of bureaucracy and literature which included mostly Arabic and Persian words and syntax (Belge, 1982; Yücel, 1982; Lewis, 1999). Opinions differ on whether this goal was achieved to a significant degree or not. However, for Lewis (1999) the language reform amounted to a 'catastrophic success' because he considered it to impoverish Turkish by eliminating many Arabic and Persian words without being able to replace them with equally meaningful Turkish words.

[4] David Barton (1994) found that Freirean critical approaches (Freire, 1972, 1974) started literacy education with an analysis of one's social position and unequal power relations in the classroom and society, whereas socio-cultural approaches to literacy are critical in the sense that they can relate

to theories of social inequality and help people enjoy different possibilities of literacy, including but not limited to school-based literacy.

[5] Alan Rogers (2000) pointed out that in most adult-literacy programmes in the 'developing' countries the primary-school classroom model of teaching was used: illiterate adults were gathered in a classroom and taught with the same textbook as if they all had the same literacy level and concerns. He observed that many such participants could not transfer the skills learned in the classroom to the outside world. Thus instead of trying to create groups of illiterate adults to be taught in classrooms, he suggested doing literacy work with groups that already existed, such as developmental groups that were formed for economic or cultural activities, religious groups and local political groups. He gave several examples of such groups that learned/improved literacy skills through real-life tasks, e.g., a group of Tamil Nadu women decided to take over the lease of the quarry they worked in and worked together to increase their literacy skills to do this.

[6] It can be suggested that the use of literacy in the plural is a critique of the school-based model of literacy that sees it as a unitary and universal notion. The term 'literacies' attracts attention to the fact that people use written language in different ways in different social situations (Ewing, 2003). Thus literacy can mean being able to write down your address, labelling family photographs, signing your name, being able to work in an office or being able to recite passages of Koran through phonic recognition and memorisation without being able to understand Arabic otherwise.

References

Addison, F.P. (2001) Using Scots Literacy in Family Literacy Work, in J. Crowther, M. Hamilton & L. Tett (Eds) *Powerful Literacies,* pp. 155-165. Leicester: National Institute of Continuing Education.

Alkan, M.Ö. (2000) Modernization from Empire to Republic and Education in the Process of Nationalism, in K.H. Karpat (Ed.) *Ottoman Past and Today's Turkey,* pp. 47-132. Leiden: Brill.

Altınyelken, H.K. (2010) Teachers' Principled Resistance to Curriculum Change: a compelling case from Turkey. http://dare.uva.nl/*document*/202725 (accessed 1 July 2011).

Ana-Kız Okuldayız (2011) *Ana-Kız Okuldayiz Okuma Yazma Kampanyası.* [Mother-Daughter to School Literacy Campaign] http://www.anakizokuldayiz.com (accessed 15 April 2011).

Attwood, G., Castle, J. & Smythe, S. (2004) 'Women are Lions in Dresses'. Negotiating Gender Relations in REFLECT Learning Circles in Lesotho, in Anna Robinson-Pant (Ed.) *Women, Literacy and Development: alternative perspectives,* pp. 139-158. London: Routledge.

Auerbach, E.R. (1989) Toward a Social-Contextual Approach to Family Literacy, *Harvard Educational Review*, 59(2), 165-181. http://www.eric.ed.gov (accessed 20 May 2010).

Bartlett, L. (2007) To Seem and to Feel: situated identities and literacy practices, *Teachers College Record*, 109(1), 51-69. http://www.tc.columbia.edu/faculty/bartlett/publications/pdf/109_1tcr.pdf (accessed 5 December 2009).

Barton, D. (1994) *An Introduction to the Ecology of Written Language*. Oxford: Blackwell.

Barton, D. & Hamilton, M. (1998) *Local Literacies: reading and writing in one community*. London: Routledge.

Batuhan, A. (2007) Education For All by 2015: will we make it? Turkey Country Case Study. UNESCO. http://unesdoc.unesco.org/images/0015/001555/155505e.pdf (accessed 7 July 2010).

Belge, M. (1982) *Türkçe Sorunu* [The problem of Turkish]. Çukurova Üniversitesi Türkoloji Araştırmaları Merkezi [The Center for Turkology Studies, Çukurova University]. http://turkoloji.cu.edu.tr/GENEL/24.php (accessed 28 July 2012).

Bilir, M. (2005) Türkiye'deki eğitim (okuma-yazma) kampanyalarının halk eğitimi açısından değerlendirilmesi [An evaluation of education (literacy) campaigns in Turkey in terms of adult education], *Ankara University Journal of Faculty of Educational Sciences*, 38(2), 103-125.

Çayır, K. (2009) Preparing Turkey for the European Union: nationalism, national identity and 'otherness' in Turkey's new textbooks, *Journal of Intercultural Studies*, 30(1), 39-55.

Crowther, J. (2004) 'In and Against' Lifelong Learning: flexibility and the corrosion of character. *International Journal of Lifelong Education*, 23(2), 125-136.

Constitution of Turkish Republic, Art. 42. http://www.anayasa.gen.tr/1982ay.htm (accessed 20 July 2012).

Crowther, J., Hamilton, M. & Tett, L. (2001) Powerful Literacies: an introduction, in J. Crowther, M. Hamilton & L. Tett (Eds) *Powerful Literacies*, pp. 1-13. Leicester: National Institute of Continuing Education.

Crowther, J. & Tett, L. (2001) Democracy as a Way of Life: literacy for citizenship, in J. Crowther, M. Hamilton & L. Tett (Eds) *Powerful Literacies*, pp. 94-108. Leicester: National Institute of Continuing Education.

Curriculum Review Commission (2005) *Report on the New Curricula: grades 1-5*. Istanbul: Education Reform Initiative. http://www.sabanciuniv.edu/ipm/eng/Yayinlar/.../ERIReportontheNewCurricula.pdf (accessed 7 July 2010).

Duman, A. & Williamson, B. (1996) Organisation, Constraints and Opportunities: an analysis of adult education in Turkey, *International Journal of Lifelong Education*, 15(4), 286-302.

Ercan, F. (1998) 1980'lerde Eğitim Sisteminin Yeniden Yapılanması: Küreselleşme ve Neo Liberal Eğitim Politikaları [Reconstruction of the education system in the 1980s: globalization and neoliberal education policies], in Fatima Gök (Ed.) *75 Yılda Eğitim* [Education through 75 years], pp. 23-38. Istanbul: İş Bankası Yayınları.

Escobar, A. (1995) *Encountering Development: the making and unmaking of the third world.* Princeton: Princeton University Press.

Esen, Y. (2007) Sexism in School Textbooks prepared under Education Reform in Turkey, *Journal for Critical Education Policy Studies*, 5(2). http://www.jceps.com/index.php?pageID=article&articleID=109

Ewing, G. (2003) The New Literacy Studies: a point of connection between literacy research and literacy work, *Literacies*, 1. http://www.literacyjournal.ca/literacies/1-2003/analysis/2/1.htm (accessed 25 July 2012).

Freire, P. (1972) *Cultural Action for Freedom.* Harmondsworth: Penguin.

Freire, P. (1974) *Education for Critical Consciousness.* London: Continuum.

Friedrich, M. (2000) Functional Participation: questioning participatory attempts at reshaping African gender identities. The Case of REFLECT in Uganda, in Anna Robinson-Pant (Ed.) *Women, Literacy and Development: alternative perspectives,* pp. 219-231. London: Routledge.

Fortna, B. C. (2011) *Learning to Read in the Late Ottoman Empire and the Early Turkish Republic.* London: Palgrave Macmillan.

GDSW (2008) Policy Document: women and education. Ankara: General Directorate on the Status of Women. http://www.ksgm.gov.tr/Pdf/egitim_ingilizce.pdf (accessed 10 January 2011).

Gök, F. (2004) Eğitimin Özelleştirilmesi, [Privatisation of education], in N. Balkan & S. Savran (Eds) Neoliberalizmin Tahribatı [Damage of neoliberalism], pp. 94-110. Istanbul: Metis Yayınları.

Güngör, R. (2006) Adaptation of the Education Participation Scale (EPS) for Participants in Level II Literacy Courses. MA thesis, Boğaziçi University, Istanbul.

Hamilton, M., Macrae, C. & Tett, L. (2001) Powerful Literacies: the policy context, in J. Crowther, M. Hamilton & L. Tett (Eds) *Powerful Literacies,* pp. 23-45. Leicester: National Institute of Continuing Education.

Heath, Shirley Brice (1983) *Ways with Words: language, life and work in communities and classrooms.* Cambridge: Cambridge University Press.

İnce, G. (2008) Yetişkin okuryazarlık programlarının nitelik açısından değerlendirilmesi [A qualitative evaluation of adult literacy programmes]. Master's thesis, Ankara University, Turkey.

İşler, I. & Çakıroğlu, E. (2009) Teachers' Efficacy Beliefs and Perceptions regarding the Implementation of New Primary Mathematics Curriculum, in *Proceedings of CERME 6,* pp. 1704-1713. http://www.inrp.fr/editions/cerme6 (accessed 7 July 2010).

Kendrik, M.E. & Hissani, H. (2007) Letters, Imagined Communities, and Literate Identities: perspectives from rural Ugandan women, *Journal of Literacy Research*, 39(2), 195-216.

Khandekar, S. (2004) 'Literacy Brought us to the Forefront': literacy and empowering processes for Dalit community women in a Mumbai slum, in Anna Robinson-Pant (Ed.) *Women, Literacy and Development: alternative perspectives,* pp. 206-218. London: Routledge.

Kirazoğlu, C. (2003) An Evaluation of Adult Literacy Campaigns in Turkey. PhD dissertation, Boğazici University, Istanbul.

Koç, Y., Işıksal, M. & Bulut, S. (2007) Elementary School Curriculum Reform in Turkey, *International Education Journal*, 8(1), 30-39.

Lewis, G. (1999) *The Turkish Language Reform: a catastrophic success.* Oxford: Oxford University Press.

Martin, I. (2003) Adult Education, Lifelong Learning and Citizenship: some ifs and buts, *International Journal of Lifelong Education*, 22(16), 566-579.

Millican, J. (2004) 'I Will Stay Here until I Die': a critical analysis of the Muthande Literacy Programme, in Anna Robinson-Pant (Ed.) *Women, Literacy and Development: alternative perspectives*, pp. 195-205. London: Routledge.

MoNE (Ministry of National Education) (2005a) *Yetişkinler okuma yazma öğretimi ve temel eğitim programı* [Adult Literacy and Basic Education Programme]. MoNE General Directorate of Apprenticeship and Non-formal Education, Ankara. http://cygm.meb.gov.tr (accessed 10 February 2011).

MoNe (2005b) *Basic Education in Turkey: background report.* Ankara: MoNE. http://www.oecd.org/dataoecd/8/51/39642601.pdf (accessed 15 February 2011).

MoNE (2007) *Yetişkinler okuma yazma öğretimi ve temel eğitim programı (I. Ve II. Kademe)* [Adult Literacy and Basic Education Programme (Level 1 and Level 2). Ankara: MoNE General Directorate of Apprenticeship and Non-formal Education. http://cygm.meb.gov.tr (accessed 10 February 2011).

MoNE (2009) Türkiye hayat boyu öğrenme strateji belgesi ve 2009-2013 dönemi hayat boyu öğrenme faaliyet planı [Turkey Lifelong Learning Strategy Paper and 2009-2013 Lifelong Learning Action Plan]. Ankara: MoNE General Directorate of Apprenticeship and Non-formal Education. http://cygm.meb.gov.tr/duyurular/hayatboyuogrenmestratejisi/HBO%20FAAL%C4%B0YET%20PLANI.pdf (accessed 20 January 2011).

MoNE (2011a) *Çıraklık ve Yaygın Eğitim Genel Müdürlüğü: Sık Sorulan Sorular.* http://cygm.meb.gov.tr/sorulansorular (accessed 15 April 2011).

MoNe (2011b) *Milli Eğitim Bakanlığı Eğitim Teknolojileri Genel Müdürlüğü Açık İlköğretim Okulu.* http://aio.meb.gov.tr (accessed 15 April 2011).

Müller, J. (2000) From Jomtien to Dakar: meeting basic learning needs – of whom? *Adult Education and Development*, 55, 29-56.

Myhill, D. (2009) Shaping Futures: literacy policy in the twenty-first century, *Research Papers in Education*, 24(2), 129-133.

Nohl, A.M. & Sayılan, F. (2004) *Türkiye'de yetişkinler için okuma yazma eğitimi: Temel eğitime destek projesi teknik raporu* [Adult literacy education in Turkey: support to elementary education project technical report]. Milli Eğitim Bakanlığı/Avrupa Komisyonu [Ministry of Education/European Commission]. www.meb.gov.tr/duyurular/duyurular/Proj/TEDPBilgilendirme.pdf (accessed 10 July 2010).

Parla, J. (2008) The Wounded Language: Turkey's language reform and the canonicity of the novel, *PMLA*, 123(1), 27-40.

Papen, U. (2002) TVs, Textbooks and Tour Guides: uses and meanings of literacy. PhD thesis, University of London.

Riemer, F. J. (2008) Becoming Literate, Being Human: adult literacy and moral reconstruction in Botswana, *Anthropology & Education Quarterly*, 39(4), 444-464.

Robinson-Pant, A. (2000) *Why Eat Green Cucumbers at the Time of Dying: exploring the link between women's literacy and development. Nepal perspective.* Hamburg: UNESCO Institute for Education. http://www.unesco.org/education/uie/pdf/robinson.pdf (accessed 20 October 2010).

Rogers, A. (2000) Literacy Comes Second: working with groups in developing societies, *Development in Practice*, 10(2), 236-240.

Şahin, I. (2010) Curriculum Assessment: constructivist primary mathematics curriculum in Turkey, *International Journal of Science and Mathematics Education*, 8, 51-72.

Sayılan, F. (2009) Yetişkin okuma yazma öğretimi ve temel eğitim programı ve ders kitapları: eleştirel söylem analizi [Adult Literacy and Basic Education Program and literacy textbooks: critical discourse analysis], *Education Science Society Journal*, 7(26), 39-68.

Sayılan, F. & Yıldız, A. (2009) The Historical and Political Context of Adult Literacy in Turkey, *International Journal of Lifelong Education*, 28(6), 735-749.

State Planning Organisation (SPO) (2006) *State Planning Organisation Ninth Development Plan: 2007-2013*. Turkish Prime Ministry State Planning Organisation, Ankara. http://ekutup.dpt.gov.tr/plan/ix/9developmentplan.pdf (accessed 5 January 2011).

Street, B.V. (1984) *Literacy in Theory and Practice*. Cambridge: Cambridge University Press.

Street, B.V. (2001) Introduction, in B.V. Street (Ed.) *Literacy and Development: ethnographic perspectives*, 1-19. London: Routledge.

Taşçı-Günlü, S. (2008) Adult Literacy Campaigns and Nation Building, in A.-M. Nohl, A. Akkoyunlu-Wigley & S. Wigley (Eds) *Education in Turkey*, pp. 175-194. New York: Waxmann.

Taylor, N. (2008) Metaphors, Discourse and Identity in Adult Literacy Policy. *Literacy*, 42(3), 131-136.

Tett, L. (2005) Learning, Literacy, and Identity, *New Directions for Adult and Continuing Education*, 106, 27-37.

Trudell, B. & Klaas, R. A. (2010) Distinction, Integration and Identity: motivations for local language literacy in Senegalese communities, *International Journal of Educational Development*, 30, 121-129.

TUIK (2011) *Statistical Indicators: 1923-2010*. http://www.tuik.gov.tr/IcerikGetir.do?istab_id=158 (accessed 28 July 2012).

UNESCO (2000) *The Dakar Framework for Action. Education For All: meeting our collective commitments.* Paris: UNESCO. http://unesdoc.unesco.org/images/0012/001211/121147e.pdf (accessed 20 June 2012).

UNESCO (2003) Literacy for Change [Special issue]. *The New Courier*. http://unesdoc.unesco.org/images/0013/001300/130036e.pdf (accessed 20 June 2012.

UNESCO (2004) Plurality of Literacy and its Implications for Policies and Programmes: UNESCO education sector position paper. http://unesdoc.unesco.org/images/0013/001362/136246e.pdf (accessed 14 November 2007].

UNESCO (2006) *Education For All: literacy for life.* Paris: UNESCO. http://unesdoc.unesco.org/images/0014/001416/141639e.pdf (accessed 20 June 2012).

Ünlühisarcıklı, Ö. (2008) Adult and Further Education: systematic and historical aspects of non-formal education in Turkey, in A.-M. Nohl, A. Akkoyunlu-Wigley & S. Wigley (Eds) *Education in Turkey,* pp. 131-150. New York: Waxmann.

Ünlühisarcıklı, Ö. (2009) Literacy, Learners and Laws: a Turkish case study of surviving regulations, *Literacy and Numeracy Studies,* 17(3), 42-56.

Walter, P. (2004) Through a Gender Lens: explaining North-Eastern Thai women's participation in adult literacy education, *International Journal of Lifelong Education*, 23(5), 423-441.

Wickens, C.M. & Sandlin, J.A. (2007) Literacy for What? Literacy for Whom? The Politics of Literacy Education and Neocolonialism in UNESCO- and World Bank-sponsored literacy programs, *Adult Education Quarterly,* 57, 275-292.

Yıldız, A. (2006) Türkiye'de yetişkin okuryazarlığı: Yetişkin okuma-yazma eğitimine eleştirel bir yaklaşım [Adult Literacy in Turkey: a critical approach to adult literacy education]. PhD thesis, Ankara University, Turkey.

Yücel, T. (1982) *Dil devrimi ve sonuçları* [The language revolution and its effects]. Ankara: Türk Dil Kurumu Yayınları.

CHAPTER EIGHT

Gender and Education in the Arabian Gulf States

SALHA ABDULLAH ISSAN

Introduction

The six Gulf Cooperation Council (GCC) countries of the Middle East share many social norms and practices. These stem from common religious, economic, cultural, political and historical characteristics which, when taken together, result in a culture that differentiates a region from societies in other parts of the world. More specifically, in these countries where money from oil has, for years, been the major source of revenue, governments are struggling to maintain the almost-universal welfare provisions established in the 1970s. This was at a time when money was not a problem and populations were much smaller than they are today (Gause, 2000).

The educational system in the six Gulf States reflects the basic dilemma that these societies face today: how to reconcile the requirements of modernisation with their traditional values. For a long time, religion, language and history have been integral to and the main focus of public education. Whilst essential for preserving the existing culture, these disciplines must be complemented with a proper dose of modern diversity in science, technology and information technology. The current mantra – repeated incessantly by international organisations – is that without modernisation in the experience of education, 'development' cannot occur. Various international targets and goals attest to this and the Organisation for Economic Cooperation and Development (OECD) and other international agencies monitor and report on 'achievement'.

In general, the six GCC states have tried to raise the level of education and training in line with these internationally driven conceptions of 'achievement'. However, the gender-equality goal is more contentious than those relating to access to education, retention in schooling or even the provision of 'quality' education (in its very many different guises).

Indeed, most recently, education policy makers in the six states have become aware that 'quality' education requires engagement by all in society. There have been measures introduced to improve quality and diversity in education and to allow female participation in the development of their society. In fact educational attainment is, without doubt, the most fundamental prerequisite for empowering women in all spheres of society. Female education encompasses both social and economic dimensions that can contribute to female empowerment. Without education comparable to that given to males in quality and content and also relevant to existing knowledge and real needs, women will be unable to access well-paid, formal-sector jobs and advance within them. Moreover they cannot participate in and be represented in government, or gain political influence. Many international organisations repeat these views and most have held conferences in the region, attended meetings in country and published reports widely read by key players in the field of education. Their views on education become the region's views on education. USAID, the United States Agency for International Development, is one such organisation and notes:

> Education is universally acknowledged to benefit individuals and promote national development. Education expands the opportunities and life choices for both boys and girls. Worldwide, however, 42 million girls remain out of school, representing 55% of all children out of school. (USAID, 2012)

Education, as defined by USAID and other international organisations, is often regarded as an investment in human capital, which in turn raises the productivity of the labour force. Though productivity and earnings are determined, also, by a host of other factors, persistent gaps in female–male educational attainments may partly explain the gender-wage differentials. Human-capital theory suggests that education and employment are the two most important determinants of individual earnings, as equalisation of education and employment opportunities tends to equalise individual earnings (Mincer, 1974; Becker, 1993). Thus, from an economic perspective, education can raise women's status, provided the amount of earnings and equality in earnings distribution are seen to be adequate indicators of empowerment.

In drawing attention to these issues, this chapter assesses the current size of the gender gap by measuring the extent to which women in the Gulf Cooperation Council's states – Bahrain, Kuwait, Oman, Qatar, Saudi Arabia and the United Arab Emirates – have achieved equality with men in educational attainment. As noted, education is seen as a critical area and may be examined as a prime indicator of socio-political as well as economic equality.

In the present chapter, gender disparities in educational attainment are captured using data on literacy rates, enrolment rates in education and female involvement in politics and the labour force across the populations of each of the six countries. In this way, not only are the current levels of female empowerment illustrated through education, but also the potential for the future generations of women in these states. Therefore the chapter will cover the following: the concept of gender; women's conditions in each country; and the social space for 'Gendered Citizenship' in the Gulf States.

1. The Concept of Gender

Gender has always been an issue of debate when it comes to the differences between men and women in all aspects of their lives. Despite significant advancements in the overall socioeconomic status of minorities and working women, race and gender remain important impediments to their attainment of authority. Gender is defined as a 'classification of sex' (Al-Lamky, 2007, p. 49) and as 'the behavioural, cultural, or psychological traits typically associated with one sex' (Neal et al, 2005, p. 478).

Joseph (2002) argued that since classical political thinkers usually discussed the citizen in terms of an abstract person (the citizen as an 'individual' with undifferentiated, uniform and universal properties, rights and duties). The citizen appeared in much of classical political theory to be neutral in cultural and gender terms (Marshall, 1950; Benedix, 1964; Barbalet 1988; Keane, 1988a, b; Culpitt, 1992; Turner, 1993; Twine, 1994). Many writers state that because constitutions and laws are written in terms of such an abstract citizen, they may appear equitable. But recent research has revealed systematic means by which citizenship, in most countries of the world, has been a highly gendered enterprise, in practice and on paper (Pateman, 1988; Phillips, 1991, 1993; Lister, 1997; Voet, 1998). The concept of citizenship in most countries of the world often conceals inequalities or attempts to justify them on the basis of family, religion, history or other cultural terms and the GCC states are no exception.

Drawing, therefore, on the importance of viewing gender equality in terms of a 'relational process' that plays out through educational systems and the norms and values institutionalised within them, Subrahmanian (2005) argues for breaking down 'gender equality' into its constituent parts and identifying indicators relevant to each component. For this purpose, he draws on Duncan Wilson's (2003) threefold characterisation of rights in education. These are: rights to education; rights within education; and rights through education.

Thus an important dimension of educational equality requires focusing on rights through education, recognising that gender equality within education is shaped by and is in turn shaping, rights and gender equality in other dimensions of life. This involves asking to what extent education strengthens gender equality outside the sphere of education.

Recently, there has been a significant shift in approach to women's advancement and empowerment. While previously the advancement of women was regarded as important for outcomes such as economic development or population policies, it has become the case that the international community considers the empowerment and autonomy of women and the improvement of their political, social, economic and health status, as important ends in themselves. This shift in approach reflects a human-rights approach to issues of concern to women.

Parallel to this shift in approach to women's advancement has been an increased emphasis on the importance of a rights-based approach to planning and programming generally. In his reform proposals, the Secretary-General of the United Nations (UN) has made clear that human rights are a cross-cutting element that should be reflected in all United Nations policies and programmes. The High Commissioner for Human Rights also stresses that human rights are integral to all activities, including peace-making, peace-keeping, peace-building, humanitarian assistance and development. Several United Nations entities, including UNICEF, the United Nations Population Fund (UNFPA) and the United States Development Programme (UNDP) have identified the securing of individuals' human rights as a critical first step in addressing global problems and are now incorporating human rights into their policy-making processes and operational activities. There are measurable indicators that are used to rank countries regarding gender equality in the education system. These are elaborated in Table I.

Subrahmanian (2005) pointed out that the italicised indicators refer to those that are measurable, but not treated as conventional indicators. The category 'factors shaping performance' outlines those indicators that could be best developed at local level for educators to manage their own educational institutions. This is by no means an exhaustive list, just an indicative one.

In terms of citizenship equality in the Gulf region, most Arab states have permitted fathers, but not mothers, to pass citizenship on to their children. This testifies to the privileging of masculine blood in citizenship rules. The efforts to give a genealogy to citizens (especially the linkage to 'blood') have appeared to 'naturalise' being a citizen. In the process of 'naturalising' who is and is not a citizen, states have asserted a continuity to their existence that elevates both the idea of membership and the being of statehood into the realm of the sacred. Rogers M. Smith (1997) has described this process of 'naturalising' the boundaries of belonging as part of the process of creating the 'civic myth' of a state. Civic myths regulate who does and does not belong and inevitably bring with them inequalities based on gender, race, ethnicity and class.

Equal access to	Equality within	Equality through
Enrolment	Subject choice	Male/female employment across different levels of education by gender
Survival	Learning outcomes (performance in examinations)	
Completion Regularity of attendance Repetition		
Average years of schooling attained	Teacher–learner ratio	Gender differentials in wages across different levels of employment/education
Transitions of boys and girls between levels of education	Gender balance within the classroom	Political participation
Number of female and male teachers	Qualifications of teachers Level of training of teachers Factors shaping performance including: Health of students Nutritional status Child's involvement in family work Social discrimination within the classroom/ society (context-specific indicators would be necessary)	

Table I. Measurable indicators.
Source: Adapted from Subrahmanian (2005, p. 404).

The educational opportunities open to women in the Gulf region have apparently contributed to greater expectations among young women. According to the literature, education and occupation are a major impetus for social mobility among Arab women, and women throughout the Gulf Region (Abu Baker, 2010).

Despite social and cultural changes that occurred over the last three generations in the Gulf region, traditional patterns have been preserved in some areas. In many cases, the man is still considered the head of the family, and this affects how the children are raised and educated. Traditional values regarding relationships and gender roles reflect patriarchal perspectives (Haj-Yahia, 2000).

The traditional culture in the society of the Gulf States has never accepted the notion of equality between men and women. The customs and practices of sex-segregation have been firmly established in these states. Moreover, until few decades ago the role of women, as defined by society, was being a good wife and a good mother. Modern education, brought into the region through discourses at conferences and high-level ministerial meetings, is the first and most visible component of this change.

In terms of authority, work and gender, social-closure meso-level theories of discrimination are rooted in the idea that majority-group members who occupy positions of authority at work have a vested interest in maintaining their hegemony over such positions and do so by excluding candidates who differ from them in racial and gender identity. Exclusionary theories allow for both conscious and not-so-conscious acts of discrimination (Smith, 2002).

While social and economic institutions have supported modernisation policies in these states, the political systems have lagged behind. The political structure continues to be pyramidal and hierarchical. Power flows to the ruling authority from the governing bodies that occupy the apex of the pyramid. Sayegh (2004) states that Sheikhs and merchants are the beneficiaries of their family role, and they perceive themselves to be the supporters of a private-enterprise system. Below these two relatively small segments lies the large stratum of the middle class that has just felt the positive impact of modernisation. This layer consists primarily of low-level civil servants, teachers, skilled workers and owners of small businesses. At the bottom of the pyramid exists another layer of society. This sector of the population lives in a world alien to that of wealth, modernity and state-of-the-art technology. Parliaments and Consultative Councils have been introduced in these states, yet most of their members are chosen, selected or nominated from the higher segment of society.

Education is the most powerful force for change and educational policies have brought significant cultural changes to woman's status in countries of the GCC. The fairly recent phenomena of female education not only influences female aspiration and attitude towards life and social values, but also makes women critical of their environment, social system and ultimately current social order. Facilities for schools and higher education for women have created considerable numbers who have completed secondary school and who are university graduates. This young generation of women have not only surpassed their male colleagues in number but also in academic performance. Studies of educational achievement have consistently shown that females have higher expectations than males. Nonetheless, the number of women holding political and public positions is still low relative to their numbers in the population.

Widespread general education in society has certainly brought about a subtle change in the attitudes of men and women towards each other and in relationships between the sexes. Being relatively economically independent, young, educated couples feel capable of bringing up their own families without interference from members of their extended families. Educated women also have better marriage prospects compared with their uneducated sisters from similar backgrounds. Finally, since education and professional qualifications, as well as employment opportunities, have created greater self-confidence among those who are beneficiaries of this system, they no longer regard themselves as commodities in their parents' or husband's home.

Until recently, most Arab nations maintained a strict gender code of segregation in public. Less conservative societies, such as Bahrain, the UAE, Oman and Kuwait have begun to lift these codes to a certain extent. Nevertheless, there is a growing unease at the trend throughout the region of women working closely with men.

Government bodies in these states have had a hand in furthering awareness by setting goals concerned with women's rights. Some of these goals were aimed at amending legislation so as to improve women's rights, as well as to construct laws that were otherwise non-existent before. Examples of such endeavours include the law related to the ownership of land, voting and participating in elections for different councils, as well as access to all levels and kinds of education.

However, it is suggested that regardless of all these changes towards women's position in society, more effort could be made by women themselves to break down the barriers between the genders and assist in achieving – or moving towards – social, political and economic equality.

The nature of female development in these states is complex as each state has its own challenges, although they do share some similarities. The next section will highlight women's conditions in each state.

2. Gendered Life in each Gulf State

Bahrain

In Bahrain, the role of women can be determined by examining their activities in all sectors. However, there is a conflict between two views concerning women's roles: the 'religious-tribal perspective' and the 'modernising perspective'. The first advocates keeping women at home and preserving the traditional arrangement of men dominating the public sphere, while female roles are limited to the private sphere. The second promotes a partnership between men and women in public life, with citizenship rights and duties for both (Arab Reform Bulletin, 2011). Al Gharaibeh (2011) stated that in addition, there is a third element: a chasm between the principles expressed in the constitution that call for the empowerment of women, and the social, economic and political realities of modern Bahrain.

With pressure and encouragement from local non-governmental organisations (NGOs), unions and international bodies, the government has taken steps toward improving the standing of women in Bahrain in recent years. For instance, Bahrain's 2002 constitution guarantees equality between men and women 'in political, social, cultural, and economic spheres, without breaching the provisions of Islamic canon law' (Constitution of the Kingdom of Bahrain, 2002). Efforts to change the political involvement of Bahraini women showed some progress in the 2010 Gender Gap Index issued by the World Economic Forum. Bahrain was fourth among Arabian countries but still 110th internationally in the Forum's assessment of gender inequality. The Global Gender Gap Index 2009 ranked Bahrain 116 out of 134 countries in terms of the opportunities and resources it makes available to women.

The report attributed improvement for women moving into legislative positions and senior ministerial positions, but the ranking was based on 2008 figures, which corresponded to a small surge in women moving into positions of power in Bahrain. However, in the parliamentary elections conducted on 23 October 2010, only one woman was elected to the State Council in comparison to 39 men (Bahrain Elections, 2010). The constitution also provides citizens the right to education, health care, property, housing, work, the right to defend the country and the right to engage in economic activities. Although the constitution does not discriminate between people based on their gender, there are no laws that directly ban discrimination either. The Penal Code (No. 15 of 1976) does not contain any provisions that would punish individuals found guilty of discrimination against women in the workplace or in other parts of society.

Ahmed (2009) stated that Bahrain ratified the Convention on the Elimination of All Forms of Discrimination against Women (CEDAW) in 2002, but made reservations on many important provisions, including those regarding family law, the granting of citizenship and housing rights. Implementation of CEDAW has been slow, though under certain, extremely limited circumstances women have been able to pass Bahraini citizenship to their children.

Bahraini women remain unable to pass their citizenship to their non-Bahraini spouses, even though Article 7 of the Bahraini Citizenship Law of 1963 permits male Bahraini citizens to do so. Moreover, the law stipulates that children may only receive Bahraini citizenship from their father and the child of a Bahraini mother and a foreign father may not receive his mother's nationality (Bahraini Citizenship Act, 1981).

True economic equality between men and women has been difficult to achieve in Arab countries, including Bahrain, where society tends to view formal employment and business as issues for men. However, Islamic history supports the idea of economic rights for women and some point to Sayeda Khadijah, the Prophet Mohammad's first wife, as an example of a successful, economically independent businesswoman (Abdulla, 2009). Women made up approximately 19% of the country's labour force and approximately 31% of adult women were employed in 2007 (World Bank, 2008). Bahraini women are free to own property and land, subject to their individual financial constraints (Supreme Council for Women, 2007).

Ahmed (2009) affirmed the effectiveness of women's rights. NGOs, however, continue to be constrained by the rules of the Ministry of Social Development (MSD), which monitors their work and limits their international funding. In particular, NGOs are not permitted to accept funds from or donate money to foreign organisations without permission from the MSD. Religious scholars also advocate on behalf of women, but their intentions and purposes differ greatly from those of NGO members and other women's rights activists.

Women's education in Bahrain has been achieved as a step towards equality of access and opportunity. Access to education has had a profound effect: it reduced the percentage of illiterate women from 76% at the time of independence in 1971, to only 17% in 2001 and 11.7% in 2006. These statistics are nevertheless still below the world average (ALESCO, 2007).

Bahraini women clearly have good access to university education. They began to enrol in foreign universities in the 1950s when the government offered scholarships to gifted female students to complete their studies in Lebanon. In addition, parents sent their daughters to Egypt, Iraq and Syria for tertiary studies. In 2004, of the 18,000 students at Bahrain University, 66.1% were female; at Gulf University in 2002, female Bahraini students represented 63% of the total Bahraini student population (Al Gharaibeh, 2011).

While the male/female imbalance at the PhD level is apparent, in Bahrain access and equal opportunity for women have been achieved in general education in such a way that less than 12% of all women are considered illiterate (Supreme Council of the Family, 2007).

The Quality Assurance Authority for Education and Training (QAA) was launched in February 2009. The QAA reviews and assesses schools, universities and training institutes, as well as conducting national exams. The body will raise educational standards within Bahrain. The QAA operates four monitoring units: the Schools Review Unit; the

Vocational Review Unit; the Higher Education Review Unit; and the National Examinations Unit.

Kuwait

In 2005 women in Kuwait received the right to vote and run in elections as candidates. In 2009, they reached another milestone when four women were elected to the parliament for the first time in the nation's history. In 2012 one of the most poignant features of Kuwait's political scene is undoubtedly the absence of women in both the Cabinet and Parliament (Conrad, 2012). A recent graduate expressed disappointment when women were not elected for the Parliament. She said: 'I was actually really surprised that none of the women were elected this time around, and a little disappointed because I know that some of them had some great suggestions for improving the country.' Despite the existence of sexual-equality legislation, the legal advisor to Kuwait's parliamentary Women's Affairs Committee said that despite the existence of sexual-equality legislation in Kuwait, there is also a need for a comprehensive education programme and awareness campaign promoting gender equality. Although women make up 77% of the workforce in Kuwait's Ministry of Education, no gender-equality programme has yet been launched to ensure their professional gender rights.

Al-Qatari (2011) states that despite the election of four female MPs to parliament in 2009, the perception of women in Kuwaiti society is not yet anywhere near equal to the legal rights afforded to them. He quoted Al Bahar:

> The excuse many use is that the law grants women their rights, and the law equalizes them with men. This is not entirely true, and it certainly isn't true when it comes to social perceptions. This indicates that there are still so many severe issues facing women in Kuwait in terms of equality and rights, and these results just add to the long list. (p. 1)

This situation confirms Abu Baker's (2010) statement in which he highlights that changes have occurred in aspects of modernisation in relation to education, which was enforced by the Gulf States. However, patriarchal society did not internalise the fundamental nature of these changes. The specific change did not reflect immediately on gender equality and did not cause changes in women's concepts of self-esteem and gender roles.

Women do not face any extraordinary obstacles in attending universities or enrolling in diverse courses of study; they also graduate at higher rates than men. At Kuwait University, however, female students are required to maintain significantly higher grade-point averages (GPAs) than men in order to be admitted into selected fields. For instance, female students must have a 3.3 GPA to be admitted to the engineering department, while male students need only a 2.8 GPA (Al-Mughni, 2009). As women make up almost two-thirds of Kuwaiti university students, the disparity in admission requirements is officially justified as positive discrimination, intended to increase the percentage of male students in certain academic fields (Al-Khaled, 2008). Women outnumber men at the institutions of higher education in Kuwait largely because men often choose to pursue their degrees abroad and the state gives them more opportunities than women, especially in engineering and in fields required by the army and police.

Qatar

Qatar's constitution explicitly prohibits gender-based discrimination under Article 35, which reads: 'All people are equal before the law. There shall be no discrimination on account of sex, origin, language or religion.' Article 34 also provides that all citizens have equal rights and duties, thereby providing female citizens with additional legal protection against discrimination. Women who feel they have been the victims of gender-based discrimination may complain to the police, appeal through the judicial system, or approach the National Human Rights Committee (NHRC) (Breslin & Jones, 2009). However, not many women use these complaint mechanisms.

The government emphasises the importance of education for the continued economic growth of Qatar. Beginning in 2001, the Supreme Education Council spearheaded intense reform efforts for the primary, secondary and post-secondary education systems. On the outskirts of Doha, Education City now contains campuses for more than half a dozen foreign universities, including Northwestern University and Georgetown University. The entire public-education system in Qatar is segregated by gender and Qatar University has separate campuses for men and women. However, foreign universities within Education City are not required to be gender-segregated.

Article 49 of the constitution grants the right to free and compulsory education up to secondary level to all citizens. Non-citizens, however, are not entitled to free primary and secondary education. Women are slightly more likely to be literate than men; moreover, women constitute 50% of the students enrolled in secondary education and 68% of all graduates from post-secondary education in 2007 (UNESCO, 2008). Women's outstanding achievements in academia indicate that society has put credence in the idea that education will eventually lead to gender equality. Promoting education among women, however, is not enough if they are unable to find positions of power in their chosen professions or if they are not accepted by society as adequate leaders. In late 2008, women were accepted into the electrical engineering programme at Qatar University for the first time, in the hope of cutting back Qatar's dependence on foreign workers for research and development jobs. The university also recently permitted women to study architecture and chemical engineering for the first time (Breslin & Jones, 2009).

Although women's academic choices are increasing, long-standing cultural ideals regarding proper professions for women persist. Article 94 of the labour law prohibits women from undertaking dangerous or arduous work, or that which could be deemed detrimental to their health or morals; Article 95 permits the Minister for Labor to determine suitable working hours for women. Both of these provisions treat women as minors who are unable to make decisions regarding their own safety. Additionally, Qatari women remain excluded from the diplomatic service. In practice, women are employed almost entirely in the healthcare, education and clerical professions, (Felder & Vuollo 2008).

Thus, a lack of education does not appear to be a contributing factor to unemployment in Qatar. Over 64% of the unemployed cite minimal job opportunities or a lack of suitable work as the main reasons for unemployment (Qatar Statistics, 2009b). However, in line with the work of Forstenlechner and Rutledge (2010), the type of education may be more important than the level of education: education that is market-driven and based on the requirements of the employer, rather than what is traditionally offered to nationals (such as cultural studies). This is vital for integration. Perhaps more telling is the fact that 96% of Qataris report that they have not been offered a private-sector job (Qatar Statistics, 2009). However, in a departure from other studies on nationals' attitudes to private-sector employment (Al-Lamki, 1998), almost 50% of Qataris indicate that they would be willing to take a private-sector position if offered one (Qatar Statistics Labour Force Survey, 2009a). The other 50% indicate that they would not be willing to take a job in the private sector due to the perception of lower wages and, perhaps most interestingly, the low social status associated with such jobs (Qatar Statistics Labour Force Survey, 2009).

Williams et al (2011) stated that one of the largest changes in Qatar's employment situation is in the employment of Qatari women. In 2001, they represented the highest number of unemployed in the nation, with an unemployment rate of approximately 22%. Only eight years later, this number had declined to 1.9% and in 2009 only 2400 females were unemployed (Qatar Statistics Labour Force Survey, 2009). They explained the change by the increase in female role models in Qatar and a subsequent rise in workforce.

Despite huge expenditures and the high career and pay expectations among Qataris, there has been no significant success in attaining the high degree of education needed to accomplish Qatarisation plans. Educational attainment in Qatar is still not as high as it is in some other

Gulf States. Participation in post-secondary education in Qatar was estimated at 16% in 2008, compared to 32% in Bahrain (Karoly, 2010). Perhaps of even more interest is the low participation rate among males in Qatar. Although older Qatari men are more educated than their female counterparts, this is true only for those above the age 40 and the inverse is true for younger Qataris (Berrebi et al, 2009).

A large number of Qatari women complete a post-secondary education: 66% in 2007, 63% in 2008 and 60% in 2009. Although this number does appear to be dropping, it is still relatively high. In contrast, the male population that has found employment but not finished high school was 34% in both 2008 and 2009 (Qatar Statistics Labour Force Survey, 2009). While the new Qatari constitution guarantees women equality in the workplace, there are cultural barriers that may take longer to change. Despite growing aspirations among young females, there is a cultural backlash that does not support the employment of women (Stasz et al, 2007). This backlash tends to blame female labour participation for many social challenges, including a rising divorce rate (Nainar, 2009). Despite many restrictions facing Qatar's women they are struggling to change their conditions within their society.

Oman

In Oman, women have made steady progress over the past decade. Against the cultural mind-set was his Majesty the Sultan of Oman in his address to the UNESCO 33rd session when he stated 'Women will be empowered' and endorsed the Sultanate of Oman's membership in the convention for the elimination of all types of discrimination against women (*Times of Oman*, 2005, p. 1). This declaration comes at a critical historical juncture in Arab history where international pressure to improve women's lot in the region has been echoed through a number of insightful reports and initiatives. These draw attention to the lagging role of Arab women and the need to harness their potential for socio-economic and political development ([CAWTAR-UNDP, 2001; Fergani, 2002).

The goals and mechanisms for institutional arrangements were stated in *The White Book 1996* and in the Five Year Development Plans, which began in 1985. These proposals intended to secure the desired balance between economic goals and female development, in order to enhance the skills of administration personnel and of women's affairs generally. The plans also intended to augment the skills needed by personnel in order to study the strategic and practical requirements for women, with a view to determining action plans and related projects.

According to Omani law, gender discrimination is prohibited in the workplace. The law emphasises equal pay for equal work, yet women consistently encounter discrimination in the area of job promotions. The

Ministry of Higher Education survey (2011) revealed that among those who are seeking jobs with a higher-education degree, 86% are females. This indicates that although laws confirm their rights, opportunities to be recruited in the labour market are limited. In a significant move towards ensuring gender equality for women, Oman has amended its land law to give women equal property ownership rights to men. The Royal Decree (No. 125/2008) issued on 16 December 2008, assures an Omani woman the same right as an Omani man to own land without discrimination. This indicates the strength of Omani women as partners in the development process and their effective contribution. Women in Oman have made steady progress over the past decade. There are currently more women than men enrolled in higher education and at the university level, despite the presence of gender-discriminatory practices during the enrolment process. The Sultan's resolve to involve women in the development of modern Oman is reflected in such legislation as the Personal Status Law, which guarantees Omani women equal rights in education and employment. This reality is reflected in the appointment of some women as government ministers and a growing number of entrepreneurs and academics.

Omani families still practice cultural norms that always seem to hinder institutional cultures when it comes to female employment. One of these norms is that women should only be employed in positions that they consider 'natural' to their gender such as medicine and teaching. They do not accept women in political positions because they assume that they are weak in decision making and cannot endure highly demanding positions (Issan, 2010).

However, the recent appointment of a number of women to leading policy-making positions in Oman marks a significant departure from the traditionally exclusively male-dominated decision-making arena and ushers in the end of an era where exclusively patriarchal dominance was held in leadership positions. Al-Lamky (2007) states that their successful transition to elevated positions can be attributed to their early socialisation experiences, which valued education, supportive parents (particularly the father) and equal treatment with their male siblings.

Saudi Arabia

Saudi Arabia is the most conservative Arab country when it comes to relations between men and women. According to Wahhabi doctrine, women shall not have direct contact with men at work. This rule limits their career opportunities to just a few professions – mostly nursing and teaching in hospitals and schools designated for women (Górak-Sosnowska & Kubicki, 2005). This is one of the reasons why the occupational activity of Saudi women accounts for slightly more than 5% of the total national workforce, with only one in 20 women of an economically productive age in the labour market. Nevertheless, according to 2003 data (Gladys-Jakóbik & Górak-Sosnowska, 2007) native Saudi females own 20% of company shares, 15% of private companies and have about 10 billion pounds deposited in bank accounts. Therefore, perceiving the status of women only through the prisms of religion and culture and their associated barriers results in certain spheres of their activity going unnoticed. One such sphere is the business world.

Public education in Saudi Arabia is free at all levels. Girls' secondary education is now within the domain of the Ministry of Education, which, until 2002, oversaw only boys' education. The kingdom's current 10-year plan for the development of public education makes no distinction between boys and girls in goals, funding allocation, or curriculum, except to expand girls' course options to include information technology and vocational training (Kingdom of Saudi Arabia, 2005). In practice, girls continue to be denied access to sports programmes in schools, although a 2004 ministerial decree called for the creation of sports and cultural centres exclusively for women. A Saudi woman's freedom to choose her profession is limited more by social than legal norms. The vast majority of working women are employed in the public sector and of these 84.1% work in education. Additionally, 40% of the kingdom's doctors with Saudi citizenship are women (SPA, 2007).

In 2004, 79% of all PhD degrees awarded in the kingdom went to women and if the 102 all-female colleges for teachers are included, about 75% of all students are women. However, according to the Minister of Education, women constituted only one-third of students at public universities (Kingdom of Saudi Arabia, 2004). Not all universities have women's sections, and where they do, women's facilities are often inadequate. Some professors simply refuse to admit females to their programmes regardless of the policies of the university or the Ministry of Education. At the King Fahd Teaching Hospital in Al-Khobar, for example, females have not been admitted to programmes in general surgery, orthopaedic surgery or paediatrics, due to faculty resistance (Human Rights Watch, 2008).

Course options in higher education are to some extent keyed to the job market. Since women are not expected to be employed in mechanical or civil engineering, for instance, these programmes were not previously available to women in public education. However, these courses, as well as interior design and law, have recently opened for women, prompting expectations that more women will be able to obtain jobs in those fields in the future. Furthermore, study abroad offers a wider range of educational options for women. To qualify for a scholarship to study overseas, a woman should be accompanied by her legal guardian the whole time she is abroad, but in practice this requirement is not enforced. Recently, two new institutions with Western curricula, which have been designed to eventually become coeducational, have been introduced. One of these is the King Abdullah University of Science and Technology, which will be a research institution, and is initially for foreign scholars. The other is Al-Faisal University in Riyadh, which is coeducational in the sense that men and women will attend the same classes but be segregated in transit by separate corridors and entrances and in the classroom by different floor levels and glass partitions.

Women's access to education is affected by guardianship laws even though the government has moved to void some of them. Some universities require that women have their guardian's approval before they are permitted to register for classes; they then have to have permission for each individual class they choose to take. But in January 2008, the College of Education at the University of Riyadh permitted female students to register using only their civil-status cards instead of by their guardian's consent. In this instance, Doumato (2009) stated that it was the students rather than the administration who complained that the state was breaking the rules of religion by not asking for a guardian's permission. Others accused the Ministry of Education of voyeurism because male employees in the Ministry would be able to view the photographs on women's civil-status cards.

Women are now more able to participate in civic life than ever before, as high-profile women have recently been appointed to elite Ministry posts, university deanships and directorships in quasi-governmental civic organisations. Female physicians were appointed for the first time as the Deputy Director of Health Affairs for the Mecca region and as the head of the General Directorate of Nursing in the Ministry of Health (www.arabnews.com/node/243611).

However, despite the significant obstacles that seem to rule out the possibility of their participation in social life, Saudi women have great potential, which translates into opportunities to achieve high positions in the social structure.

Women could only work in fields that were deemed a women's domain, such as female education, nursing and medical care. This situation, however, resulted in a large number of unemployed graduate females and a surplus of those employed in nursing and teaching occupations. The country has been deprived of a native human resource and has made itself dependent on an expatriate male workforce to fill the gap (Abdalla, 1996).

The Elamin and Omair (2010) study was initiated to assess Saudi male attitudes towards working females. It examined the impact of some demographic variables such as marital status, employment status, education level and age on attitudes towards working females in Saudi Arabia. For that purpose a sample of 301 male participants was selected. The researchers used the new version of the Multidimensional Aversion to Women Who Work Scale (MAWWWS). The results of the study revealed that Saudi males reported very traditional attitudes towards working females, suggesting they were mainly responsible for domestic responsibilities. However, the single, unemployed, young and educated Saudi males reported less traditional attitudes towards working females compared to married, employed, old and less-educated ones. The results based on Saudi Arabia do not reveal changes in males' attitudes in favour of women's economic participation. However, as age was found to be the largest indicator of males' attitudes towards working women, traditional attitudes may gradually become more egalitarian as the new generations, based on liberal gender socialisation, replace the old one.

United Arab Emirates

Emirati women are undergoing a transition as their society, exposed to foreign influences, adapts to changing identities while protecting cultural and religious traditions. The government has worked to improve various aspects of women's rights over the last five years, although some reforms have been slow to take effect. Certain steps in the right direction are obvious: women are entering new professional fields such as engineering and information technology; there has been a rapid expansion in higher education for women; the ratio of females to males in the workforce is increasing; and women have been appointed to high-profile positions within the government and the business world. Nevertheless, restrictions still apply to some professions, and support for advancements in women's rights varies among the emirates. Moreover, societal and familial perceptions of a woman's proper role continue to pose a significant barrier to advancement.

Article 25 of the constitution provides for equality among Emirati citizens, 'without distinction between citizens of the Union in regard to race, nationality, religious belief, or social status' (Constitution of the United Arab Emirates, 1996). Although the law states that all people are equal, there is no mention of gender equality, nor are there any laws or policies designed to eliminate existing gender-based discrimination (Kirdar, 2009).

Educational-awareness campaigns, scholarships and Emiratisation laws, described below, have allowed women to make steady inroads into universities and public- and private-sector jobs in recent years. The proportion of working adult women has grown from 35% (in 2000) to 41% in 2007 (World Bank, 2008). Nevertheless, women in the UAE are significantly underrepresented in upper-level positions both in governmental institutions and particularly in the private sector. Moreover, the Labor Law (No. 8 of 1980) continues to place certain restrictions on women's employment options and rights based on gender stereotypes.

Education in the UAE is free for all nationals and compulsory for both boys and girls up to the age of 11. As of 2004, 65% of all university students were women, the majority of whom choose to study social sciences and humanities. Although these are the most recent government-published statistics, individual university figures show that women are filling an ever-increasing percentage of university slots every year. In fact, the 2007 World Bank Development Indicators approximate that the female-to-male ratio in tertiary education is three to one (World Bank, 2008).

Kirdar (2009) states that social mores and gender biases play a large part in subject choices; the long-term result has been the 'feminisation' of certain fields of study (Willoughby, 2008). Girls are particularly discouraged from studying science in the emirates outside of Dubai and Abu Dhabi. Some evidence suggests that this process has resulted in employers' devaluation of degrees in traditionally 'female' subjects, such as humanities or social sciences. This trend has been well documented internationally, but published research on the issue in the Arab world is scarce. Regardless of the rationale behind it, upon graduation women are more likely to earn less than men by virtue of the positions they tend to assume, in addition to the gender discrimination they may encounter. Women, particularly nationals, are inclined to join the public sector rather than the private sector because it is deemed more respectable by society, requires shorter working hours and shows commitment to the country.

Women in the UAE have made significant inroads into high-level government positions in recent years. With the introduction of elections for the Federal National Council, one woman successfully ran as a candidate, joining eight other women appointed to their positions on this advisory body. Additionally, amendments to federal judicial law paved the way for the appointment of female federal judges and prosecutors. However, it remains to be seen to what extent these high-level appointments will permit greater women's representation in middle-management and leadership positions in the realm of public policy.

Women are also increasingly represented in cabinet positions. In 2004, the first Emirati woman, Lubna al-Qassimi, was appointed as Minister of the Economy and Planning. In 2008 she became the Minister for External Trade. Her groundbreaking appointment in 2004 marked the first time a woman had been appointed to the Council of Ministers. As of February 2008, there were four female ministers. Additionally, the first female ambassadors were appointed in September 2008. Aside from high-profile appointments, however, evidence suggests that women are failing to achieve promotions at a rate comparable to that of men in management positions within the executive branch. In March 2008, the UAE's permanent representative to the United Nations noted that women constituted 66% of public-sector employees, but only 30% of those held 'leadership and decision-making posts' (Al-Baltaji, 2008).

3. The Meaning of 'Gendered Citizenship'

The analysis of each of the GCC states indicates the complexities in understanding the 'gender dynamic' across this region. As noted, the relevance of adopting international conceptions of 'gender' is partly educational and partly developmental. Without female involvement in all stages of education and without female achievement through education, social development is drastically restricted.

Additionally, and as noted in many United Nations Development Programme (UNDP) reports, an expansion of 'choice' is critical to development (Adely, 2009). Adely argues that there is a tension, evidenced in the *Arab Human Development Report (AHDR)* 2005, between the claim that providing education is an essential element of expanding choice and the assumptions embedded in discussions about which choices are acceptable and/or desirable for women. She suggests that these tensions point to the persistence of values derived from the mandates of global capital, albeit in the new language of neoliberal choice.

The problematic nature of this conceptualisation of development as the expansion of choices appears most clearly in discussions about women's education in the Arab world. Underlying the belief in the power of educating women is an assumption about the proper forms that development should take and the assumed preferences women will have if given 'proper capabilities'. These preferences are consistently linked to the male-dominated fields of study and waged labour. Arab women's choices have not always fitted the patterns and correlations that development researchers have come to assume and assert in their educational policies and programmes. In the AHDR 2005 as well as in the broader literature on this topic, one typically finds 'Arab women's' 12 choices cast as a problem of culture, religion and family.

It can be seen that in nearly all of the countries examined, progress is 'stymied' by the lack of democratic institutions, an independent judiciary and freedom of association and assembly. In Oman, Qatar, Saudi Arabia and the UAE, excessively restrictive rules on the formation of civil-society organisations make it extremely difficult for women's advocates to effectively organise and lobby the government for expanded rights. Ultimately, the passage of new laws that guarantee equal rights for women, such as under the Arab Charter on Human Rights, mean little if those guarantees are not fully enforced by various state authorities (Kelly, 2009).

There are consistent discussions around social beliefs about the 'proper place' of men and women. These conceptions, it is argued, limit female educational and career aspirations. However, more women than ever receive higher education because governments pay for all education costs (Roberts, 2007). Women gain scholarships just like men. More women achieve Bachelor's, Master's and PhD degrees but when they graduate, the majority find few career opportunities other than in very traditional jobs (Roberts, 2007). Governments have invested in education and this has started to open more doors for women. Private companies are encouraged to do the same. It is suggested that females achieve their academic successes in spite of obstructive social and family environments, which envelop many of them in the fallacy that a woman's destiny is the home, while learning and careers are the domain of males. Al-Lamky (2007) describes the Arabian Gulf societies as 'bastions of patriarchy and male chauvinism'. Many in these societies still believe that a woman's place is at home.

In a Muslim culture, when a person deviates from tradition, especially a woman, this is seen as an act against sacred principles. In the minds of many – men and women alike – a departure from a traditional orientation is almost a religious deviation from divine will (Al Lamky, 2007). Thus, in addition to what is clearly a form of structural gender discrimination at work, in terms of fields, levels and quality of work, there is an internalised mind-set which gives preferential treatment, justification and acceptance for men over women, especially in the professions and in politics (Phillips, 2001).

Although advances have been made for women in all Arabian Gulf nations, women have had difficult lives in many ways (Al Jenaibi, 2010). For example, especially in recent times when there has been the fear of too much Western influence, there has been conservative pressure for women to become even more 'religious'. Because women are seen as the keepers of morality, they have been expected to make more of a show of their loyalty to Islam. On the other hand, women have gained ground in certain professions in the Arabian Gulf, especially in those jobs that seem best suited to them.

The major 'gender paradox' (World Bank, 2004) in the region was found in the high rates of educational attainment alongside low rates of economic participation. Although more women are entering education and studying the sciences, this shift is still viewed as insufficient because young women are not choosing the 'right' sciences. A UNDP report provides data on enrolment in engineering programmes in nine Arab countries. Only in Bahrain do we find that 20% of engineering students are female (AHDR, 2005).

In addition, the gender gap may contribute to the fact that women face difficulties in their workplace. Apparently, men do not object to women working for them, but they object when women are their superiors. One study found that 'if professionally inclined, their participation is expected to be in the areas of education, health (mainly nurses) and other support or clerical jobs primarily at the lower end of organizational hierarchies; leadership positions are typically reserved for men' (Al Lamky, 2007). There is clear discrimination against women, whose abilities are often doubted and who are always treated unequally to men (Al Jenaibi, 2010). Al Jenaibi found that in the UAE, the word 'gender' is not widely used, yet it is through assumptions and perceptions of gender roles that women are controlled in their workplace. So whilst there have been many changes in education and the Arab family, it is suggested that these are mainly instrumental, not normative (Abu Baker, 2010).

This is evident in female-owned businesses. Women in the Gulf are becoming more involved in business (Gladys-Jakóbik & Górak-Sosnowska, 2007) often establishing their own companies. It is suggested that the business environment provides women with more challenges and opportunities for self-fulfilment. Due to their higher levels of education, lifestyle changes and gradual social reforms, more women are beginning to work for self-satisfaction (Dechant & Al-Lamky 2005).

Enabling factors for empowerment	Constraining factors for empowerment
(1) Commitment at the highest national level and incorporation of gender goals in development plans	Lack of policies and procedures for implementation of these declarations
(2) International pressure to empower women, i.e. United Nations initiatives	Restrictive traditional and patriarchal social attitudes towards women
(3) Constitutional rights for gender equality	Absence of regulatory body to ensure compliance with the law's tacit discriminatory practices at work
(4) Universal education at all levels	Implicit gender-based specialisations and preferential admission criteria for males in higher-education institutions
(5) Increasing visibility of women in managerial and decision-making positions	Lack of human-resources (HR) strategies to promote inclusiveness
(6) Increasing training and educational opportunities for women	Lack of focused training to manage diversity or promote inclusiveness
(7) Establishment of authorities and organisations for women	An administrative body which lacks strategic authority to affect change

Table II. Enabling and constraining factors for gender empowerment in GCCCs. Source: Adapted from Al Lamky (2006, p. 59).

Conclusion

From the above it can be seen that there are enabling factors that encourage the empowerment of women as well as constraining ones. They are summarised in Table II.

Although the gender gap in educational attainment has significantly narrowed in the GCC countries and women have gained access to higher-paying professions in greater numbers, it remains uncertain what their occupational futures will be. Despite the multitude of market opportunities and the progress in human-capital accumulation which these opportunities presumably afford, women's educational outcomes, particularly the economic return to education, remain persistently different from those of their male counterparts.

It can be concluded that there are key and common barriers to 'localisation' throughout the countries of the GCC (Williams et al, 2011). But given the foregoing, it is quite apparent that the future development of countries in the region depends not only on removing barriers but on establishing structures, procedures and processes which enable men and women to become citizens in development rather than 'gendered citizens'. In fact, the latter seems to mitigate against the achievement of current global definitions of development.

References

Abdalla, I. (1996) Attitudes towards Women in the Arabian Gulf Region, *Women in Management Review*, 11(1), 29-39.

Abeer, Mishkhas (2007) Violence against Women Is Still a Problem. D Ignatius – humiliationstudies.org

Abu Baker, K. (2010) Strategies for Closing the Educational Gaps amongst Palestinian Couples in Israel, *Journal of Women of the Middle East and the Islamic World*, 8, 1-27.

Adely, Fida J. (2009) Educating Women for Development: the *Arab Human Development Report 2005* and the problem with women's choices, *International Journal of Middle East Studies*, 41, 105-122.

Ahmed, Dunya Ahmed Abdulla (2009) *Women's Rights in Bahrain*. http://www.freedomhouse.org

Al-Baltaji, Dana (2008) The Gender Issue. Kipp Report. http://www.kippreport.com/article.php?articleid=1153

Al Gharaibeh, F. (2011) Women's Empowerment in Bahrain, *Journal of International Women's Studies*, 12(3), 96-113.

Al-Jenaibi, Badreya (2010) Differences between Gender Treatments in the Work force/Les différences de traitement entre les sexes dans la population active, *International Journal of Academic Research*, 6(2) (30 June), 63-74.

Al-Khaled, A. (2008) Kuwaiti Women's Civil Rights at Issue, *Kuwait Times*, 14 April. http://www.kuwaittimes.net/read_news.php?newsid=OTY1ODM2NzAw

Al-Lamki, S.M. (1998) Barriers to Omanization in the Private Sector: the perceptions of Omani graduates, *International Journal of Human Resource Management*, 9(2), 377-400.

Al-Lamky, Aysa (2007) Feminizing Leadership in Arab Societies: the perspectives of Omani female leaders, *Women in Management Review*, 22(1), 49.

Al-Mughni H. (2009) Kuwait. Women's Rights in the Middle East and North Africa. http://www.freedomhouse.org

Al-Qatari, Hussain (2011) Education Vital for Gender Equality, *Kuwait Times*, 13 July.

Al-Salamah, Abdullah & Wilson, Rodney (2001) The Implications for Employment Conditions of Foreign Direct Investment in Saudi Arabia: lessons from the Saudi Arabian basic industries corporation. *Managerial Finance*, 27(10/11), 123-139.

ALESCO (Arab League Educational, Cultural and Scientific Organization; Arab Women Organization) (2007) Arab Women and the Mediterranean: a partnership and development in the world of convertibles, in Aisha Al Teeb (Ed.) *Proceedings of the International Symposium held in Malta (20-21 February 2007)*. Tunisia: ALESCO Publication.

Arab Reform Bulletin (2011) 20 January, 3:30 p.m. http://www.carnegieendowment.org/arb/?fa=showIssue&backIssue=7/1/2008

Bahrain Elections (2010) 25 January, 12:00 a.m. http://jazeeranews.net/news/world-news/11345-bahrain-elections2010.html

Bahraini Citizenship Act (1981) 16 September 1963, Article 5. Last amendment 1981. http://www.unhcr.org/refworld/docid/3fb9f34f4.html

Barbarlet, J.M. (1988) *Citizenship: Rights, Struggle and Class Inequality*. Milton Keynes: Open University Press.

Becker, G.S. (1993) *Human Capital: a theoretical and empirical analysis with special reference to education*, 3rd edn. Chicago: University of Chicago Press.

Benedix, Richard (1964) *Nation-Building and Citizenship: studies of our changing social order*. New York: Wiley.

Berrebi, C., Martorell, F. & Tanner, J. (2009) Qatar's Labour Markets at a Crucial Crossroad, *Middle East Journal*, 63(3), 421-447.

Breslin, J. & Jones, T. (2009) Qatar: women's rights in the Middle East and North Africa. http://www.freedomhouse.org

Bureau of Democracy, Human Rights, and Labor (2009) 2008 Human Rights Report: Qatar Country Reports on Human Rights Practices. http://www.state.gov/j/drl/rls/hrrpt/2008/nea/119125.htm

CAWTAR (2001) *Globalization and Gender: economic participation of Arab women*. Tunisia: Center of Arab Women for Training and Research.

Conrad, L. (2012) Kuwaiti Women Express Shock at Absence on Political Scene, *McClatchy – Tribune Business News,* 19 February. http://search.proquest.com/docview/922164240?accountid=27575

Constitution of the Kingdom of Bahrain (2002) Law No. 17 of 2002, Article 5(b), http://www.pogar.org/publications/other/constitutions/bahrain-02e.pdf

Constitution of the United Arab Emirates (1996) http://www.helplinelaw.com/law/uae/constitution/constitution01.php

Culpitt, Ian (1992) *Welfare and Citizenship: beyond the crisis of the welfare state.* London: Sage.

Dechant, K. & Al-Lamky, A. (2005) Toward an Understanding of Arab Women Entrepreneurs in Bahrain and Oman, *Journal of Developmental Entrepreneurship,* 10 (2), 123-140. http://search.proquest.com/docview/208427486?accountid=27575

Doumato, E.A. (2009) Saudi Arabia: women's rights in the Middle East and North Africa. http://www.freedomhouse.org

Elamin, A.M. & Omair, K. (2010) Male Attitudes towards Working Females in Saudi Arabia, *Personnel Review,* 39(6), 746-766.

Felder, D. & Vuollo, M. (2008) *Qatari Women in the Workforce.* Rand-Qatari Policy Institute). http://www.rand.org

Fergani, N. (Ed.) (2002) *Arab Human Development Report: creating opportunities for future generations.* New York: United Nations Development Programme.

Forstenlechner, Ingo & Rutledge, Emilie (2010) Unemployment in the Gulf: time to update the 'social contract', *Middle East Policy,* 17(2), 38-51.

Gause, G.F. (2000) Saudi Arabia over a Barrel, *Foreign Affairs,* 79(3), 80-94.

Gladys-Jakóbik, J. & Górak-Sosnowska, K. (2007) Women of the Gulf: the situation in the labour market and business. Trans. Abdullah Yusuf Ali, *Kobieta i Biznes,* (1-4), 17-25. http://search.proquest.com/docview/230470754?accountid=27575

Górak-Sosnowska, K. & Kubicki, M. (2005) Women of the Gulf: the situation in the labour market and business, in M. Dziekan &. Konczak (Eds) Kobiety na rynku pracy w panstwach Zatoki: utopia czy rzeczywistoác, pp. 17-25. Warsaw: School of Economics.

Haj Yahia, M.M. (2000) Wife Abuse and Battering in the Socio-cultural Context of Arab Society, *Family Press,* 39(2), 237-255.

Issan, Salha A. (2010) Preparing for the Women of the Future: literacy and development, *Journal of Women of the Middle East and Islamic World (HAWWA),* 8, 120-153.

Joseph, C. (2002) *A Contextual Exploration of Justice: culture, citizenship, and community.* Oxford: Oxford University Press.

Karoly, L. (2010) The Role of Education in Preparing Graduates for the Labour Markets in the GCC Countries. A paper for the 15th Annual Conference of the Emirates Center for Strategic Studies, February 17, 2010. Rand Working Paper Series, Wr.742, http://ssm.com

Keane, John (1988a) *Democracy and Civil Society.* London: Verso.

Keane, John (1988b) Despotism and Democracy: the origins and development of the distinction between civil society and the state, in John Keane, (Ed.) *Civil Society and the State*. London: Verso.

Kelly, Sanja (2009) *Recent Gains and New Opportunities for Women's Rights in The Gulf Arab States: women's rights in the Middle East and North Africa*. http://www.freedomhouse.org

Kingdom of Saudi Arabia (2004) Saudi Education Minister on Universities and Curricula. *Al Hayat*, 23 April.

Kingdom of Saudi Arabia (2005) *Executive Summary of the Ministry of Education Ten-Year Development Plan (2004-2014)*, 2nd edn. Riyadh: Kingdom of Saudi Arabia.

Kirdar, Serra (2009) *United Arab Emirates: women's rights in the Middle East and North Africa*. http://www.freedomhouse.org

Lister, Ruth (1997) *Citizenship: feminist perspectives*. New York: New York University Press.

Marshall, T.H. (1950) *Citizenship, Social Class and Other Essays*. Cambridge: Cambridge University Press.

Mincer, J. (1974) *Schooling, Experience and Earnings*. New York: Columbia University Press.

Ministry of Higher Education, Sultanate of Oman (2011) *Oman Graduates Survey*. Muscat: Mazoon Press.

Mohammed, N.S.A. (2002) Population and Development of the Arab Gulf States: the case of Bahrain, Oman and Kuwait, in S.H. Nasr (Ed.) *The Heart of Islam: enduring values for humanity*. San Francisco: HarperCollins.

Nainar, S.M.M. (2009) Working Women and Qatar's Divorce Rate, *Gulf Times*, 24 February.

Neal, M., Finlay, J. & Tansey, R. (2005) 'My Father knows the Minister': a comparative study of Arab women's attitudes towards leadership authority, *Women in Management Review*, 20(7), 354-375.

Pateman, Carole (1988) *The Sexual Contract*. Stanford: Stanford University Press.

Phillips, Ann (1991) *Engendering Democracy*. Cambridge: Polity Press.

Phillips, Ann (1993) *Democracy and Difference*. Cambridge: Polity Press.

Phillips, D. (2001) *Online Public Relations*. London: Kogan Page.

Qatar Statistics Authority (2009a) Qatar Labour Standards. www.qsa.gov.qa

Qatar Statistics Authority (2009b) Qatar Statistics 2009. www.qsa.gov.qa

Roberts, L. (2007) Arab Women Defy Western Stereotypes, 18 September). http:///www.ArabianBusiness.com

SPA (2007) Saudi UN Representative hails 'Growing Role' of Women, Saudi News Agency (SPA), 8 March.

Sayegh, F.A. (2004) Post-9/11 Changes in the Gulf: the case of the UAE, *Middle East Policy*, 11(2), 107-124. http://search.proquest.com/docview/203767916?accountid=27575

Smith, Rogers M. (1997) *Civic Ideals. Conflicting Visions of Citizenship in U.S. History*. New Haven: Yale University Press.

Smith, R.A. (2002) Race, Gender, and Authority in the Workplace: theory and research, *Annual Review of Sociology*, 28, 509-542.

Stasz, C., Eide, E.R., Martorell, F., Salem, H., Constant, L., Glodman, C.A. et al (2007) *Identifying Priorities for Post-secondary Education in Qatar*. Resarch Brief. Chicago: Rand.

Subrahmanian, R. (2005) Gender Equality in Education: definitions and measurements, *International Journal of Educational Development* 25 (2005), 395-407.

Supreme Council for Women (2007) *Statistics on Bahraini Women*. http//www.scw.gov.bh/media/pdf/statistics-Bahraini-Women.pdf

Supreme Council of the Family (2007) *Women Education*. Manama: Bahrain Publication.

Times of Oman (2005) HM: women will be empowered (October), 1.

Turner, Bryan (1993) Contemporary Problems in the Theory of Citizenship, in Bryan Turner (Ed.) *Citizenship and Social Theory*. pp. 1-18. London: Sage.

Twine, Fred (1994) *Citizenship and Social Rights: the interdependence of self and society*. London: Sage.

United Nations Development Programme (UNDP) & Watkins, Kevin (2009) Human Development Report 2005 – International Cooperation at a Crossroads – Aid, Trade and Security in an Unequal World. dspace.cigilibrary.org

USAID (2012) *Gender Equality in Education. Approach to Gender Equality*. http://www.usaid.gov

UNESCO (2008) *Qatar, Literacy, 2005-2007*. Montreal: UNESCO Institute for Statistics. http://www.uis.unesco.org

Voet, Rian (1998) *Feminism and Citizenship*. London: Sage.

Williams, J., Bhanugopan, R. & Fish, A. (2011) Localization of Human Resources in the State of Qatar: emerging issues and research agenda, *Education, Business and Society: Contemporary Middle Eastern Issues*, 4(3), 193-206.

Willoughby, J. (2008) Segmented Feminization and the Decline of Neopatriarchy in G.C.C. Countries of the Persian Gulf, *Comparative Studies of South Asia, Africa, and the Middle East*, 28(1), 184-199.

Wilson, D. (2003) *Human Rights: promoting gender equality in and through education*. Background paper for EFA GMR 2003/4.

World Bank (2004) *Gender and Development in the Middle East and North Africa: women in the public sphere*. Washington, DC: World Bank.

World Bank (2008) *World Development Indicators*. http://web.worldbank.org/WBSITE/EXTERNAL/DATASTATISTICS/0,,contentMDK:21725423~pagePK:64133150~piPK:64133175~theSitePK:239419,00.html

CHAPTER NINE

Crossborder Education in the Gulf Countries: changes and challenges

JANE KNIGHT

Introduction

Internationalisation is one of the major forces impacting and shaping higher education as it changes to meet the challenges of the twenty-first century. Overall, the picture of internationalisation that is emerging is one of complexity, diversity and differentiation. One aspect of internationalisation which is particularly important and controversial is crossborder education. Crossborder education refers to the movement of people, knowledge, programmes, providers, policies, ideas, curricula, projects and services across national or regional jurisdictional borders.

Changes to the higher-education landscape in the Gulf countries are startling and much of the transformation is due to crossborder academic mobility. For example, as of 2012, the United Arab Emirates is home to 37 international branch campuses. Oman has developed its higher-education sector by mandating new private universities and colleges to affiliate with foreign institutions for collaborative programmes. King Abdullah University of Science and Technology (KAUST) in Saudi Arabia has recruited renowned faculty and the brightest students from around the world with the provision of top-notch research facilities and generous scholarship schemes. Qatar is promoting itself as a regional education hub by inviting US and British Universities to offer their degree programmes in its Education City. Bahrain is home to three well-established branch campuses and has announced plans to develop a Higher Education City and Science and Technology park. Kuwait has developed several twinning programmes with foreign institutions and has two branch campuses. Of course, all countries have substantial incoming and outgoing student mobility. These new developments are eloquent testimony to the central role that crossborder education has in the transformation and vitalisation of the higher-education sector in the Gulf region.

While it is clear that the scope and volume of crossborder education are growing there are still many unanswered questions about its impact. Does crossborder education actually increase access to higher education? As the number and types of crossborder providers and delivery modes grow is the quality of the academic offering ensured? Is crossborder education and research based on strong partnerships that respect national context and priorities? While the benefits can be numerous, there are also risks and unintended consequences. These can include the brain-drain effect, diploma mills, commercialisation and commodification, elitism, and cultural homogenisation and tensions.

The purpose of this chapter is to explore the rationales, scope and scale of the three generations of crossborder education in the context of the Gulf Countries. Academic mobility has significantly expanded in size and substance during the past four decades. The first part of the chapter examines the multi-faceted phenomenon of crossborder education. It provides a definition and differentiates the term from internationalisation, borderless, transnational and offshore education. The three generations of crossborder education are analysed in detail so as to provide a basic understanding of programme and provider mobility, the new development of education hubs as well as related issues and challenges. Attention is given to examining the rationales and perspectives of different stakeholders: students, foreign institutions and host-country institutions. In the second part of the chapter the modes and motivations of crossborder education for each of the six Gulf countries is discussed. The differences and similarities among the countries are highlighted. The third and final section of the chapter looks at some of the emerging issues, challenges and unintended consequences of crossborder education in general and in particular for the Gulf region. The concluding remarks acknowledge the benefits and risks of crossborder education and the need to be open to the huge potential of crossborder education, but not at the expense of academic quality and integrity.

Crossborder Education: definition and three generations

Definition

Crossborder education refers to the 'movement of people, knowledge, programs, providers, policies, ideas, curricula, projects, research and services across national or regional jurisdictional borders' (Knight, 2007a). Crossborder education is often mistakenly confused with the term internationalisation. It is important to understand that crossborder education is only one part of the complex process of internationalisation.

As Figure 1 illustrates there are two interdependent pillars of internationalisation: at-home or campus-based and abroad/crossborder education. This chapter focuses on crossborder education while acknowledging the strong connection with and implications for campus-based internationalisation.

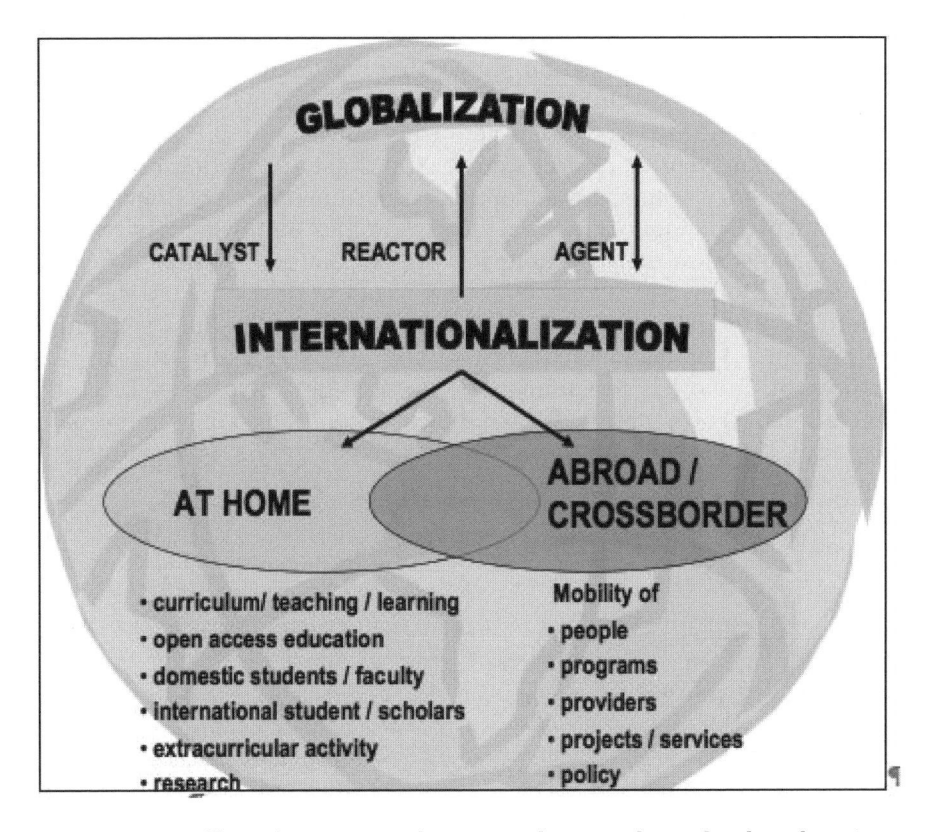

Figure 1. Two pillars of internationalization: at home and crossborder education.

As crossborder education is often used interchangeably with transnational, borderless and offshore education, it is enlightening to explore these terms and to juxtapose the concepts of borderless education and crossborder education. Borderless education acknowledges the disappearance of all types of borders – time, disciplinary, geographic – while the latter term actually emphasises the existence of borders, especially the geographic and jurisdictional. Both approaches reflect the reality of today. In this period of distance and e-learning education, geographic borders seem to be of little consequence. Yet, we can detect a growing importance of borders when the focus turns to regulatory responsibility, especially as related to quality assurance, funding and accreditation. Offshore education is self-explanatory but is

Jane Knight

not often used by landlocked countries. For non-native English speakers, it is often difficult to discern the difference between transnational and international education. Thus, crossborder education is the preferred term and is used in this chapter.

Three Generations of Crossborder Education

Any study of higher education shows that academic mobility has been happening for a very long time. Scholars and knowledge have been moving around the world for centuries. But, late in the twentieth century, the movement of programmes and higher-education institutions across borders became more popular and numerous. No longer were there isolated incidences of foreign programmes and providers resident in a small number of countries: the numbers started to grow exponentially. By 2005, some countries began to develop a critical mass of foreign providers, programmes and students, and the third generation in the form of education hubs, cities and zones began to appear. The purpose of Table I is to summarise the highlights of each of the three generations. Worth noting is that these generations are not mutually exclusive. In the following sections, each generation is examined in depth so as to understand the differences and similarities among them and to raise some of the issues and challenges associated with each category.

Crossborder education	Primary focus	Description
First Generation	*Student/people mobility* Movement of students to foreign country for education purposes	Full degree or for short-term study research, field work, internship, exchange programmes
Second Generation	*Programme and provider mobility* Movement of programmes or institutions/companies across jurisdictional borders for delivery of education	*Programme Mobility* Twinning Franchised Articulated/Validated Joint/Double Award Online/Distance *Provider Mobility* Branch Campus Virtual University Merger/Acquisition Independent Institutions

Third Generation	*Education Hubs* Countries attract foreign students, researchers, workers, programmes, providers, R&D (research and development) companies for education, training, knowledge production, innovation purposes	*Student Hub* Students, programme, providers move to foreign country for education purposes *Talent Hub* Students, workers move to foreign country for education and training and employment purposes *Knowledge/Innovation Hub* Education researchers, scholars, HEIs, R&D centres move to foreign country to produce knowledge and innovation

Table I. Three generations of crossborder education.

The First Generation: people mobility

Student and scholar mobility has been occurring for as long as universities have been in existence. In fact, the concept of universe in the term university is proof of the global dimension. The startling change in student mobility is that the numbers have multiplied exponentially in the last 50 years. For example, international students in foreign countries expanded from 238,000 in the 1960s (Chen & Barnett, 2000) to 3.3 million in 2008 (OECD, 2010). Of course, the numbers of students, the modes of mobility (full degree abroad, exchange, internships, semester/year abroad) the destination countries, and the driving rationales have changed dramatically. It is estimated that 7.8 million students will be enrolled in foreign countries for their tertiary education by 2025 (Boehm et al, 2002). These statistics indicate that student mobility will continue to expand, but new forms of crossborder education are needed to meet this demand.

Table II shows the inbound and outbound mobility of students in the Gulf region. While student mobility is active in the Gulf countries this chapter does not analyse in depth the growth in student mobility or the changes in destination countries and programme enrolments. More emphasis is placed on second- and third-generation activities.

The Second Generation: programme and provider mobility

In the second generation of crossborder education the programmes and providers are mobile, not the student. In the early 1990s the movement of programmes and providers across borders began to increase substantially and have an impact on the number of students who could access foreign higher-education programmes and qualifications without leaving home.

Country	Gross outbound enrolment ratio in 2009* %	Total number of outbound students	Total number of inbound students
Bahrain	5.3	3,608	8,640**
Kuwait	5.6	12,070	7,984
Oman	1.7	4,868	1,745
Qatar	1.9	2,440	3,715
Saudi Arabia	1.3	31,157	19,906
United Arab Emirates	2.7	7,719	34,122

Notes: Top five destinations for mobile students and outbound mobility ratio.
*The gross outbound enrolment ratio shows the magnitude of a phenomenon that students enter tertiary programmes outside of their country of origin.
**Data from 2010.

Table II. Student mobility in the Arab Gulf countries 2009.
Source: Adapted from UESCO (2009).

As Table III illustrates, there are different rationales driving the movement of academic programmes and higher-education providers across borders.

Rationales and impact	Enrolled students in receiving (host) country	Institution/provider in sending country	Institution/provider in receiving country
Increased access/supply in home country	Ability to gain foreign qualification without leaving home. Can continue to meet family and work commitments	Attracted to unmet need for higher education and training and/or invitation to establish presence in foreign country	Competition, collaboration or co-existence with foreign providers
Cost/income	Less expensive to take foreign programme at home as no travel or accommodation costs. But tuition fees of quality foreign providers	Strong imperative to generate a profit for cross-border operations as well as increased profile.	Varied rationales and impacts depending on whether local institution/provider is competing or cooperating with foreign providers.

	may be much higher than local HEIs.		Can include development of new talent, revenue generation or increased regional profile
Selection of courses and programmes	Increased access to courses/ programmes in high demand by labour market	Tendency to offer high-demand courses which require little infrastructure or investment unless infrastructure is provided by host country	Need to offer broad selection of courses which may not have high enrolments and/or have major lab or equipment requirements
Language/ cultural and safety aspects	Can have access to courses in foreign and/or indigenous language. Remain in familiar cultural and linguistic environment.	Language of instruction and relevance of curriculum to host country important issues. If foreign language used additional academic and linguistic support may be needed	Provide courses and programmes according to local cultural and linguistic norms and practices but consistent with admission requirements and quality standards of home institution
Quality	Can be exposed to higher- or lower-quality course provision	Depending on delivery mode, quality may be at risk. Assurance of relevant and high-quality courses may require significant investment	Presence of foreign providers may be a catalyst for innovation and improvement of quality in courses, management and governance
Recognition of qualification	Foreign qualification has to be recognised for academic and employment purposes	May be difficult for academic award and for institution to be recognised in foreign country	Recognised home providers have an advantage. Foreign providers may wish to collaborate for award granting powers

| Reputation and profile | Due to massive marketing campaigns international profile is often mistakenly equated with quality of provider/ programme | Profile and visibility are key factors for high enrolments and strategic alliances | Home (domestic) providers are challenged to distinguish between foreign providers with high/low profile and high/ low quality |

Table III. Stakeholder perspectives on programme and provider mobility.

It is informative to examine the perspectives and expectations of the students, the foreign institution providing the education (i.e., sending country higher-education institution [HEI]), and the host country. These perspectives apply to the six countries addressed in this chapter but not in a uniform way. There are stark differences in why and how crossborder education is used in the Gulf region. This demonstrates that one model of crossborder does not fit all countries. The local context, culture and national priorities dictate the crossborder-education approach. This will be explored in more depth in a later section of the chapter which discusses the crossborder approach and activities of each country.

To understand the phenomenon of programme and provider mobility it is helpful to examine each mode of movement and the associated issues.

Programme Mobility

Crossborder mobility of *programmes* can be described as 'the movement of individual education/training courses and programmes across jurisdictional borders through face to face, distance or a combination of these modes. Credits towards a qualification can be awarded by the sending foreign country provider or by an affiliated domestic partner or jointly.' Franchising, twinning, double/joint degrees and various articulation models are the more popular methods of crossborder programme mobility (Knight, 2007a). A short description of each follows.

Franchise: An arrangement whereby a provider in the source country A authorises a provider in country B to deliver their course/programme/service in country B. The qualification is awarded by the provider in Country A. Arrangements for teaching, management, assessment, profit-sharing, awarding of credit/qualification are customised for each franchise arrangement and must comply with national regulations (if they exist) in Country B.

Twinning: A situation where a provider in source country A collaborates with a provider located in country B to develop an articulation system that allows students to take course credits in country B and/or source country A. Only one qualification is awarded by the provider in source country A. Arrangements for twinning programmes and awarding of degrees usually comply with national regulations of the provider in the source country A.

Double/Joint Degree: An arrangement where providers in different countries collaborate to offer a programme for which a student receives a qualification from each provider, or a joint award from the collaborating partners. Arrangements for programme provision and criteria for awarding the qualifications are customised for each collaborative initiative in accordance with national regulations in each country.

Articulation: Various types of articulation arrangements between providers situated in different countries permit students to gain credit for courses/programmes offered by all of the collaborating providers. This allows students to gain credit for work done with a provider other than the provider awarding the qualification.

Validation: Validation arrangements between providers in different countries allow Provider B in the receiving country to award the qualification of Provider A in the source country. In some cases, the source-country provider may not offer these courses or awards themselves, which may raise questions about quality.

Virtual/Distance: Arrangements where providers deliver courses/ programmes to students in different countries through distance and online modes. These arrangements may include some face-to-face support for students through domestic study or support centres.

It is clear that a critical factor in programme mobility is 'who' awards the course credits or ultimate credential. As the movement of programmes proliferates, there will undoubtedly be further changes to national, regional and even international regulatory frameworks. For instance the quality-assurance organisations in Bahrain, Oman and UAE are cognisant of the fact that more attention has to be paid to foreign programmes being offered independently or in affiliation with domestic institutions.

The question of 'who grants the credits/awards' will be augmented by 'who recognizes the provider' and whether or not the programme has been 'accredited or quality assured' by a bona fide body either domestically of internationally. Of central importance is whether the qualification is recognised for employment or further study in the receiving country and in other countries as well. The perceived legitimacy and recognition of the qualification at home and abroad are fundamental issues yet to be resolved.

The last decade has seen the introduction of twinning and franchise programmes in Bahrain, Kuwait and Oman and to a lesser extent in the other Gulf countries. The benefits of these arrangements to students and host institutions as well as the foreign providers are many and varied. However, issues related to quality of teaching, relevance of course content, admission requirements, testing and evaluation, and qualifications of teaching staff must be addressed. Double/joint/combined degree programmes differ from twinning and franchise programmes in that the course curriculum is jointly designed and delivered by the partner institutions. This means that a foreign curriculum is not imported; instead, it is jointly developed.

A joint degree programme awards one joint qualification upon completion of the collaborative programme requirements established by the partner institutions. The duration of the programme is normally not extended and thus students have the advantage of completing a joint programme in the same time period as an individual programme from one of the institutions. They normally involve student mobility or professor mobility. Strategies to integrate distance and virtual education into the programmes are being explored. One of the issues concerning joint degree certification is that many countries do not legally allow the stamps of two different institutions on the actual certificate. The risk of not being able to award legally a joint qualification is leading to the dubious practice of awarding two individual degrees for the same workload or course credits of one programme. Several Gulf countries including Oman, Bahrain and Kuwait are facing the legal realities and challenges involved in awarding joint degree programmes.

Given that in the Gulf countries, several modes for programme mobility involve affiliations and partnerships, the issue of ownership of intellectual-property rights to course design and materials is relevant. What are the legal roles and responsibilities of the participating partners in terms of academic, staffing, recruitment, evaluation, financial and administrative matters? While the movement of programmes across borders has been taking place for years, it is clear that the new types of providers, partnerships, awards and delivery modes are challenging national and international higher-education policies.

Provider Mobility

Crossborder mobility of *providers* can be described as 'the physical or virtual movement of an education provider (institution, organization, company) across a jurisdictional border to offer education/training programs and/or services to students and other clients' (Knight, 2007a). The difference between programme and provider mobility is one of scope and scale in terms of programmes/services offered and the local presence (and investment) by the foreign provider. Credits and qualifications are awarded by the foreign provider (through foreign, local or self-accreditation methods) or by an affiliated domestic partner. Different forms of crossborder provider mobility are as follows:

Branch Campus: Provider in country A establishes a satellite campus in Country B to deliver courses and programmes to students in Country B. (This may also include Country A students taking a semester/course abroad). The qualification is awarded by the provider in Country A.

Independent Institution: Foreign Provider A (a traditional university, a commercial company or alliance/network) establishes in Country B a stand-alone HEI to offer courses/programmes and awards. There is no usually no 'home' institution in Country A.

Acquisition/Merger: Foreign Provider A purchases a part of or 100% of a local HEI in Country B.

Study Centre/Teaching Site: Foreign Provider A establishes study centres in Country B for students taking their courses/programmes. Study centres can be independent or in collaboration with local providers in Country B.

Affiliation/Networks: Different types of 'public and private', 'traditional and new', 'local and foreign' providers collaborate through innovative types of partnerships to establish networks/institutions for the delivery of courses and programmes in local and foreign countries through distance or face-to-face modes.

Virtual University: Provider that delivers credit courses and degree programmes to students in different countries through distance education using predominantly the Internet technology mode, generally without face-to-face support services for students.

In the Gulf region, the most popular mode of provider mobility is branch campuses, as more than 50 have been established in the last 15 years. The Arab Open University affiliated with the United Kingdom's Open University and based in Kuwait is the largest virtual provider.

The virtual and physical movement of providers to other countries raises many of the same registration, quality-assurance and recognition issues that programme mobility does, but there are additional factors to consider if local/foreign partnerships are involved. Setting up a physical presence requires that attention is paid to national regulations regarding the status of the entity, total or joint ownership with local bodies, tax laws, for-profit or non-profit status, repatriation of earned income, boards of directors, staffing, granting of qualifications, selection of academic programmes and courses and so on. For some countries, for instance in Oman, it means that regulations are developed to monitor closely new providers coming into the country or the development of affiliation arrangements with local institutions. In other instances, free zones such as those in Dubai, tax incentives and physical infrastructure are provided and non-compliance with national regulations is the norm. However, given concerns about quality and sustainability of foreign education providers, free zones are now developing new procedures for selection, licensing and quality assurance (Fox & Al Shamisi, forthcoming 2013). Qatar uses yet another model as the foreign branch campuses located in Education City are fully funded by the Qatar Foundation, but the academic requirements, programme design and quality assurance are aligned and monitored by the home-institution quality-assurance process.

The Third Generation: education hubs

Education hubs are the latest development and constitute the third wave of crossborder education initiatives. Education hubs build on and can include first- and second-generation crossborder activities, but they represent a wider and more strategic configuration of actors and activities. An education hub is a concerted and planned effort by a country (or zone or city) to build a critical mass of education/knowledge actors and strengthen its efforts to exert more influence in the new marketplace of education. The concept of a national education hub rests on the assumption that it is a country's plan and efforts to position itself within the region and beyond as a reputed centre for higher education and research. Therefore an education hub is not an individual branch campus, or a large number of international students, or a science and technology park. It is more than that. The proposed working definition is generic enough to apply to all levels of education hubs (city, zone, country) even though this chapter only focuses on country-level hubs: 'An education hub is a planned effort to build a critical mass of local and international actors strategically engaged in crossborder education, training, knowledge production and innovation initiatives' (Knight, 2011a).

As of 2012, there are six countries around the world which are seriously trying to position themselves as an education hub and two of them are located in the Gulf region: the United Arab Emirates and Qatar. There are others who may be using the term hub as a branding label or are in early stages of development. Bahrain can be described as an emerging hub as there is no clarity on the plans or investments to date. There is no single model or one-size-fits-all approach for establishing an education hub. Each country has its own set of drivers, approaches and expectations. It is worth noting that to date, all education-hub countries are relatively small and share an interest in shifting from a natural-resources or manufacturing economy to one that places more emphasis on knowledge and service industries (Knight, 2011a).

The reasons for developing a hub are critical as they drive objectives, strategies, progress indicators and outcomes. Table IV presents the rationales and expectations of education hubs for three different stakeholder groups: students; foreign institutions/providers;

and the host government/sponsor. It is revealing to see the areas of overlap and divergence. The major point of convergence is an increase in skilled labour and further opportunities for employment.

Stakeholder group	Rationales and expectations
Student (local and international)	Access to higher- and further-education opportunities Foreign academic credential Specialised programme not offered domestically Employment and career path International outlook
Foreign institutions and providers	Status-building and increased competitiveness Income generation New research partnerships with private and public bodies Recruit faculty and students for home campus Contribute to capacity-building efforts in host country
Sponsor and host government	Prepare and recruit skilled workforce Support knowledge-based industries Attract foreign direct investment Establish geo-political status and soft power in region Modernise domestic higher-education sector

Table IV. Rationales and expectations of different stakeholder groups.

The diversity of rationales, actors and activities characterising education hubs is clear. In order to capture these differences and allow for a more nuanced understanding and exploration of education hubs, a typology of three categories of hubs is suggested (Knight, 2011b). The three types of hubs include: student hub; talent hub; and knowledge/innovation hub. The typology is based on the rationales and nature of the activities not on the location, level or scope of hubs. The typology will become more robust when hard information on strategic plans, laws, policies, enrolment data and outputs are available but at this early stage of hub development this information does not exist for some countries.

The Student Hub is the most focused and prevalent type of education hub. The key activity is the education and training of local, expatriate and international students. In addition to recruiting students it also focuses on attracting foreign higher education institutions to offer franchised and twinning programmes or establish branch campuses in order to increase access for all types of students. The primary objectives for student hubs are: (1) to generate revenue from international student fees; (2) to provide increased access to higher education for students; (3) to modernise and internationalise domestic higher education institutions; and (4) to build profile and increase competitiveness within the regional higher-education sector and beyond.

The Talent Hub focuses on student education and training but differs from the Student Hub because the overarching goal is to develop a skilled workforce; thus foreign students are encouraged to remain in the host country for employment purposes. International higher-education institutions as well as private training/ education companies are encouraged to offer academic programmes and professional-development opportunities aimed at international and national students as well as local employees. The overall goal is human-resource development. The driving key objectives are: (1) to educate and train students to be skilled labour/knowledge workers for knowledge and service-led economy; and (2) to establish geo-political status in the region and beyond. The education/training institutions and companies are often, but not necessarily, co-located in a zone in order to share facilities and promote collaboration amongst themselves and with industry. In order to develop a critical mass there can be more than one co-location site in a country. United Arab Emirates is an example of a talent hub with several education zones developed across the country to house the 37 foreign branch campuses and numerous international training companies.

The Knowledge/Innovation Hub broadens its mandate beyond education and training to include the production and distribution of knowledge and innovation. Foreign actors including universities, research institutes, and companies with major research and development activities, are attracted through favourable business incentives to establish a base in the country and to collaborate with local partners to develop applied research, knowledge and innovation. The primary objectives are to: (1) help build a knowledge and service-based economy; (2) educate and train skilled labour for knowledge/innovation; (3) attract foreign direct investment; and (4) increase regional or global economic competitiveness and soft power. Collaboration among the key players – foreign and local education institutions, industries, research centres and companies – is a key factor to building a knowledge and innovation hub. Qatar is an example of a country trying to establish itself as a knowledge/innovation type of education hub, but its current status could be described as more of student or talent hub.

Education hubs are full of lofty expectations and fraught with potential challenges. There are a myriad of issues that require further reflection and examination by researchers, policy makers and the hub sponsors. The UAE approach to hub development through free or specially designated zones differs from the Qatar approach, which involves inviting and funding foreign institutions to deliver a specific programme. Issues vary by the approach and type of hub but include regulatory, policy and operational questions related to an array of topics including: registration and quality assurance of education and training providers; recognition of qualifications for further study and employment in different countries; university–industry partnerships;

intellectual property rights for new knowledge and innovation; employment and immigration policies incentives to attract foreign education providers and companies; relevance of teaching/training methods in light of cultural diversity; and compliance with regional and international trade laws. (Knight, forthcoming 2013).

Analysis of Country Crossborder Approaches and Activities

Bahrain

Bahrain, a small country with under a million inhabitants, has giant aspirations in terms of higher education. The first branch campus was established in 2002 by AMA University in the Philippines. By 2011, total enrolment had reached 4000 students registered in a variety of Information Technology-related programmes. New York Institute of Technology established a campus in 2003 and almost a decade later has about 730 students in undergraduate programmes and another 150 at the graduate level. Of particular interest is that about 77% of students are from Bahrain with another 22% from the region. The majority of courses offered are in Business Management, Computer Engineering and Information Technology. The Royal College of Surgeons from Ireland established its branch campus in 2004 and offers health-related courses in medicine and nursing. As of 2012 it has approximately 1000 students registered with less than half (44%) being from Bahrain (Lawton & Katsomitros, 2012). Clearly there has been some success in attracting both foreign providers and students to Bahrain and this may have led to Bahrain's interest in developing itself as a regional education hub.

In 2007, Bahrain announced its intention to become a higher-education hub at a total cost of US$1 billion by establishing Higher Education City and a Science and Technology Park (Munden, 2009). The Bahrain Executive Development Board (BEDB) made the announcement after agreeing to undertake jointly this major initiative with the Kuwait Finance and Investment Company. These are ambitious plans for a small state like Bahrain, but to date there is little information on the status and progress of this development. However, it is still interesting to examine the rationales that underpin the planning of these initiatives as they are still relevant to its crossborder education activities and aspirations. The drivers and anticipated benefits of the Higher Education City include: (1) to provide a technologically skilled workforce for the current and future labour market in Bahrain and the region; (2) to encourage innovation; (3) to leverage increased direct investments into the Kingdom; and (4) to reposition the Kingdom as a regional specialist centre in higher education. As of 2012, Bahrain continues to label itself as an Education Hub due to its heightened efforts to attract foreign students (Bahrain Daily Tribune, 2012) but there are still no signs of a national plan or serious investment to build the announced Higher Education City.

Jane Knight

Kuwait

Kuwait has a diversified approach to crossborder education. It hosts two branch campuses, both of whom have been approved by the Council of Private Universities and Ministry of Education. Kuwait Maastricht Business School was established in 2003 and offers an MBA programme on a part-time basis. Algonquin College of Applied Arts and Science from Canada is in the process of developing a branch campus in cooperation with a private company in Kuwait called Orient Education services. The planned programmes are at the diploma level in computer-technology and business-management related programmes. Students can complete their full programme in Kuwait an receive the Algonquin College credential or participate in 'Two plus Two' format which allows students to take the first two years of the programme in Kuwait and the final two years in Canada.

A second mode of crossborder education is through the affiliation model. The Gulf University for Science and Technology was established in 2002 in partnership with the University of Missouri in St Louis. This was the first private university in Kuwait and after a decade of operation it has a college of Arts and Sciences and a College of Business Administration (GUST, 2011). Other international affiliated programmes and institutes include the American University of Kuwait, established in 2003 in partnership with Dartmouth College, the American College of the Middle East affiliated with Purdue University, and the Kuwait branch of the Arab Open University linked to the United Kingdom Open University (Private Universities Council, 2005). In 2007, the University of Bangor from Wales (United Kingdom) signed an agreement with the newly established British University of Kuwait, but as of 2011 it has not yet admitted any students.

In terms of student mobility, the gross outbound enrolment ration in 2009 was 5.6%, which represents 12,070 students going abroad to study versus 7984 incoming students. The top destination countries for Kuwaiti students include neighbouring Bahrain (4852). USA (1998), Jordan (1954), UK (1546) and lastly Australia (254) (UNESCO, 2009). It is interesting to note that in comparison to other Gulf countries, Kuwait has the largest outbound enrolment ratio and that almost half stay within the region for their studies.

Oman

The Sultanate of Oman has taken an innovative approach to the expansion of higher education by mandating that each private institution develop an affiliation with a foreign university for the development of twinning, franchise, articulated or joint/double degree programmes. Thus, the 25 private institutions have developed partnerships with over 50 foreign institutions. The number of foreign affiliations per Omani private college ranges from one – the German University of Technology in Oman is linked with RWTH Aachan University in Germany, for example – to 13 affiliations from all corners of the world for Nizwa University. Worth noting is that more than half of all the affiliations are with institutions in the United States, the United Kingdom, Germany and Austria but there are more than ten with partners in the region including Lebanon, Jordan and India. The medium of instruction is English, with several institutions teaching in Arabic as well. These international collaborative programmes cover all disciplines and several professional studies such as dentistry, engineering, medicine and business administration. While the majority of programmes are at the foundation, diploma or Bachelors level, there are also several graduate level programmes (MOHE, 2010). There is no question that these private universities in collaboration with their foreign partners have substantially increased access for the large percentage of young Omanis who are keen to have tertiary-level education. In Oman there is only one public institution, the Sultan Qaboos University; a second one, Oman University, is being developed.

Oman differs from the other Gulf States by not hosting any foreign branch campuses. Instead, they have concentrated on establishing foreign affiliations to develop twinning and joint/double degree programmes. By choosing this approach, they have arranged that most – but not all – the qualifications offered are Omani, not foreign. In cases where the credential is awarded by the foreign partner, all quality standards and procedures for assessment, grade approval, and so on are regulated by the foreign affiliate.

In terms of student mobility, Oman has a relatively low outbound-enrolment ratio at 1.7% in 2009. There are 4869 outbound students compared to 1745 incoming. The top three preferred destinations are Jordan, UK and Australia (UNESCO, 2009).

Qatar

Qatar was the first country in the Middle East to act on the concept of developing an Education City. More than a decade ago it developed its strategy for Qatar Education City (QEC). The idea originated with the Emir and the Qatar Foundation was mandated to implement the ambitious plan. As of 2012, QEC is a 2500 acre well-equipped complex fully functioning with eight foreign universities offering a variety of undergraduate and graduate programmes.

There are two foreign institutions (North Atlantic College and Texas Community College) functioning outside of the QEC, bringing the total in Qatar to ten.

The Qatar Foundation (QF) for Education, Science and Community Development is a private, non-profit organisation established in 1995 by the Emir of Qatar. The QF is committed to human-resource development through a network of innovative centres and partnerships, all dedicated to making the knowledge society in Qatar a reality. The QF believes that a highly educated population is a key prerequisite for success in the knowledge economy. Their commitment is to provide quality education at all levels to prepare today's generation for their leadership role in a global society.

In terms of their higher-education mandate, the QF has been strategic and highly selective in inviting foreign universities to become partners in their endeavour. To date, six US universities, one French and one United Kingdom institution are operational in Qatar Education City. The critical factor for selection is an internationally recognised curriculum and expertise in disciplines that are central to broadening Qatar's range of higher-education programmes. Given that each university has a niche area of curriculum, there is no overlap or competition in academic programmes among the international higher-education institutions operating in Qatar Education city. It operates on a differentiated academic model which is responsive to the clearly articulated Qatar priority of developing human-resource requirements for the twenty-first-century knowledge economy. The US universities currently operating in Education City include Virginia Commonwealth University, Weill Cornell Medical College, Texas A&M University, Carnegie Mellon University, Georgetown University School of Foreign Service, Northwestern University plus University College London from the United Kingdom and the International Business School (HEC) from Paris.

These eight institutions are co-located in the complex, each with their own state-of- the-art building but sharing some common facilities, thus creating a campus-like setting for the students. All institutions maintain admission standards equal to their home campus, which has presented some challenges to enroling qualified Qatari students, especially males. At the current time, enrolments are half domestic students and half regional/international (Bains, 2009).

In 2009, The Qatar Science and Technology Park (QSTP) was launched as a complementary initiative to Qatar Education City. It is anticipated that by 2013 it will be fully operational with the tenant companies such as Microsoft, General Electric and Shell conducting commercially oriented research and development in collaboration with the academic institutions and researchers from QEC. It is estimated that Qatar has invested more than US$800 million to date in the QSTP and over US$2 billion in QEC (Witte, 2010). This illustrates the sizable investment Qatar is making to transform itself into an education hub and grow the knowledge economy. Whether it is a sustainable model is yet to be seen but it is doubtful that it is an approach that can be replicated by other countries, given the enormous financial investment made to date.

Saudi Arabia

Unlike other Gulf countries, Saudi Arabia does not host any branch campuses, although there has been a media announcement that the Georgia Institute of Technology plans to establish a research institute and postgraduate programme (Sawahel, 2010). Unlike other branch campuses in the region, the emphasis is more on research than education programmes. However, Saudi Arabia is active in crossborder education through other modes, especially student mobility and faculty recruitment. In 2009, the outbound enrolment ratio was 1.3%, which translates into 31,157 outgoing students and 19,906 inbound international students (UNESCO, 2009). The top five destination countries for Saudi students were the United States (12,453), the United Kingdom (5203), Australia (3676), Jordan (3008) and Bahrain (1639). Saudi students appear to prefer Western English-speaking countries over the neighbouring countries of Jordan and Bahrain. Interestingly, this is exactly opposite to the preferences of Kuwaiti students.

The new King Abdullah University of Science and Technology (KAUST) is presenting itself as an international showcase institution by attracting top-notch faculty, establishing institutional agreements, and offering generous scholarships to the brightest of students from around the world. It has developed Academic Excellence Alliances with foreign institutions such as Cambridge, Stanford, University of California Berkeley, University of Texas at Austin and Imperial College London. Through these alliances, KAUST awards approximately US$25 million to partner universities in exchange for their advice and suggestions on different aspects of governance and programme design. The Global Research Partnership programme is an innovative initiative aimed at attracting researchers to KAUST and helping to establish collaborative research initiatives with foreign research centres through funding of US$25 million over five years for each approved programme. In addition, highly respected scholars are identified in key focus areas and are funded up to US$10 million over five years to strengthen KAUST's capacity and production in niche research initiatives. These scholars remain part of their home institution but are required to spend specific time periods at KAUST during the year to conduct research, collaborate with resident researchers and mentor graduate students and scholars.

Saudi Arabia is clearly committed to international collaboration for student mobility, faculty recruitment, research and advice for modernising and internationalising its higher-education system. The ability to provide substantial financing is making it attractive to foreign students, researchers and institutions to collaborate with KAUST. Whether this mode of international cooperation is sustainable without generous financial support from the Saudi side remains to be seen, but there is clear evidence that Saudi Arabia is giving increased priority to attracting and paying for the best advice, brains and research opportunities from around the world.

United Arab Emirates (UAE)

UAE is in the process of moving from an oil-based economy to a knowledge/services oriented economy. This requires major investments to develop the necessary infrastructure and to attract businesses from the region and beyond. A key priority is having skilled and professional workers to support the growing knowledge economy. Of the seven emirates making up the United Arab Emirates (UAE), four – Dubai, Abu Dhabi, Ras al Khaimah and Sharjah – are currently active in recruiting international universities, faculty, students and knowledge industries in an attempt to position UAE as the premier education hub in the Gulf region. As of 2012, UAE has the largest number of foreign branch campuses of any country in the world. While it may be home to 37 branch campuses, the enrolments are relatively small; many are expatriate students who have spent most of their life in UAE and do not have access to federal institutions (Lawton & Katsomitros, 2012).

Dubai sees higher education as a critical sector for developing brain power for their new knowledge-based economy. Fundamental to their strategy is the recruitment of reputable international higher-education institutions that can lend their brand equity, offer their academic programmes and provide experienced faculty to teach national and international students. It is somewhat surprising that higher-education institutions are primarily being recruited as business partners to educate and train future knowledge workers and less for their research and innovation expertise. In contrast, the Emirate of Abu Dhabi, which has recruited the well-known Sorbonne University from Paris as well as New York University, is trying to present itself as a cultural zone yet one still interested in training international students as potential human capital for its economic aspirations. UAE is a complex arrangement of individual emirates developing plans to be an education hub without an explicit overall national vision or plan.

The owner/sponsor of Dubai International Academic City and Knowledge Village is TECOM Investments, a subsidiary of Dubai Holdings. Knowledge Village (KV) is home to many business partners oriented to short-term training and professional development by private firms. The newer Dubai International Academic City is part of the Education Business Cluster currently home to over 25 foreign institutions of higher learning. Total enrolment in both free zones as of 2012 was estimated at 15,000 students representing 102 nationalities (Fox & Al Shamisi, forthcoming 2013). Academic programmes range from one to four years and include engineering, computer science, finance, media, fashion and design, biotechnology, environmental studies, quality management and business management programmes. For academics who question whether higher education should be treated as a commodity, this US$3.27 billion business venture is concrete proof of UAE's commitment to developing education as a profitable commercial industry (Knight, 2011a).

Given that institutions located in the free zones of Dubai are exempt from national quality assurance and accreditation regulations, the Knowledge and Human Development Authority (KHDA) established the University Quality Assurance International Board (UQAIB) in 2008. The primary task of the UQAIB is 'to ensure that branches of universities and colleges accredited by foreign associations comply with the same standards of academic quality found at the "home" campus programs' (KHDA, 2011). This assumes of course, that the home institution has been accredited by a bona fide accreditation agency. The mandate of the Board includes: firstly, reviewing the applications of all institutions applying to the Dubai Free Zones and making recommendations to the licensing board of the Free Zone Authority, and secondly, approving the academic programmes of licensed institutions. The UQAIB is an ambitious undertaking but a necessary one.

The 2008 world economic crisis put the aspirations of UAE to be a recognised education hub into question, but it appears not into jeopardy, as the numbers of programmes at the branch campuses is steadily growing in spite of the struggles to attract sizeable numbers of students. At greater risk is recruiting a continuously increasing number of foreign students from the region and training them as skilled labour for the service and knowledge industries that Dubai is building.

Emerging Issues, Challenges and Unintended Consequences

Student Access

Does crossborder education help countries satisfy the growing demand for higher and continuing education? Many would answer 'yes', and that increased access for students is a driver for all forms of crossborder education. But there remains the critical issue of equity of access and whether it will be available only to those who can afford it or have the language skills (primarily English). No precise data exists on the rate of participation of students in crossborder programmes at the national or international levels. Only a handful of countries around the world collect reliable data on enrolments in crossborder education programmes, although this situation is improving, especially in the Gulf countries.

In the Gulf region, a key question is the number of students from the host country (expatriates or citizens) benefiting from increased access versus the number of foreign students recruited from the region or beyond. Each country differs. The three international branch campuses in Bahrain cater to both local and regional students. This aligns with its desire to attract foreign talent for expanding its service- and knowledge-oriented economy. Oman is using international foreign partnerships and affiliations as a way to provide increased access for local students who are qualified for tertiary education but who have to date had limited access. UAE presents yet another scenario as many of the 37 branch campuses cater to the expatriate students who want to stay in UAE for higher education, but do not have access to domestic higher-education institutions. As the number of foreign institutions and programmes are increased and diversified in UAE, the enrolment profiles are changing. As of 2012 more and more expatriate, Emirati and regional students are gaining access to foreign higher-education programmes. Qatar represents yet another scenario, where fewer than half of the students registered in the programmes offered through the institutions housed in Education City are Qatari. Meeting the academic and language requirements continues to be a challenge for local students. Therefore, regional students as well as students from the home campuses who study a year abroad in Qatar make up the majority of the enrolments. Of course, this picture varies across the different programmes available in Education city (Witte, 2010).

Quality Assurance of Crossborder Education

In the last decade, increased importance has been given to quality assurance at the institutional and national levels. This is especially true in the Gulf region (Babiker, 2010). Table V shows that all quality assurance and accreditation bodies in the six countries have been established since 2000.

New regional quality networks such as the Arab Network for Quality Assurance in Higher Education (ANQAHE) have also been established (Al-Atiqi & Alharbi, 2009). The primary task of these agencies in the six Gulf countries has been quality recognition and assurance of domestic higher-education provision by public and/or private higher-education institutions. However, the increase in crossborder education by foreign institutions has introduced a new challenge (and gap) in the field of quality assurance. Historically, national quality-assurance agencies have generally not focussed their efforts on assessing the quality of imported and exported programmes. The question now facing the sector is how to deal with the increase in crossborder education by traditional higher-education institutions and the new private commercial providers who are not normally part of nationally based quality-assurance schemes (Knight, 2010).

UAE, specifically Dubai, is an interesting case study in terms of quality assurance for foreign providers. Almost all the international branch campuses in Dubai have been established in a free zone: either Knowledge Village or International Academic City. By definition a free zone means that they are exempt from the regulations of the Commission for Academic Accreditation, a federal body. Therefore, in 2008 the HKDA established its own quality body and review process known as the University Quality Assurance International Board (UQAIB). The mandate of this new organisation covers Dubai only, which means that the international branch campuses in the other emirates are not subject to any review process other than those provided by the home institution.

	Agencies/organisations	Arrangements/ mechanisms
Bahrain	Higher Education Review Unit of the Quality Assurance Authority for Education and Training, established in 2008	Establishes framework for reviews Institutional and programme review Capacity building
	Higher Education Council, established in 2006	Approve licence for private HEIs
Kuwait	Private University Council of the Ministry of Higher Education, established in 2000	Establish framework for accreditation Approve/suspend licence Institutional and programme accreditation and review Degree, certificate and diploma recognition Each operating private HEI mandated to be affiliated with an international partner; and programme mandated to have international accreditation
Oman	Oman Academic Accreditation Authority Originally formed as Oman Accreditation Council in 2001 and restructured as OAAA in 2010	Establishes national qualifications framework Institutional reviews, standards assessment, accreditation and licensing Programme evaluation Recognition of imported programmes that are offered by foreign HEIs and accredited by well-known international agencies
	Directorate General of Private Universities and Colleges, established in 2000	QA of private HEIs

193

	Oman Quality Network, established in 2006 and sponsored by OACCC	Assists HEIs in sharing information and practices of QA
Qatar	Institutional Standards Office of the Supreme Education Council	Establish policies and criteria for QA License, accredit and monitor private programmes and HEIs
	Supreme Education Council, established in 2002	
Saudi Arabia	National Commission for Academic Accreditation and Assessment	Establishes national qualifications framework for accreditation and quality assurance Accredit and follow processes of QA
United Arab Emirates	Commission for Academic Accreditation (federal body), established in 2000	Establishes quality framework Institutional licensing and programme accreditation for private HEIs
	University Quality Assurance International Board (for Dubai), established in 2008	Provide the KHDA with guidance on quality of HE in Dubai's Free Zones Reviews and makes recommendations of the new licensing applications to KHDA Approves new programmes and branch campuses Audits and renews validation for branch campuses and programmes

Table V. Quality assurance (QA) agencies in the Gulf region.
Source: Adapted from Lee (2011).

Recognition of Qualifications

Increased academic mobility raises the issue of credential recognition to a more prominent place in international-education policy. The credibility of higher-education programmes and qualifications is extremely important for students, their employers, the public at large and of course for the academic community itself. It is critical that the qualifications awarded by crossborder providers are legitimate and will be recognised for employment or further studies both at home and abroad. To establish a credential review and assessment agency is a challenge facing many countries of the world, including those in the Gulf region.

The General Agreement in Trade in Services (GATS) and Higher Education

GATS has been a wake-up call for higher-education leaders around the world. Higher education has traditionally been seen as a 'public good' and 'social responsibility'. But with the advent of a new international trade agreement, higher education has also become a tradable commodity or more precisely, in terms of GATS, an internationally tradable service. GATS is often seen as the catalyst for the increased growth in commercial higher education between countries. Many educators would argue that GATS is responsible for these new developments. But others would contend that the opposite is true by pointing out that one of the consequences of increased private for-profit education at the national and international level has actually led to education being a multi-billion dollar business and thus a profitable sector to be covered in trade agreements. (Knight, 2007b) Academic mobility (students, programmes, providers) is considered by many as a huge commercial business and is expected to increase exponentially as the demand for higher and continuing education escalates. GATS has been seen by many as presenting new opportunities and benefits, but by others as introducing new risks. Thus, while international academic mobility is not new, the presence of international trade law to regulate it is new and causing interesting debates within the higher-education community.

Capacity Building

It is clear that crossborder education can be considered a double-edged sword. On one hand it can increase access for local (and in many cases also regional) students. But, by importing foreign programmes and providers, one can question the relevance of the curriculum to local context and needs. More importantly, it often does not help to develop the human capacity of the domestic higher-education institutions and faculty to design and offer these programmes themselves. Critics of crossborder education believe that relying on foreign expertise to prepare and teach courses introduces issues of dependency, sometimes neo-colonisation, and also sustainability.

Brain Drain/Gain/Train

For all of the Gulf States the training and retaining of required skilled labour is a top priority. This challenge is made more complex by the fact that one third of the population in the Gulf countries is under 15 years of age and another third is between 15 and 29. This is compounded by the reality that over 25% of these young people are unemployed (IFC, 2011). The development and deployment of domestic (and/or foreign brain) power is thus an increasingly important issue due in part to the need to keep the youth employed and productive as well as the increasing competitiveness for human capital in the knowledge economy.

While 'brain drain and brain gain' are well-known concepts, research is showing that students are increasingly interested in taking a degree in country A, followed by a second degree or perhaps internship in country B, leading to employment in country C and probably D, finally returning to their home country after eight to 12 years of international study and work experience. Hence, the emergence of the term 'brain train' (Knight, 2008). From a policy perspective, higher education is becoming a more important actor and is now working in closer collaboration with immigration, industry and the science and technology sectors to build an integrated strategy for attracting and retaining knowledge workers. In the Gulf region, the convergence of a young population, the transition to a knowledge and service economy, and professional labour mobility is introducing new challenges and opportunities for the higher-education sector; at the same time it is also encouraging unprecedented competition for educating and retaining the best and the brightest of students and scholars as well as exploring ways for strategic brain drain (Al-Barwani et al, 2009). A key issue is ensuring that the curriculum is relevant and responsive to the needs of the labour market while still recognising the importance of respecting local culture and customs and most importantly that higher education is, and has to be, more than skills development for future careers.

It is impossible to gaze into a crystal ball to forecast the future, but if the experiences of the last decade are harbingers of the future it is likely that competition for the brightest of students and scholars will only increase, bringing with it benefits for some countries and higher-education institutions and losses for others. Perhaps technology and social networking will bring new opportunities for brain sharing that will mitigate the overall effect of winners and losers, but the current obsession with global rankings and the economic-competitiveness agenda suggests otherwise. The great brain race through student mobility is likely to be in active mode for a while.

Double Degrees: double the benefit or double counting?

Interest in these double-degree programmes is increasing in the Gulf region, but so is concern about the necessary academic requirements and the validity of a double or multiple degree qualification. For many academics and policy makers, double-degree programmes are welcomed as a natural extension of exchange and mobility programmes. For others, they are perceived as a troublesome development leading to double counting of academic work and the thin edge of academic fraud. A broad range of reactions exist for a number of different reasons: the diversity of programme models; the uncertainty related to quality assurance and qualifications recognition; and finally, the ethics involved in deciding what academic workload or new competencies are required for the granting of a joint, double, multiple or consecutive (i.e., BA and MA or MA and PhD) degrees.

The value of a qualification/credential is at the root of the murkiness surrounding the 'acceptability or legitimacy' of double/multiple degrees. Many would argue that attributing the same courses or workload towards two or more degrees from two or more institutions devalues the validity of a qualification. Others believe that if students meet the stated learning outcomes/competencies required to obtain a qualification regardless of where or how the competencies were acquired, the credential is legitimate. This logic infers that double/multiple degrees, based on a set of core courses or competencies plus additional requirements of the collaborating institutions are academically sound and legitimate. It is argued that the process for recognising these qualifications requires more attention, not the completion requirements per se. Both arguments have validity but the variety of models used prevents a clear resolution to the question of 'legitimacy'. Doubt remains. (Knight, 2011c)

Education Hubs: fad, brand or innovation?

Education hubs are important new developments. They represent a new generation of crossborder education activities where critical mass, co-location and connection between international/local universities, students, research institutes and private industry are key. But are they just a fad? Are they more rhetoric than reality? A common perception is that being recognised as an education hub will increase a country's reputation, competitiveness and geo-political status within the region and beyond. Are education hubs nothing more than a branding exercise designed to increase status and a sense of soft power?

To ensure that education hubs are more than a brand and can achieve their goals and become sustainable requires substantial planning, policy preparedness, human resources, infrastructure and financial investment. It remains to be seen whether student-education hubs are sustainable given the intense competition among countries for fee-paying students, or whether talent hubs are feasible in light of immigration policies and unemployment rates for domestic workers. Finally, it is still unknown whether knowledge/innovation-type education hubs can be developed successfully through university–industry collaborations. Ensuring that education hubs are sustainable and an innovative new development represents the next challenge facing countries keen to shift to a knowledge- and service-based economy and gain a competitive edge and profile in the region and beyond.

Jane Knight

Cultural Diversity or Homogenisation: cultural tensions?

Debates on the impact of crossborder education on indigenous knowledge and cultural diversity often provoke strong positions and sentiments. Some take a positive view of the ways that modern information and communication technologies as well as the movement of people, ideas and culture across national boundaries promote the fusion and hybridisation of culture. Others contend that these same forces are eroding national cultural identities and leading to cultural homogenisation, most often in the form of Westernisation. And still others speculate that crossborder mobility of students, providers and programmes will only increase cultural tensions within host institutions and countries.

Concluding Remarks

Words like diversity, innovation, complexity, confusion, risks, benefits, opportunities and challenges have been used repeatedly in this chapter to describe the development and evolution of crossborder education in general, and in the Gulf countries more specifically. The mobility of students, professors, knowledge and values has been part of higher education for centuries, but it has only been in the last two decades that there has been significant growth in the mobility of programmes and providers and the establishment of education hubs.

These new developments present many new opportunities: for increased access to higher education; for strategic alliances between countries and regions; for the production and exchange of new knowledge through academic/industry partnerships; for the mobility of graduates and professionals; for human-resource and institutional capacity building; for income generation; for the improvement of academic quality; and for increased mutual understanding. The list of potential benefits is long and varied. But so is the list of potential risks. Risks can include: an increase in low-quality programmes and providers; a potential decrease in public funding if foreign providers are providing increased access; courses being driven by short-term needs of the labour market, non-sustainable foreign provision of higher education if profit margins are low; foreign qualifications not recognised by domestic employers or education institutions; elitism in terms of those who can afford crossborder education, overuse of English as the language of instruction; little importance being given to collaborative research; and national higher-education policy objectives not being met. These present major challenges to the education sector in the Gulf region. It is important to acknowledge the huge potential of crossborder education, but not at the expense of academic quality and integrity.

References

Al-Atiqi, I.M. & Alharbi, L.M. (2009) Meeting the Challenge: quality systems in private higher education in Kuwait, *Quality in Higher Education*, 15, 5-16.

Al-Barwani, T., Chapman, D.W. & Ameen, H. (2009) Strategic Brain Drain: implications for higher education in Oman, *Higher Education Policy*, 22, 415-432.

Babiker, A. (2010) Proceedings from the Arab Regional Conference on Higher Education 2009: licensing and supervision of private higher education institutions in Arab States. Cairo: UNESCO. http://unesdoc.unesco.org/images/0018/001892/189272m.pdf (accessed 15 April 2012).

Bahrain Daily Tribune (2012) Higher Education Hub, *Bahrain Daily Tribune*, 14 March. http://www.dt.bh/newsdetails.php?newsid=130312192317&key=301110213450 (accessed 15 April 2012).

Bains, E. (2009) *Qatar Education City's Key Institutions*. Meed Supplements, 21 September. http://www.meed.com/supplements/education-citys-key-institutions/3000797.article (accessed 15 April 2012).

Boehm, A., Davis, D., Meares, D. & Pearce D. (2002) *The Global Student Mobility 2025 Report: forecasts of the global demand for international education*. Canberra: IDP.

Chen, T. & Barnett, G. (2000) Research on International Student Flows from a Macro Perspective: a network analysis of 1985, 1989 and 1995, *Higher Education*, 39, 435-453.

Fox, W. & Al Shamisi, S. (forthcoming 2013) United Arab Emirates Education Hub: a decade of development, in J. Knight, *International Education Hubs: emerging models from Asia, Africa and the Gulf States*. Rotterdam: Springer.

Gulf University for Science & Technology (GUST) (2011) UMSL Cooperation. https://www.gust.edu.kw/about-us/umsl_cooperation (accessed 15 April 2012).

IFC (2011) *Education for Employment: realizing Arab youth potential*. Washington, DC: International Finance Corporation.

Knight, J. (2007a) Cross-Border Tertiary Education: an introduction, in OECD *Cross-border Tertiary Education: a way towards capacity development*, 21-46. Paris: OECD, World Bank and NUFFIC.

Knight, J. (2007b) *Implications of Crossborder Education and GATS for the Knowledge Enterprise*. Commissioned Research Paper for UNESCO Forum on Higher Education, Research and Knowledge. Paris: UNESCO.

Knight, J. (2008) *Higher Education in Turmoil: the changing world of internationalization*. Rotterdam: Sense Publishers.

Knight, J. (2011a) Quality Dilemmas with Regional Education Hubs and Cities, in S. Kaur, M. Sirat & W. Tierney (Eds) *Quality Assurance and University Rankings in Higher Education in the Asia Pacific: challenges for universities and nations*. Penang: Universiti Sains Malaysia Press.

Knight, J. (2011a) Education Hubs: a fad, a brand, or an innovation, *Journal for Studies in International Education,* 15(3), 221-240.

Knight, J. (2011b) *Three Types of Education Hubs: student, talent, knowledge. Are Indicators Useful or Feasible?* London: Observatory on Borderless Higher Education.

Knight, J. (2011c) Doubts and Dilemmas with Double Degree Programs, *Revista de Universidad y Sociedad del Conocimiento (RUSC)*, 8(2), 297-312. http://rusc.uoc.edu/ojs/index.php/rusc/article/view/v8n2-knight (accessed 15 April 2012).

Knight, J. (forthcoming 2013) *International Education Hubs: emerging models from Asia, Africa and the Gulf States.* Rotterdam: Springer.

KHDA (2011) *The Higher Education Landscape in Dubai.* Dubai: Knowledge, Human Development Authority.

Lawton, B. & Katsomitros, A. (2012) *International Branch Campuses: data and developments.* London: Observatory of Borderless Higher Education.

Lee, H. (2011) *Quality Assurance of Higher Education in the Gulf Region.* Unpublished paper, University of Toronto, Canada.

MOHE (2010) *Higher Education: a window to the future.* Directorate General of Private Universities and Colleges, Ministry of Higher Education. Muscat: Sultanate of Oman.

Munden, D. (2009) Bahrain Top Research Hub, *Gulf Daily News,* 29 September. http://www.iiss.org/whats-new/iiss-in-the-press/september-2009/bahrain-top-research-hub/ (accessed 15 April 2012).

Organisation for Economic Cooperation and Development (OECD) (2010) *Education at a Glance 2010.* http://www.oecd.org/document/52/0,3343,en_2649_39263238_45897844_1_1_1_1,00.html (accessed 15 April 2012).

Private Universities Council (2005) Licensed Private Institutions in Kuwait. http://puc.edu.kw/en/index.php?TP=einstitutions (accessed 15 April 2012).

Sawahel, W. (2010) Saudi Arabia: first foreign accredited degrees plan, *University World News,* 3 October, p. 142. http://www.universityworldnews.com/article.php?story=20101003072341593 (accessed 15 April 2012).

UNESCO (2009) Top Five Destinations for Mobile Students and Outbound Mobility Ratio. http://www.uis.unesco.org/Education/Pages/tertiary-education.aspx (accessed 15 April 2012).

Witte, S. (2010) *Inside Education City: the persistent demographic and gender imbalance in Qatar.* London: The Observatory on Borderless Higher Education.

Sources of Further Information

Bahrain Economic Development Board (BEDB) (2008) *Education and Training.* http://www.bahrainedb.com/education-training.aspx (accessed 15 April 2012).

Coulter, K. (2009) Saudi Arabia unveils co-ed 'House of Wisdom'/Postcards from Saudi Arabia: the KAUST inauguration, *GlobalHigherEd*, 5 October. http://globalhighered.wordpress.com/2009/10/05/the-kaust-inauguration (accessed 15 April 2012).

Denman, B.D., & Hilal, K.T. (2011) From Barriers to Bridges: an investigation on Saudi student mobility, *International Review of Education*, 57, 299-318.

Donn, G. & Al Manthri, Y. (2010) *Globalisation and Higher Education in the Arab Gulf States.* Oxford: Symposium Books.

Lewin, T. (2009) University Branches in Dubai are Struggling, *New York Times*, 27 December. http://www.nytimes.com/2009/12/28/education/28dubai.html (accessed 15 April 2012).

Sawahel, W. (2009) Malaysia: knowledge hub in progress, *University World News*, 94, 27 September. http://www.universityworldnews.com/article.php?story=20090925024920661 (accessed 15 April 2012).

Wilkins, S. (2011) Who Benefits from Foreign Universities in the Arab Gulf States, *Australian University Review*, 53(1), 73-83.

Notes on Contributors

Gari Donn is the Executive Director of the United Nations House in Scotland. She is the Convenor of UNA Scotland and Chair of the Edinburgh Peace Initiative. Dr Donn also works at the University of Edinburgh where she researches, supervises PhD students and lectures on postgraduate programmes in International Education. Her research focuses upon the political economy of globalisation, international education and higher-education policy making notably in countries of the Middle East, Asia and sub-Saharan Africa. She acts as adviser to ministries of education. She is an active member of the UK National Commission for UNESCO Scotland Committee and Soroptimist International in Edinburgh.

Yahya Al Manthri is the Chair of the State Council of Oman, having been previously the Minister for Higher Education, Minister for Education and Vice Chancellor of the Sultan Qaboos University in Oman. As a senior diplomat in the 1980s, Dr Al Manthri was a member of the Omani delegation to the UN and Deputy Governor of Dhofar, the Southern Province. He has represented his country at international events organised by UNESCO, the International Arab Union and the Arab Bureau for Education in the Gulf States.

Sajid Ali is an Assistant Professor at the Aga Khan University's Institute for Educational Development, Karachi. He has a PhD in Education Policy from the University of Edinburgh, an MEd in Leadership and Policy from Monash University, and a Masters in Sociology from the University of Karachi. Dr Ali is a recipient of various academic awards including the Commonwealth Youth Leadership Award (2003), Australian Development Award (2003), Edinburgh Research Award (2006) and South Asian Visiting Scholar Oxford University (2011). Dr Ali has taught at Hamdard, Karachi and Aga Khan Universities as well as at the University of Edinburgh. His research interests include globalisation and education policy, educational governance, education reforms, and the privatisation of education and the teacher labour market.

Mohammed Alrozzi is a Palestinian research professional who specialises in youth and young childhood. He was born and continues to live in Gaza in the Palestinian Territories. Mohammed completed his undergraduate study at Bethlehem University, where he was awarded a BSc in Occupational Therapy. In 2011 he completed his Masters degree in Childhood Studies at the University of Edinburgh. He has worked with many international non-governmental organisations and UN agencies, including Mercy Corps, Terre des Hommes, the Norwegian Refugee Council and UNICEF. He is currently the Child Participation Coordinator at World Vision – Gaza. Through his work experience, Mohammed has developed an extensive multidisciplinary expertise in child-protection issues, education in post-conflict settings and aspects of psychosocial wellbeing at times of crisis. He is particularly interested in researching the politics of education.

Brooke Barnowe-Meyer is a PhD candidate at the University of Edinburgh. Born and raised in the Pacific Northwest of the United States, Brooke completed her undergraduate studies at the University of Washington in Seattle (BA Political Science, 2005) before pursuing postgraduate study at the University of Edinburgh (MSc Education, 2010). Her PhD studies focus on the role of policy networks and social entrepreneurs in the development and implementation of health-education programmes in sub-Saharan Africa. Her research and professional interests include globalisation and education, international policy borrowing, sexual and reproductive-health education and HIV/AIDS prevention.

Tanya Kane graduated with a PhD in Social Anthropology from the University of Edinburgh in 2011. Her thesis examined the transfer of a US pedagogical model to the Arabian Gulf against the wider context of the globalisation of higher education. Dr Kane's anthropological fieldwork was conducted at Weill Cornell Medical College in Qatar where she explored Arab student experiences of the US-style medical curriculum. A former schoolteacher, with a BEd from the University of Toronto, BA from Queens University, and an MA in Classics and Archaeology from McMaster University, Tanya has taught in Canada and the United Kingdom. Her research interests include globalisation, education, medicine, neoliberalism and knowledge-based economies, especially in relation to the countries of the Middle East.

Sana Al Balushi is the Director General of the National Career Guidance Center at the Ministry of Education in the Sultanate of Oman. She has worked as the Director of the Technical Office for Studies and Development, running the International Educational Programmes Office. She works as an educational expert with education-reform projects, and in that capacity has supervised a number of consultancies and works closely with international agencies. She is a qualified teacher in English language at elementary, preparatory, secondary, college and university levels. She received her PhD in Education (Curriculum Design and Evaluation) from the University of Louisville (Kentucky, USA). Her research is in the areas of education reform and English as a second language. She is a member of a number of policy-making committees and represents the Sultanate of Oman on international consultative bodies.

David Griffiths qualified with an MA (Honours) Degree from Dundee University in Scotland. He worked as teacher and Principal Teacher for 15 years in schools in Edinburgh. He served as a Curriculum Development Officer with Lothian Region for four years and as an Examination Officer with the Scottish Examination Board for six. He worked as the Lead Consultant on a three-year Scottish Qualifications Authority project to reform assessment practices in schools in Oman. For the last 12 years he has been employed as an Educational Adviser to the Ministry of Education in the Sultanate of Oman. He is the author of several school textbooks.

Özlem Yazlık is a PhD candidate at the University of Edinburgh, Scotland. Her PhD is on women's identity-related participation and engagement in adult-literacy and basic-education courses in Turkey. Her research interests focus on conceptions of literacy and identity, adult-literacy programmes, women's literacy, feminist methodologies and gender and education in Turkey. She worked as a teacher of English for both children and adults in Turkey. She also worked as a project officer in the community-based educational projects of international non-governmental organisations in the earthquake-stricken Iranian city of Bam and Pakistani Kashmir. She continues her involvement in feminist activism in Turkey through her voluntary translation and publication-research work in the Mor Çatı Women's Shelter Foundation.

Salha Issan graduated with an MEd degree from Hull University, United Kingdom and a PhD in Comparative Education from the Institute of Education, University of London. Her research continues to be in comparative education. She has lectured and supervised postgraduate students in educational administration at Bahrain University, Sultan Qaboos University, Oman and Cairo University. She is external examiner for PhD dissertations for the University of Malaya, Institute of Graduate Studies. Professor Issan has worked as a consultant for the Ministry of Education and Ministry of Higher Education in Sultanate of Oman. She has presented research papers in comparative education at conferences around the world. During her period as Dean at SQU, she introduced accreditation and evaluation of programmes in education. She has participated in multiple international research projects, including the Service Learning Project in collaboration with four renowned US universities.

Notes on Contributors

Jane Knight works at the Ontario Institute for Studies in Education, University of Toronto, where the focus of her research is on institutional, national, regional and international dimensions of higher education. Through her work in over 65 countries with universities, governments, UN agencies and foundations a comparative, developmental and international perspective is brought to her research, teaching and policy work. Dr Knight is the author of numerous publications on internationalisation concepts and strategies, quality assurance, institutional management, trade and cross-border education. She is the co-founder of the African Network for the Internationalisation of Education and sits on the advisory boards of many international organisations and journals.